Fabric of Enchantment

Fabric of

Batik fro

From the Inger McCabe Elliott Collect

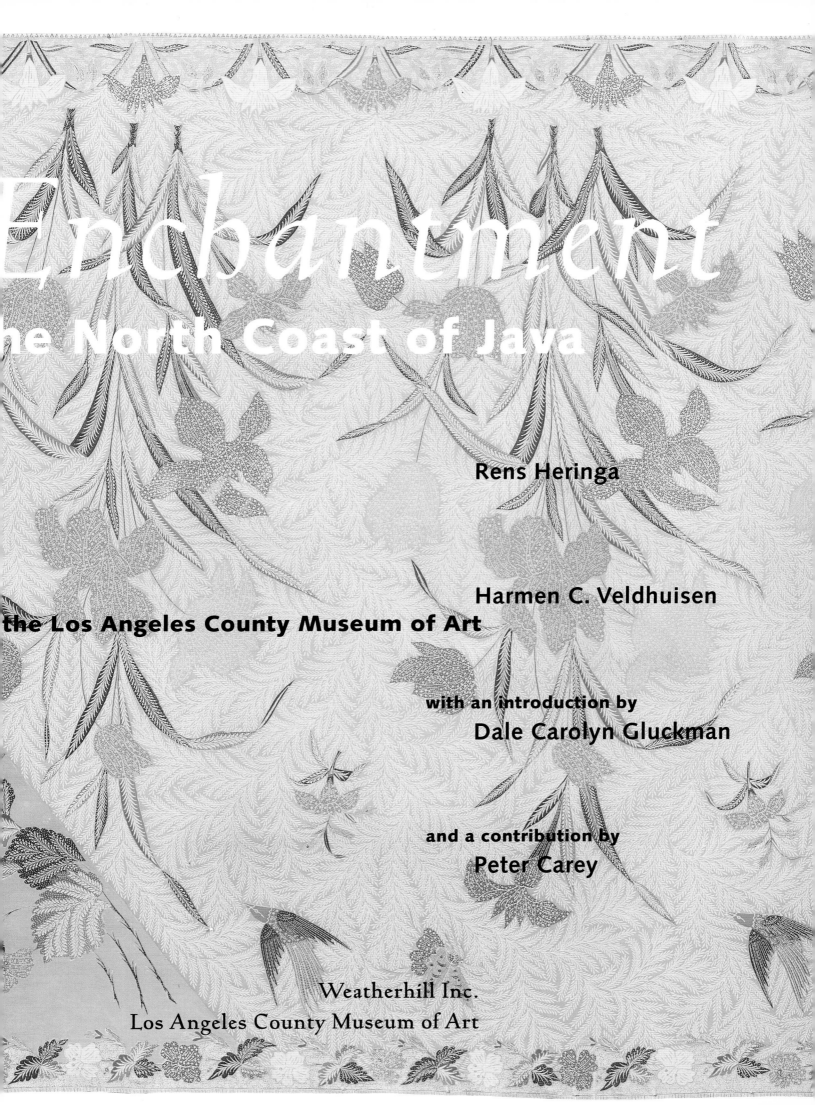

Enchantment

the North Coast of Java

Rens Heringa

Harmen C. Veldhuisen

the Los Angeles County Museum of Art

with an introduction by
Dale Carolyn Gluckman

and a contribution by
Peter Carey

Weatherhill Inc.

Los Angeles County Museum of Art

Copublished by the Los Angeles County Museum of Art,
5905 Wilshire Boulevard, Los Angeles, California 90036,
and Weatherhill, Inc., 568 Broadway, Suite 705, New York City,
New York 10012.

Published in conjunction with the exhibition *Fabric of
Enchantment: Batik from the North Coast of Java from the Inger
McCabe Elliott Collection*, held at the Los Angeles County
Museum of Art October 31, 1996–
January 26, 1997.

The exhibition was organized by the Los Angeles County
Museum of Art and supported in part by grants from the
National Endowment for the Arts and the Costume Council
of the Los Angeles County Museum of Art. Additional
support was provided through the Andrew W. Mellon
Curatorial Support Endowment Fund.

10 9 8 7 6 5 4 3 2 1   1996 1997 1998 1999 2000

Library of Congress Catalog Card Number: 96-076331
ISBN: 0-8348-0372-0 (clothbound)

Front and back covers: hip wrapper (details), Java, Semarang,
c. 1850, catalogue no. 17

Title page: hip wrapper, Java, Pekalongan, c. 1930, catalogue
no. 57.

Regarding dimensions: for all textiles width (weft) precedes
length (warp). All textiles were measured in the metric system
with mathematical conversion to the imperial system.

Printed in Singapore.

CONTENTS

FOREWORD

◆

THE LOS ANGELES COUNTY MUSEUM OF ART became one of the first art museums to recognize the beauty and importance of Indonesian textiles when it presented *Textile Traditions of Indonesia* in the fall of 1977. During the following decade the museum's collection, which had formed the core of that landmark exhibition, continued to grow with judicious acquisitions. *A Singular Beauty: Ceremonial Textiles from the Islands of Indonesia*, the museum's second Indonesian textile exhibition, opened on September 6, 1990, as part of the nationwide Festival of Indonesia (1989–90); it drew entirely from the holdings of the department of costumes and textiles. *Fabric of Enchantment: Batik from the North Coast of Java*, offers the museum its third opportunity to present the sophisticated textile arts of Indonesia to the public, making a significant scholarly contribution to the field of Indonesian textile studies.

Although the textiles of Sumatra, Java, Bali, Kalimantan, and the outer islands were well represented in the museum's collection, it contained only a few key pieces of north coast Javanese batik. It was with great pleasure and excitement, therefore, that the museum in 1991 accepted Inger McCabe Elliott's generous gift of her extensive collection of Southeast Asian textiles, primarily north coast batik. With the assistance of the Costume Council, support group of the department of costumes and textiles, the database and photographic documentation of the collection were purchased, greatly facilitating the preparation of both the exhibition and catalogue.

Hip wrapper (detail)
Java, Pekalongan, c. 1935
Catalogue no. 52

The relationship between donor and museum is ideally a close and personal one, resulting in an ongoing dialogue. Such has been the case with Ms. Elliott. From the beginning, communication has been regular and lively, for she is no ordinary collector, but one who has had an intimate working relationship with her collection, both personally and professionally. Her enthusiastic support of the "cause" of north coast batik, too long overshadowed by its nearest relative, central Javanese batik, has enriched us all.

The exhibition *Fabric of Enchantment* highlights selections from the Inger McCabe Elliott batik collection, for which this volume serves as the catalogue. Dale Carolyn Gluckman, associate curator of costumes and textiles, herself an authority on South Asian textiles, has brought together an outstanding trio of scholars from Great Britain and the Netherlands to shed new light on these colorful, intricate, and sometimes fanciful textiles, textiles that have many stories to tell about their creators and wearers; their images and meanings; their historical context and social milieu. Perhaps the most interesting story for the modern reader is that of the artistic flowering of a culturally and ethnically diverse society whose major creative expression was on cloth. Some fifty years later, its examination here has particular resonance for a sprawling Pacific Rim city on the west coast of the United States.

Andrea L. Rich
President and chief executive officer
Los Angeles County Museum of Art

PREFACE

FOR MUCH OF MY PROFESSIONAL LIFE I saw the world in black-and-white. Soldiers dying in Southeast Asia—black-and-white; Ted Kennedy on the campaign trail—black-and-white; Puerto Rican school children trapped in a Harlem barrio—black-and-white. I was a photojournalist, and those were my colors.

Then one day more than thirty years ago my black-and-white world exploded into glorious color. It happened in a hole-in-the-wall Hong Kong curio shop—that moment when the splendors of Java's north coast batik burst upon me. It was an epiphany of sorts.

Leaping out from among the store's tacky porcelain tigers and drab colonial sea charts was a wondrous textile cosmos, where lions roar ferociously, ducks paddle serenely, mythical animals defy gravity, and surreal flowers unfold their brilliant petals.

The batik artists of Java's north coast splash color and form with controlled—and often uncontrolled—abandon. They break rules: they blend pink, yellow, brown, and aqua without evoking the garishness of Las Vegas neon. Somehow their batik reminds one of eighteenth-century Versailles, not twentieth-century Miami Beach.

Entranced by what I had first glimpsed in Hong Kong, I set out on a new mission: to unravel the mystery of batik. I made my way to Indonesia and

Hip wrapper (detail)
Java, Pekalongan, c. 1950–60
Catalogue no. 63

8

before long was working with Javanese artists, helping them design new patterns and rearrange old ones, mixing colors never before used in batik and demonstrating that it was possible to produce batik in longer lengths of fabric so that it could be used not only for clothing but also for upholstery and drapery. In time, my company, China Seas, Inc., helped open new markets for batik in Europe, Asia, and North America.

As you will see in this volume, geography, history, and religion all were crucial to the evolution of batik. For hundreds of years Java has lain at a crossroads of trade, near the routes sailed by Marco Polo, Ferdinand Magellan, Sir Francis Drake, and St. Francis Xavier. Trade brought with it a succession of religions—Hinduism, Buddhism, Islam—and successive waves of colonization. Each left its imprint on the culture of Java and on its finest art form, batik.

My collection draws almost exclusively from the exuberant fabrics of north coast Java, the Pasisir, an area almost forgotten by earlier batik scholars, who concentrated on the courtly textiles of central Java. Making sense of these cloths has proven to be a formidable challenge, requiring both visual skills and historical insight.

Did a certain batik resemble another in color, design, technique? Chances are that they came from the same region, the same town, the same period, even the same maker. Delving deeply into historical tracts as well as visual memory, I was gradually able to put most of the pieces into what seems to be an appropriate cultural, geographic, and historic context.

The book that resulted, *Batik: Fabled Cloth of Java* (published in 1984 by Clarkson N. Potter), serves as the curatorial basis for my collection. The batik presented spans more than a hundred years, from the 1850s to 1990—from the earliest recognized batik designers and entrepreneurs to some anonymous geniuses whose work I found exquisite and daring.

During this long and sometimes arduous search, I traveled on four continents, crawled through cobwebbed attics, slogged through slithering mud, batted away flying cockroaches, and was apprehended by gun-toting policemen when I arrived unannounced in remote villages. I pestered scholars and friends alike in the hope of collecting and showing what had never been seen before.

A quarter of a century later I felt the need to share these works with a larger audience and began a search for a long-term home for my collection and its accompanying photographs and database. My concerns were that the museum that received it would "care" about such a collection, that it be a teaching institution, that the textiles would be exhibited regularly, and that the museum could comfortably support such a large collection.

I thought that the Los Angeles County Museum of Art satisfied all these stipulations—and more. It is appropriately part of the Pacific Rim and even has a special department devoted to costumes and textiles. To be perfectly candid, Rusty Powell, who was then the director, Edward Maeder, former curator, and Dale Gluckman, associate curator of costumes and textiles, and I got along famously. Sometimes major decisions become very simple indeed.

I hope you will share my joy in these astonishing works of art.

Inger McCabe Elliott

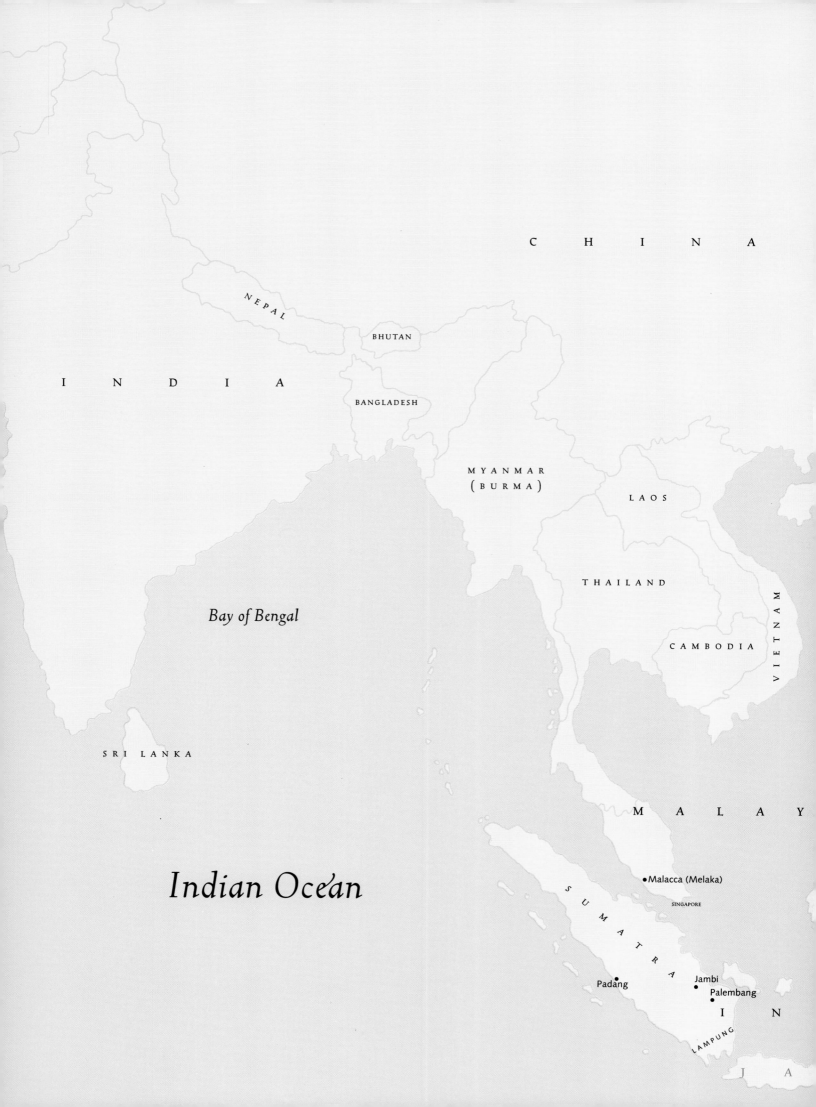

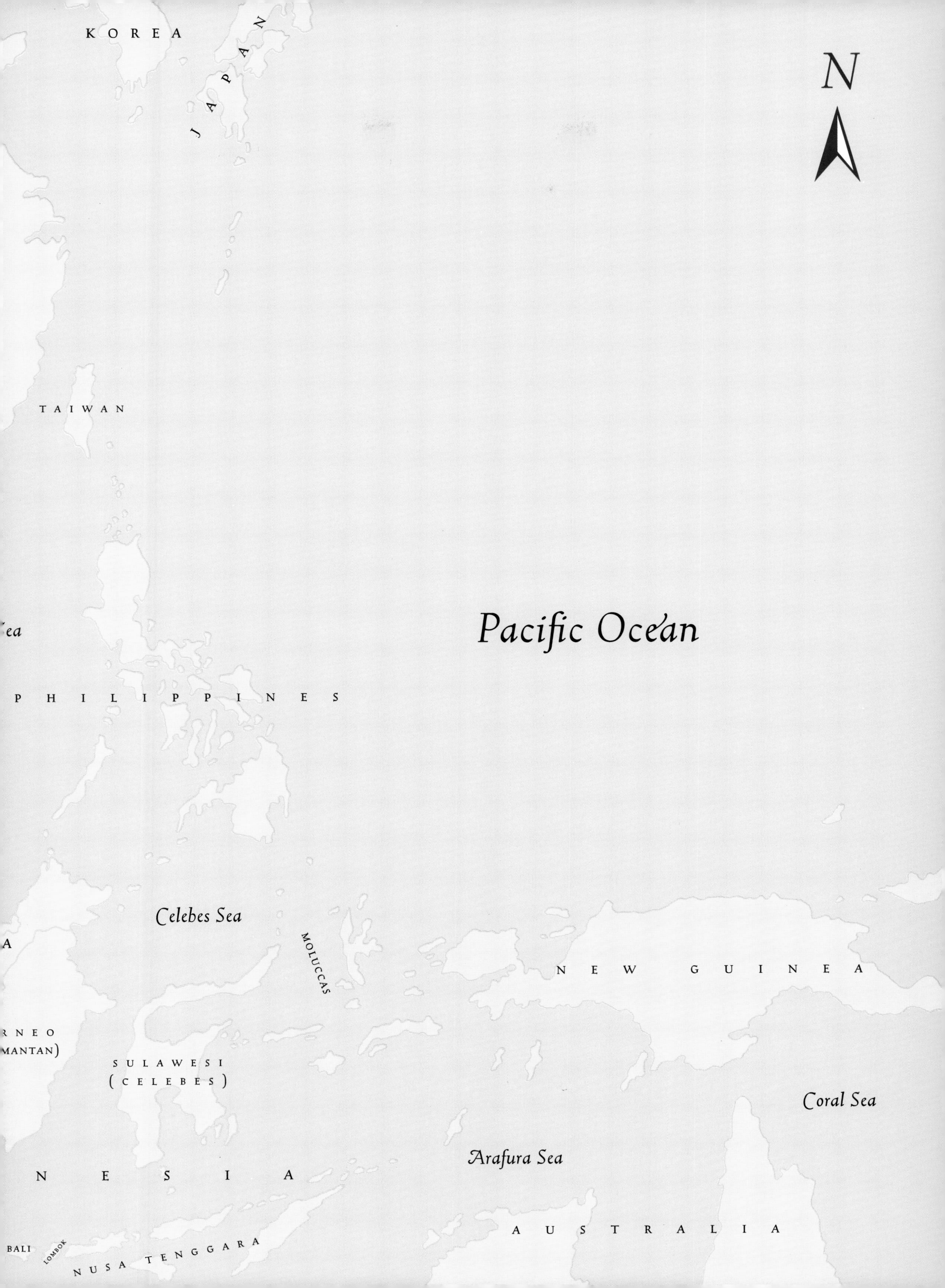

KOREA

JAPAN

TAIWAN

ea

PHILIPPINES

Pacific Ocean

Celebes Sea

MOLUCCAS

NEW GUINEA

A

RNEO
MANTAN)

SULAWESI
(CELEBES)

Coral Sea

N E S I A

Arafura Sea

BALI

LOMBOK

NUSA TENGGARA

A U S T R A L I A

N

SUMATRA

SUNDA STRAITS

Banten (Bantam) •

• Jakarta (Batavia)

Indramayu •

NORTH COAST (

Java

Cirebon •

Tegal
•

Pekalon

Kedungwur

• Bandung

J

A

• Ciamis

Tasikmalaya •

Banyumas •

WEST JAVA

CEN

Indian Ocean

N

))

Japara

Pati
(Pathi)
Kudus Juana Lasem
Rembang

Demak

Semarang

Tuban Paciran

M A D U R A

Gresik

Surabaya

Brantas *river*

Kartasura
Pajang
Surakarta (Solo)

Sidoarjo

Pasuruan

Panarukan

ta Yogyakarta

B A L I

EAST JAVA

INTRODUCTION

•

Dale Carolyn Gluckman

As a rule <u>batik</u> textiles preserved in museum

The Javanese word batik, which has been assimilated

into the English language, is treated as an English word in this publication with the result

that the plural is formed by the addition of **s**. Strictly interpreted, the word only refers to the wax-resist technique;

in common English usage, however, the term has come to refer both to the technique

and to the fabric decorated with it. This publication follows that convention.

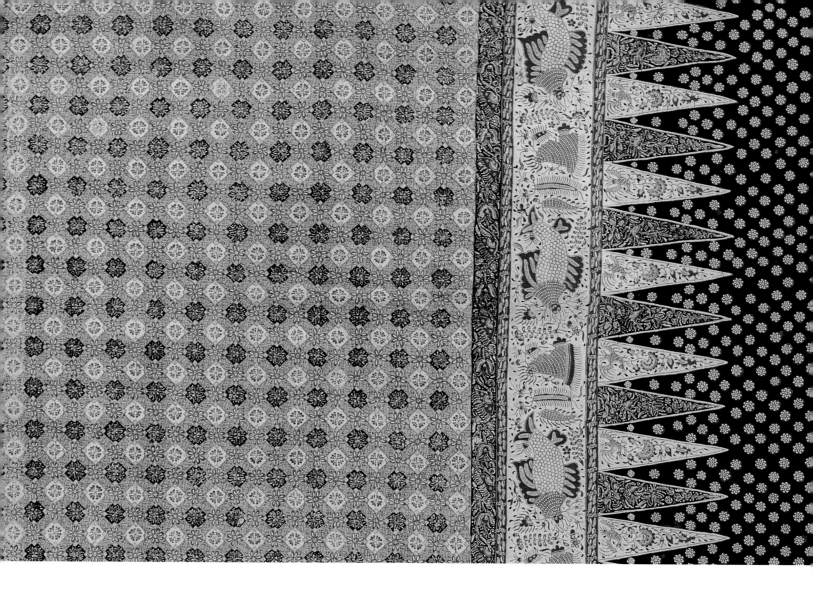

ctions are not fully representative of the variety of styles and the multiplicity of production centers that once existed along the Pasisir (north coast of Java). The majority of batik collections in Dutch museums were begun toward the end of the last century and generally favor central Javanese batiks.[1] American museums, several of whose Indonesian collections date to the early years of this century, also underrepresent *batik Pasisir*.[2] This lacuna is the result of preconceptions about what constituted "real" Javanese batik and the narrow focus of early European interest in batik production.

　　The batik of central Java came to be seen by Europeans as the quintessential Javanese textile and, as such, became the cloth most frequently collected and donated to Western museums. Dutch authors writing at the beginning of this century, typified by

G. P. Rouffaer and J. E. Jasper, assumed that the central Javanese Principalities were the homeland of Javanese batik; it necessarily followed that the colorful batik of the Pasisir must have been a later development, modified by various "foreign influences": Indian, Chinese, and European.[3] Those authors did not deem these "hybrids" Javanese; their aesthetic judgment of them was largely negative. Further, their preconceived ideas led these authors to the conclusion that the floral and figural designs on *batik Pasisir* had no symbolic significance for the wearers, in contrast to the complex abstract imagery on the blue, brown, and cream batik of the central Javanese courts.[4] These prejudices and assumptions held sway among Western scholars until fairly recently; only in the last several years have they been challenged by

Hip wrapper (detail)
Java, Lasem, c. 1900
Catalogue no. 1

Rens Heringa and Harmen C. Veldhuisen, who have expanded upon their research for this publication.[5]

The early emphasis on central Javanese batik is not found in more recently formed private collections, including that of Inger McCabe Elliott. These are often heavily weighted toward north coast batik, while other, better-known types are conspicuously absent.[6] This has come about for several reasons. The attitudes established by Rouffaer, Jasper, and others meant that very few of the north coast batiks brought to the Netherlands by Indo-Europeans were sought by museums. Instead, they remained stored in cabinets and trunks until their heirs sold them, directly or indirectly, to private textile collectors. By the late 1960s the demand for old batik cloth began to increase among museums and collectors. Prices rose in Jakarta, the main antiques market in Indonesia. Consequently, many older north coast batik textiles still in the possession of Peranakan[7] families were offered for sale and now preponderate in collections of recent origin. When the supply of old *batik Pasisir* began to decline in Java in the 1980s, dealers from Jakarta turned elsewhere in their search. Many of them were Minangkabau, the dominant ethnic group in the highlands of west Sumatra, with extensive trade contacts throughout that island, where heirloom Pasisir batiks, produced in Lasem on the north coast, could still be found (FIGURE 1). Soon these cloths began appearing on the Jakarta antiques market.

Textiles in Southeast Asia have served many functions, from ritual gifts to currency, but their primary use has been as clothing for both the living and the dead. This holds true for the majority of batiks in the Inger McCabe Elliott collection; the remainder functioned as ceremonial or religious hangings, baby carriers, or domestic textiles. The cloths discussed in this volume must be examined from a number of perspectives to be fully appreciated. To place them within a cultural and historical context, Peter Carey's contribution to this publication sets the stage upon which the story of the makers and wearers of *batik Pasisir* can be told. Next, Rens Heringa explores the origins of the batik process from contemporary survivals of earlier comparable resist techniques and highlights the seminal influence of the Pasisir on

central Javanese batik during the Mataram sultanate (fl. seventeenth century). Harmen C. Veldhuisen then recounts the transformation of batik production from a home craft into a commercial enterprise catering to a variety of markets. Finally, Heringa chronicles the impact of social events on the dress styles of the various ethnic groups whose members were the primary consumers of Pasisir batik. These essays are followed by a descriptive catalogue of eighty-two batiks selected from Elliott's generous gift to the museum.

The catalogue entries analyze key pieces in order to tell the story of the development of north coast batik. A careful reading reveals a methodological framework for approaching a Javanese batik.

First, how was it made? The batik process is a technique of textile decoration that involves the application of a resist substance (a wax mixture in Java) to protect particular areas of a design from dye penetration (see Appendix 3). Was the design created by the *tulis* or the *cap* method? That is, was the wax resist applied to the cotton or silk fabric with the bamboo and copper-spouted stylus (*canting*) used for freehand drawing? Or, was it put on with two or more copper stamps (*cap*), the dimensions of the stamp creating a unit of the pattern, or repeat, which should be apparent on close examination? The Javanese say that one can distinguish a *cap* from a *tulis* batik by the quality of the lines that form the motifs: *batik tulis* is "alive" with variation and movement; *batik cap* is more static and rigid. Batiks can also be *kombinasi*, a combination of the *tulis* and *cap* techniques[8] (see catalogue no. 29).

Second, where and by whom was it made? The place of manufacture of a batik textile can often be deduced from a careful study of its colors and patterning details. The city or town can be read in the particular shades for which a locale was famous: Lasem red versus Pekalongan red, for example. Some entrepreneurs can be identified by their house style, characterized by such qualities as a preference for certain colors or motifs, a particular technical perfection, or a special visual effect (FIGURES 2A–C).

FIGURE 1
Hip wrapper (detail)
Java, Lasem, c. 1870
Catalogue no. 5

Third, when was it made? Dating relies on evolutionary changes in the overall layout and in individual pattern details. The entries in the catalogue have been arranged by the authors to illuminate this development. Because a style, once introduced, continued in production over a long period, the entries are not arranged in a strict chronological sequence, but rather in the order that best exemplifies design modifications. Like any collection, Inger McCabe Elliott's, although extensive, is not exhaustive. Veldhuisen and Heringa, therefore, have occasionally utilized other textiles from the museum's collection to aid the reader in gaining a fuller understanding of the stylistic evolution of Pasisir batik. One key to the date of production of a batik textile that should be mentioned is the use of synthetic dyes, developed in Germany in the late 1850s and first imported into Java about 1890. Many Peranakan entrepreneurs began using these dyes because they were more vivid and offered a wider range of colors than vegetable sources. Peranakan customers in particular seem to have been partial to these bright colors. After 1900 the use of synthetic dyes markedly increased, although vegetable dyeing continued; from 1920, when the Peranakan became the primary clientele for *batik tulis*, synthetic dyes virtually replaced natural ones.9

A fourth and final consideration is who wore it and for what reason? Scholars from many disciplines have studied dress, analyzing it as a form of silent communication conveying messages about gender, age, rank, class, religion, wealth, status, lineage, kin, regional and ethnic identity, and clan or group affiliation.[10] The wearing of batik on Java is a prime example of clothing as a mode of communication. The catalogue entries that follow show a relationship between the makers and the wearers of north coast batik centering on an acute awareness of the symbolic content of many designs. The varying and distinctive ways in which members of a particular group within the polyglot Pasisir society manipulated aspects of Hindu, Chinese, Islamic, and European imagery on their clothing perhaps give the greatest insight into that world.

Indonesia's geographic location has influenced its textiles, including Pasisir batik, in two ways. One is its proximity to mainland Southeast Asia, with which it shares many cultural traits; the other is its position between the Indian Ocean and the South China Sea. Messages expressed on batiks frequently reflect the underlying philosophical concept of dualism at the heart of the Southeast Asian (and particularly the Javanese) cosmos, according to which the universe is comprised of opposed pairs: light and dark, night and day, male and female, upper and lower worlds.[11] Thus, in Indonesia "daily routines and ritual activities are ordered into two comparable yet opposing elements basically defined as male and female."[12] Some of the interpretations of layout, patterns, colors, and specific imagery on batiks discussed in this volume should be considered in the context of an ancient meaning system in which, for instance, an upper world of birds and other flying creatures is juxtaposed to a lower

FIGURE 2A
Carolina von Franquemont's distinctive blue-green
Hip wrapper (detail)
Java, Semarang, c. 1850
Catalogue no. 17

FIGURE 2B
Eliza ("Lies") van Zuylen's precise execution and flawless background
Hip wrapper (detail)
Java, Pekalongan,
c. 1900–1910
Catalogue no. 32

FIGURE 2C
Oey Soe Tjoen's use of shading for three-dimensional effect
Hip wrapper (detail)
Java, Kedungwuni, c. 1950
Catalogue no. 56

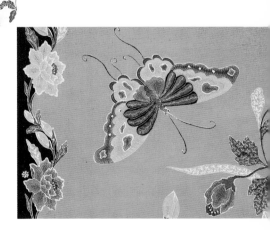

FIGURE 3
Hip wrapper (detail)
Java, Semarang, c. 1910
Catalogue no. 9

FIGURE 4
Trade textile (*patola*)
India, Gujarat, Patan,
late nineteenth century
Double-ikat, plain weave silk;
natural dyes
87.6 x 228.6 cm
(34 1/2 x 90 in.)
Los Angeles County
Museum of Art,
gift of Earllene Weiss,
M.89.146

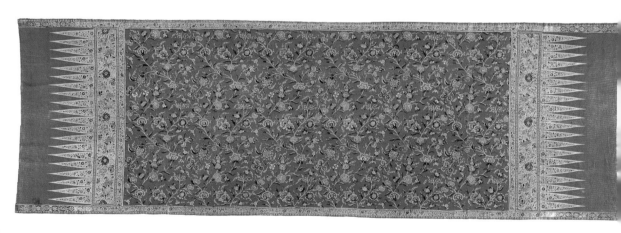

one of fish, snakes, and sea serpents (FIGURE 3).[13]
Not all Pasisir batiks lend themselves to this type of
analysis, but many in this catalogue do.

Indonesia's location at the crossroads of Indian
and Chinese culture and
trade is seen in its successive dominant religions
(Buddhism, Hinduism,
and Islam), its artistic
heritage, and in key ele-
ments of its textile vocabulary. From India came
two particular types of
trade textiles: woven silk,
double-ikat *patola* cloths
from western India
(Gujarat) (FIGURE 4) and
painted and resist-dyed
cottons primarily from the Coromandel coast[14]
(FIGURE 5). Both Heringa and Veldhuisen discuss
the similarities and differences between these heirloom cloths and Pasisir batik. From China came
trade ceramics and textiles, which enriched an
indigenous design vocabulary. Over time the
symbolic associations of particular images, such as
the butterfly or *qilin* (a mythical animal), blended
with Javanese concepts to form a unique set of interpretations sometimes at variance with standard
Chinese meanings.[15]

In this publication the principal authors present complementary perspectives. Rens Heringa
illuminates the social persona of the wearer and
the information emanating from a particular cloth
for those who can read its subtle messages. Harmen
Veldhuisen, by contrast, focuses on the batik entrepreneurs and takes a detailed look at the shifts in
color, design, and style that mark changing tastes
and clientele. This dual approach provides the first
broad-based study of a fascinating society and its
extraordinary textile artistry.

FIGURE 5
Trade textile (*tapib sarasa*)
India, Coromandel coast,
1750–1800
Hand-drawn mordants and
wax resist on handwoven
cotton (worked on one side);
natural dyes
117 x 349 cm
(46 x 137 3/8 in.)
Los Angeles County Museum
of Art, Costume Council
Fund
AC1996.60.1

NOTES

I am very grateful to Harmen Veldhuisen for sharing his thoughts and unpublished research concerning many of the issues discussed in this essay. His observations on the Jakarta batik market, the elements of connoisseurship, and collecting trends have been especially helpful. Rens Heringa too has contributed her perceptive thoughts. Any errors, however, are entirely my own.

1. Several European museums have batiks collected before 1860. These include the Museum für Volkerkunde, Vienna (1 example, collected in 1859); Koninklijke Museum voor Kunst en Geschiedenis, Brussels (4, c. 1840); Ethnography Department of the Nationalmuseet, Copenhagen (1, before 1843; 10, 1843–50); Museum of Mankind, London (1 surviving, c. 1816) (drawn from "Indonesian Textiles in European Collections," in *Indonesian Textiles, Symposium 1985*, eds. Gisela Völger and Karin von Welck, vol. 14 of *Ethnologica* [Cologne: Rautenstrauch-Joest Museum, 1991], 199–231).

2. Notable exceptions of batiks in American collections predating 1900 include those at the American Museum of Natural History, New York City (1, 1879); Peabody Essex Museum, Salem, Massachusetts (2, 1839 and 1882); Museum of Fine Arts, Boston (3 north coast: 2,1893; 1, 1895). The MFA represents a typical museum collecting pattern with 41 north coast batiks and 228 central Javanese batiks (statistics drawn from "An Introductory Survey of Indonesian Textiles in American Museums," in *Indonesian Textiles*, 1979 Roundtable on Museum Textiles, ed., Mattiebelle Gittinger [Washington D.C.: Textile Museum, 1980], 337–440).

3. G. P. Rouffaer, "De voornaamste industriën der inlandsche bevolking van Java en Madoera," *Koloniaal-Economische Bijdragen* (1904); J. E. Jasper and Mas Pirngadie, *De batikkunst*, vol. 3 of *De inlandsche kunstnijverheid in Nederlandsch Indië* (The Hague: Mouton, 1916). I am grateful to Harmen Veldhuisen for calling my attention to these references.

4. Perhaps encouraging this view was the fact that the rulers in the Principalities tightly controlled the right to wear certain patterns, a circumstance Westerners found particularly fascinating. In addition, during European occupation the *kraton* (palace complexes) became increasingly obsessed with carrying out sacred rituals that required the use of certain batik and other textiles.

5. Harmen Veldhuisen (*Batik Belanda 1840–1940* [Jakarta: Gaya Favorit, 1993]) has shown that the batik tradition on the north coast is, in fact, older than that of the Principalities. The view that *batik Pasisir* has no meaning was first refuted by Rens Heringa ("Dye Process and Life Sequence: The Coloring of Textiles in an East Javanese Village," in *To Speak with Cloth: Studies in Indonesian Textiles*, ed. Mattiebelle Gittinger [Los Angeles: Museum of Cultural History, University of California, Los Angeles, 1989]); that refutation was amplified in Danielle C. Geirnaert and Rens Heringa, *The A.E.D.T.A. Batik Collection* (Paris: Association pour l'Etude et la Documentation des Textiles d'Asie, 1989).

6. Of the more than six hundred Southeast Asian textiles in Elliott's generous gift to the Los Angeles County Museum of Art, the largest portion are Javanese batik, mostly from the north coast.

7. The modern term *Peranakan* literally means person of mixed descent. Historically, however, it has had two meanings. The first referred to the Muslim Chinese from Guangdong who settled in Indonesia in the fourteenth and fifteenth centuries; the second, and somewhat later, reference was to any locally born descendant of a Chinese father and local mother. These people formed a discrete community in Southeast Asia distinguished by the use of the vernacular language for daily communication and a particular cultural identity blending Chinese and local Southeast Asian elements. This has given rise to the term *Peranakan Cina* (Chinese Peranakan) as well as *Peranakan Arab* (Arabian father and local mother). In this publication for the sake of clarity *Peranakan* is used to indicate Chinese of mixed descent and *Indo-Arabian* for persons of that heritage.

8. Another test is to examine carefully the pattern for slight misalignments of contiguous stamps or the repetition of tiny errors that indicate a flaw in the copper *cap*.

9. This can be deduced from a survey of the batiks preserved among Peranakan Chinese on the north coast, according to Harmen Veldhuisen (personal communication, July 1995).

10. See for example, Margot Blum Schevill, *Costume as Communication* (Bristol, Rhode Island: Haffenreffer Museum of Anthropology, Brown University, 1986), 7.

11. There is some evidence that this concept of cosmic dualism had already begun to form in Southeast Asia as early as the Metal Age (B.C.E. 3500 in Thailand, c. B.C.E. 1000 elsewhere in Southeast Asia). Robyn J. Maxwell, *Textiles of Southeast Asia: Tradition, Trade and Transformation* (Melbourne: Oxford University Press and Australian National Gallery, 1990), 93.

12. Ibid., 94. Textiles, regardless of intended wearer, are "female"; metal objects, ivory tusks, and water buffalo are "male" in ritual gift exchanges.

13. On color symbolism see Heringa, "Dye Process," 107–30; for a discussion of the other points raised here see Maxwell, *Textiles of Southeast Asia*, 94–98.

14. For a discussion of the impact of Indian textiles on Southeast Asia see Mattiebelle Gittinger, *Master Dyers to the World: Technique and Trade in Early Indian Dyed Cotton Textiles*, exh. cat. (Washington, D.C.: Textile Museum, 1982), 137–55.

15. For a further discussion see Maxwell, *Textiles of Southeast Asia*, 239–44.

THE WORLD OF THE PASISIR

Peter Carey

The *Pasisir*, as the north coast of Java was kn

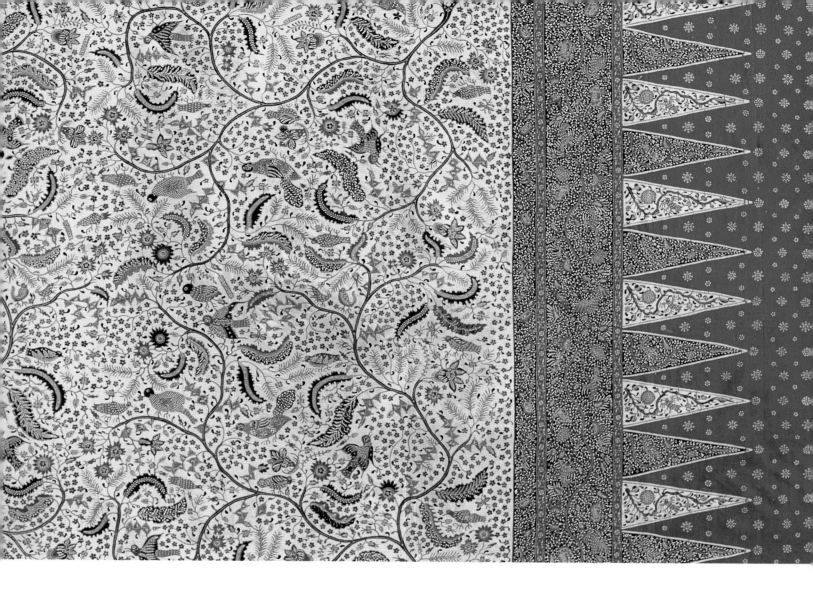

Hip wrapper (detail)
Java, Lasem, c. 1900–1910
Catalogue no. 2

FIGURE 6 (right)
Street of Chinese shops in the
Arab quarter of Semarang,
c. 1900.
Koninklijk Instituut voor
Taal-, Land- en
Volkenkunde, Leiden

m precolonial times, derived its name from the Javanese word for coastal region. Although it later came to refer to any area distant from the great court centers of the Javanese interior, such as Majapahit (fl. 1292–1450) and seventeenth-century Mataram, it was the north coast that became the cradle of the unique culture that gave the Pasisir its special character. This culture had its heyday between the fall of Majapahit in the early sixteenth century and the establishment of full Dutch colonial rule following the Javanese defeat in the Java War (1825–30). Sustained by the lifeblood of international commerce, which linked it to the great trade marts of southern India, China, and the Indian Ocean, the Pasisir stood at the maritime hub of Southeast Asia. It became the meeting place for travelers, merchants, and men of religion from the farflung corners of the Orient. It was here that the overseas Chinese made their first home and where Arabs and Gujaratis from western India began to proselytize the new faith of Islam, a world religion peculiarly suited to the needs of the trading communities. The life and soul of the Pasisir, these foreign communities lay at the heart of the polyglot north coast world that so impressed the first European explorers in the fifteenth and sixteenth centuries (FIGURE 6).

The First Islamic States in Java, 1450–1600

As the once mighty Hindu-Buddhist empire of Majapahit in east Java began to wane in the late fourteenth century, the north coast states began to assume a new political prominence.[1] Java had long been renowned for its riches, the product of a bountiful climate. "The wealth of this island is unbelievable," wrote Rijklof van Goens (1619–82), a senior Dutch East India Company official in the mid-seventeenth century, "nature having planted there everything except gold and silver that men upon this earth might ever wish from the Lord God."[2] Prominent among its products were rice and timber, the former supplying both Java and much of eastern Indonesia, where it was exchanged for spices, and the latter supporting a flourishing shipbuilding industry on the north coast. In 1500, of Java's estimated three million inhabitants, at least half lived on the Pasisir, with most concentrated in the fertile river valleys and coastal plains in a wide 330-mile arc from Cirebon in the west to Panarukan in the east. It was here that the specific culture of the north coast took root during the course of the fifteenth and sixteenth centuries.

Islam had already won adherents in Java by the fourteenth century, and by the seventeenth it was to become the religion of the vast majority of Javanese with the remaining Hindu-Buddhist communities being relegated to pockets in the interior. Reaching Java by way of India, Islam spread—usually peacefully—by Arab, Bengali, Chinese, Gujarati, and Malay merchants. A late sixteenth-century Javanese-Islamic text speaks of the difference that was then discernible between the adherents of traditional Javanese belief systems and followers of Islam, with membership of Javanese society now increasingly a matter of religion and culture rather than ethnicity.[3] As the Portuguese apothecary Tomé Pires (1468–c. 1539) observed of the north coast rulers in the early sixteenth century:

These . . . pates [patihs, i.e., lords of the Pasisir] are not Javanese of long standing in this country, but they are descended from Chinese, from Parsees and Kling [i.e., Keling, a generic name historically applied to Indian traders or settlers in Southeast Asia], and from the nations we have already mentioned [i.e., Arabs, Bengalis, Gujaratis, and Malays]. However, brought up amongst the bragging Javanese, and still more on account of the riches they have inherited from their ancestors, these men have made themselves more important in Javanese nobility and state than those of the hinterland.[4]

Among the most influential of this group were the Muslim Chinese, the so-called *Peranakan Cina* (Chinese with local roots), who hailed from the maritime provinces of China, Fujian and Guangdong. Many had converted to Islam, a practice that involved circumcision and the saying of the *Sahadat*, or Muslim profession of faith. In the Dutch colonial period (1600–1942) most men also abandoned their stiff hair buns and tonsured their heads, leaving only a long pigtail at the back in order to escape the tax levied by the United East India Company (Vereenigde Oost-Indische Compagnie, or VOC) on all those who still wore their hair in the style of the defunct Ming dynasty (1368–1644).[5]

As the power of the Majapahit waned, these so-called shaven Chinese extended their political influence, turning what had once been local offices, such as harbor master, into the basis of quasi-independent sovereign authority in their north coast harbor principalities. Examples of Muslim Chinese influence on the fifteenth-century Pasisir are numerous. The sultanate of Gresik, founded by Muslim Chinese traders fleeing from post-1368 Ming persecution in Fujian, was one such harbor state where the Peranakan were prominent. So too was Cirebon, where the ruler was related to the part-Chinese Sunan Bonang (Makdum Ibrahim; fl. c. 1490–c. 1512), one of the celebrated nine "apostles of Islam."[6]

These states adopted many of the techniques and traditions of Majapahit, with master craftsmen being brought from east Java to work on court buildings and mosques (FIGURE 7).[7] The old east Javanese *wayang* shadow play, gamelan orchestras, and

FIGURE 7
Hindu-Buddhist architectural influence can be seen in the tower and double roof of the minaret of the mosque at Kudus, c. 1880–81.
Note the Chinese porcelain embedded in the walls.
Koninklijk Instituut voor Taal-, Land- en Volkenkunde, Leiden

FIGURE 8A
The *kapitan cina* of Semarang
in official robes, c. 1890.
Koninklijk Instituut voor
Taal-, Land- en
Volkenkunde, Leiden

FIGURE 8B
Haji Ibrahim, the senior
mosque official in Pati, 1904.
Koninklijk Instituut voor
Taal-, Land- en
Volkenkunde, Leiden

kris (Javanese daggers with intricate meteorite inlay) were all taken over and developed by Pasisir rulers. Likewise, new Javanese Islamic literary genres grew out of the influence of Arabic and Persian classics.[8]

By the sixteenth century a particular pattern of urban settlement was already discernible in the Pasisir ports, with certain quarters (*kampung*) being set aside for different ethnic groups, such as the Arabs, Balinese, Bugis, Gujaratis, Keling, and Madurese, each of whom had their own heads (*kapitan*) to mediate their disputes and liaise with the local ruler's officials (FIGURES 8A–B).

The Coming of the Europeans, 1500–1800

The commercial wealth of Java's north coast, especially its access to the cash crops of the island's interior—cotton, cubeb, ginger, peas, and pepper—plus its abundant rice production and teak forests, attracted the attention of the early European navigators and merchant adventurers. After their capture of the great Malay trading emporium of Melaka (Malacca) in 1511, the Portuguese were drawn into the Pasisir world by their trade with the spice islands of eastern Indonesia. Intermarriage with the local population gave birth to a mestizo community, which owed as much to its Indonesian and Peranakan Cina roots as to its Lusitanian heritage, producing women of fabled beauty, who became the consorts of

senior European officials right down to the late colonial period. The Iberians also left their mark on the Pasisir economy through the introduction of New World crops—maize, sweet potatoes, tobacco—the introduction of Mocha coffee from the Middle East, and the widespread circulation of Spanish (Mexican) silver dollars, which, alongside Chinese copper (later lead) cash, became the main currency in the increasingly monetized trade of the north coast.

Despite their easygoing social mores, the seven thousand Portuguese east of the Cape of Good Hope in the sixteenth century were pressed hard by the naval power of the Pasisir principalities with their powerful allies in the Indonesian-Malay world. In 1512 the sultan of Demak was reported to have sent a fleet of one hundred ships and twelve thousand men to attack Portuguese Melaka, an exploit that was twice repeated by another Pasisir ruler, Queen Kalinyamat of Japara in 1551 and 1574. Although their carracks and caravels were able to beat off these attacks, the Portuguese soon fell victim to the superior naval organization and military power of the northern Europeans, particularly the Dutch. The creation of the VOC gave the Dutch a huge advantage over their European competitors since the company was vested by the Dutch parliament, the Netherlands States-General, with quasi-sovereign powers, enabling it to enlist personnel, establish fortresses, wage war, and conclude treaties.

The arrival of the Dutch had a profound effect on the balance of power in the Pasisir. The lucrative trade in imported Indian textiles and Javanese rice with the spice islands had been the mainstay of the harbor principalities' wealth. The Dutch drive for monopoly—something that they effectively achieved by the 1670s—led to the collapse of the Pasisir country trade with eastern Indonesia. But just as the Dutch were establishing themselves in west Java from 1601, first at the pepper port of Banten

FIGURE 9
The market at Banten, Java.
From G. P. Rouffaer
and J. W. IJzerman, eds.,
*De eerste schipvaart der
Nederlanders naar Oost-Indië
onder Cornelis de Houtman
1595–1597*
(The Hague, 1915).

(Bantam) (FIGURE 9) and then in 1619 at Jakarta (FIGURE 10),9 developments were occurring in Java which were to fundamentally alter political relationships in the island. Already in the late sixteenth century the rise of the new states of Pengging and Pajang in the interior had signaled a shift in influence away from the coast toward the agrarian hinterland. With the establishment of the kingdom of Mataram in the 1580s the whole of the Pasisir from Cirebon to Surabaya fell under the sway of this central Javanese power. In a series of bloody campaigns, culminating in the five-year siege of Surabaya in 1620–25, Pasisir resistance was broken, and Mataram's armies turned to confront the Dutch in their new capital of Batavia (Jakarta), which narrowly survived two sieges in 1628–29.

The seventeenth century thus witnessed the emergence of two new powers, Mataram and the VOC, whose rivalry would have a lasting effect on the north coast communities. Among the most important of these were the forcible removal of Pasisir cultural artifacts to the central Javanese courts, the changing position of the Chinese, the imposition of Dutch trading monopolies (1677–78), the establishment of new administrative structures, and the arrival of new waves of Chinese and Arab,

La ville de BATAVIE.
vrbs BATAVIA.

particularly Hadhrami,10 settlers. These changes would determine the character of the Pasisir until well into the nineteenth century, when the demands of the colonial economy would signal the start of a new era.

Despite its military success Mataram was no match for the Pasisir when it came to matters of art and culture. By the early seventeenth century the port city of Surabaya at the eastern extremity of the Pasisir was at the height of its power, a great walled town with fortifications encircling an area twenty-three miles in circumference, its political influence stretching as far afield as Pasuruan and Blambangan in Java's Eastern Salient (Oosthoek), the upper Brantas valley, and West Borneo (Kalimantan).11

Such political prestige was accompanied by a great cultural efflorescence, which reached its peak

FIGURE 10
View of Jakarta (Batavia).
From Joan Nieuhof,
*Het Gezantschap der
Neerlandtsche Oost-Indische
Compagnie aan den grooten
Tartarischen Cham den tegen-
woordigen Keizer van China*
(Amsterdam, 1670).
Mitchell Library,
State Library of
New South Wales

FIGURE 11
Masked dance performance,
Surabaya, 1905.
Koninklijk Instituut voor
Taal-, Land- en
Volkenkunde, Leiden

FIGURE 12 (right)
Port of Rembang, c. 1900,
important for its teak trade
and shipbuilding.
Koninklijk Instituut voor
Taal-, Land- en
Volkenkunde, Leiden

in the first quarter of the seventeenth century. It was at this time that the east Javanese romances dealing with the fictional history of Majapahit and the Panji tales relating the adventures of Radèn Panji Ino Kertapati and a Kedhiri princess became popular in the shadow play and masked dance performances along the Pasisir (FIGURE 11).[12] Cultural attainments of this magnitude were naturally coveted by Mataram, which now sought to emulate the cultural style of its defeated Pasisir rivals with Surabaya and north coast artificers being pressed into service as architects and builders for the Mataram ruler's new court at Karta. In much the same way Demak a century earlier had brought craftsmen and artisans to help build the mosques and court compounds of the new Pasisir kingdoms.[13]

With the Pasisir now ruled directly from Mataram (twenty of the kingdom's forty-eight provinces were situated on the north coast, with Pekalongan and Surabaya producing particularly significant returns for the royal exchequer), a system of administration was established whereby the north coast regents acted as revenue collectors for the Javanese state. These administrative developments opened up important opportunities for the Muslim Chinese, deemed by Mataram to be more reliable and less beholden to the erstwhile ruling dynasties of the Pasisir than the Javanese. Just how entrenched the Chinese had become by the mid-seventeenth century can be seen in the privileged legal status accorded them in the Javanese law codes, which stipulated that the fine (*diyat*, literally "blood money") for killing a Chinese was to be twice that for murdering a Javanese.[14]

By the third quarter of the seventeenth century the Pasisir was already passing under the political sway of the Dutch and their Chinese allies: a series of treaties with the Mataram court in 1677–78 led to the direct cession of Semarang (destined to become the seat of Dutch government on the north coast from 1678 to 1808). The lure of incomes from the Pasisir ports (FIGURE 12), monopolies over the purchase of rice and sugar, and the import of textiles and opium made control of this area particularly attractive to the Dutch.

The economic opportunities opened by these treaties soon attracted new waves of Chinese immigration to the Pasisir. Developments in China itself quickened this process: the fall of the Ming dynasty in 1644 and the reopening of Chinese trade with Southeast Asia in 1683 following successful Qing campaigns in Formosa created ideal conditions for an increased flow of Chinese immigrants from the southern maritime provinces to the Pasisir. Hokkiens (inhabitants of Fujian who had settled in Southeast Asia) from the neighborhood of Amoy and Cantonese from Canton and Macao were most prominent here. Many of these newcomers found their way from Batavia to Semarang and other north coast ports. According to Ong Tae-hae, a low-ranking Fujianese mandarin who spent nearly a decade, from 1783 to 1791, on the north coast working as a schoolmaster in Pekalongan, this quickened flow of immigrants led over time to ever deeper cultural and social assimilation.

When the Chinese remain abroad for several generations without returning to their native land, they frequently cut themselves off from the instruction of the sages: in language, food and dress, they imitate the natives, and studying foreign books [the Qur'an?], they do not scruple to become Javanese, when they called themselves islam (Sit-lam). They then refuse to eat pork and adopt altogether native customs. [The Chinese] having multiplied, the Dutch have given them into the hands of a Captain [i.e., kapitan cina] who superintends this class.[15]

Such assimilation, however, was no guarantee of political security. Indeed, as the numbers of Chinese on the Pasisir rose (by the mid-eighteenth century there were fifteen thousand in the colonial capital and its immediate environs alone), so the fears of the greatly outnumbered Dutch increased. In October 1740 a general massacre of the Chinese in Batavia cost the lives of ten thousand Chinese and sparked a conflict that affected most of the north coast, leading eventually to the cession to the VOC of the whole of the remainder of the Pasisir by the last Mataram ruler in 1749 and political partition of central Java between Yogyakarta and Surakarta in 1755. The Dutch were now the principal power in Java.[16]

The mid-eighteenth-century crisis led to the consolidation of a separate Dutch administration on the Pasisir with the appointment (from 1746) of governors and directors of Java's Northeast Coast (Noord Oost Kust), whose authority stretched from Cirebon to Madura. Until its abolition in 1808 this governorship offered huge opportunities for personal enrichment for senior VOC officials and remained "as much of a mystery to the Government in Batavia, as the Semarang Governor wished to make it."[17] It also spawned a unique Eurasian society that saw the development of the institution of the *nyai* (Indonesian/Javanese housekeeper, mistress, or common-law wife), whose sartorial tastes owed much to the Javanese world. The modified version of the *sarung* (tubular hip wrapper) and *kabaya* (long-sleeved blouse) became de rigueur among elite Indo-Dutch ladies, who so horrified the British during their short-lived interregnum (1811–16), when they saw them attending official receptions "in their underwear"—the *sarung* being viewed as a petticoat and the *kabaya* as a chemise.[18] Just how intimate Dutch officials could be with Javanese ways at this time can be seen in the remark of the senior Dutch representative at the central Javanese courts, Johannes Gerardus van den Berg (in office 1799–1806), who boasted, "I count myself lucky that in my youth I was able to learn Javanese well and now I know it better than my mother tongue."[19] And then there was the remarkable episode involving the governor of Java's northeast coast, Nicolaas Hartingh (in office 1754–61), in which he reciprocated the presentation by Sultan Hamengkubuwana I

(r. 1749–92) of one of his unofficial wives (a present for his crucial role in arranging the 1755 partition) by sending the Yogyakarta ruler a woman from the VOC territories in Blambangan.[20]

An important feature of late eighteenth-century Pasisir society was the great influx of Hadhrami Arabs, who now swelled the populations of the special Arab commercial quarters in the north coast towns.[21] Arabs from South Yemen, a notoriously inhospitable and impoverished homeland, had been emigrating to the Indonesian archipelago from at least the sixteenth century, but disturbances in the Middle East attendant on the rise of the puritanical Islamic Wahhabī sect now forced many more to seek refuge overseas. Endowed with considerable business acumen, the Hadhrami communities flourished: by the 1850s, when there were some fifteen thousand Hadhramis on the Pasisir, over one-third of all the oceangoing shipping in Java was owned by Arabs, with Gresik being their principal home port.

By this time the political face of the Pasisir had been changed by the establishment of the Dutch colonial state. This process had been in train since the period of Marshal H. W. Daendels's governor-generalship (1808–11). Holland's only Napoleonic marshal, Daendels began a thorough overhaul of the corrupt administration of the former VOC, introducing a system of Napoleonic-style prefects (later residents) in the Pasisir and placing the local Javanese administrators under firmer Dutch control.[22]

These reforms were continued by Sir Thomas Stamford Raffles during the British interregnum. Raffles initiated a land-tax system and attempted the abolition of the old VOC system of forced deliveries of rice, cotton, sugar, and coffee by Javanese peasants through the north coast ports. Unfortunately such bold administrative changes were introduced too hastily, and Javanese producers soon fell into debt with Chinese moneylenders, many of them based in Semarang and other key Pasisir towns, who alone had the resources to extend cash for the payment of the land tax.[23] Widespread peasant discontent precipitated the five-year conflict known as the Java War, which by 1830 had cost the lives of two hundred thousand Javanese and damaged one-quarter of all cultivated land in central and east Java.[24] Although slightly outside the main areas of conflict, the Pasisir did not escape unscathed: both Semarang and Rembang experienced local uprisings, in 1825 and 1827–28 respectively, which caused many casualties among the resident Chinese Peranakan communities.[25]

The war was a shock to the Dutch, forcing them to take measures to recoup their huge financial losses (estimated at 20 million florins) and reinforce their authority over the whole of Java, including the hitherto independent princely territories. The year 1830 thus marked the end of a process, maturing since Daendels's administration: the change from the "trading era" of the VOC to the high colonial period (1830–1942), which lasted until the Dutch defeat at the hands of the Japanese (FIGURE 13).

prices, the money thus earned being used by the peasants to pay their land tax. The impact of this "system," which lasted until 1870, when a new agrarian law opened Java's agricultural economy to private European investment and the development of privately owned estates, has been much debated by historians.[26] Some have seen it as a catalyst for economic modernization, with the peasant economy undergoing rapid monetization as it underwent incorporation into the wider world economy. Others have seen it as a deeply divisive epoch, with a handful of richer peasants and village heads benefiting from new opportunities, but the vast majority sinking ever deeper into debt, with widespread impoverishment and famine as cash crops, such as coffee,

FIGURE 13
Europeans in the white cotton jackets of the civil servant's uniform, the *jas tutup*, and *sarung*, 1880s.
The seated gentlemen at far left and right wear Pasisir batik.
National Library, Singapore

The "cultivation system" of Governor-General Johannes van den Bosch (in office 1830–34)—in fact, not so much a system as a series of local arrangements with Javanese village heads—defined the new colonial relationship between ruler and ruled. Javanese peasant producers were now required to set aside one-fifth of their land for cash crops, which were then delivered to the government at fixed

indigo, and sugar, encroached on available ricelands. Certainly there were disasters, such as the famine in Demak in 1849–50, which led to a quarter of the population of two hundred eighty thousand either succumbing or fleeing the regency, but there are also signs that many rural areas were undergoing unprecedented economic and demographic expansion, a development mirrored in the quadrupling of

Java's population between 1815 and 1875 (from 4.7 to just over 18 million).

Nowhere were these changes more apparent than in the great port cities Batavia, Semarang, and Surabaya and the entrepots of the Pasisir, which served as the main export and processing centers for Java's cash crops; there a new urban society came into existence during the course of the nineteenth century. The revolution in communications attendant on the development of railways linking the north coast with the Javanese interior was especially important. The building of the Netherlands-Indies Railway (NIS) Company's Semarang principalities (i.e., Surakarta and Yogyakarta) railroad between 1867 and 1873 and the steam tramways, which linked Semarang with Surabaya in 1884, with Cirebon in 1895, and eventually with Batavia in 1914, greatly accelerated the movement of goods and people. By 1883, just a decade after the completion of the NIS line, it was estimated that nearly one million passengers, or 10 percent of the total population in the Semarang-Surakarta-Yogyakarta triangle, were traveling by train, many of them peasants making their way to the Pasisir ports to sell their produce.[27] The construction industry, which relied heavily on the labor of unmarried men, also underwent a huge expansion. Workers flocked from the hinterland to find employment on the north coast, where extensive building projects were being undertaken to expand harbor facilities and road, rail, and canal communications.[28] By 1914 the great cities of the north coast had taken on a new character, with sprawling working-class residential areas growing up in the shadow of the new commercial centers and dockyards.

The outbreak of World War I exposed the fragility of the Pasisir economy. Although Holland was not itself a belligerent, it soon found that trade with its distant Indies colony was jeopardized by German naval activity in the Indian Ocean. Huge stocks of cash crops built up in the north coast ports, which were only cleared after 1918, when, following a brief postwar boom, prices began to tumble on world markets. The rise of Indonesian nationalism, with the foundation of the Indonesian Nationalist party in 1926–27 under the leadership of Sukarno (1901–70) and the increasingly strident demands of the Indonesian Communists, all led to a loss of investor confidence in the Indies. While some Dutch settlers and officials took refuge in right-wing politics—the Dutch fascist leader, Anton Mussert (1894–1946), enjoyed a wide following in the colonies—members of the Pasisir Chinese and Arab communities looked to developments in their own homelands, where great events were afoot. At his trial for sedition in 1930 Sukarno warned the Dutch of a coming Pacific war that would sweep away their colonial empire in Southeast Asia and in which Japan, the new Asian power, would be their nemesis. Certainly Japanese inroads into the Pasisir economy were spectacular in the late 1920s and early 1930s, as cheap Japanese goods flooded local markets and undercut Dutch imports, particularly in textiles. By 1933 the Dutch had introduced protectionist measures, but by then it was too late: the depredations of the Great Depression, Japanese competition, and the increasing alienation of the local population from Dutch rule meant that the days of the European colonial order in the Indies were numbered. With the Dutch defeat at the hands of the Japanese in March 1942, the quickening of Indonesian political aspirations during the short-lived Japanese occupation (1942–45), and the revolutionary struggle against Holland (1945–49), the way was open for the triumph of Indonesian nationalism and the birth of the independent republic. In the heady dawn of the new postcolonial order there was to be no space for separate regional identities. The world of the Pasisir, which had sustained such a unique cosmopolitan culture for so long, was now part of the new Indonesian state. A remarkable chapter of Indonesian history was at an end.

NOTES

1. Historians continue to debate the reasons for this shift from the east Javanese heartland to the north coast, but it is clear that trade with the spice islands of eastern Indonesia and the spread of Islam were both important influences.

2. H. J. de Graaf, ed., *De vijf gezantschapsreizen van Rijklof van Goens naar het hof Mataram, 1648–1654* (The Hague: Martinus Nijhoff, 1956), 181.

3. G. W. J. Drewes, ed. and trans., *An Early Javanese Code of Muslim Ethics* (The Hague: Martinus Nijhoff, 1978), 36–37.

4. Armando Cortesão, ed. and trans., *The Suma Oriental of Tomé Pires and the Book of Francisco Rodrigues* (London: Hakluyt Society, 1944), 1: 182.

5. Peter Carey, "Changing Perceptions of the Chinese Communities in Central Java, 1755–1825," *Indonesia* 37 (April 1984): 12 n. 51.

6. H. J. de Graaf and Th. G. Th. Pigeaud, *De eerste Moslimse vorstendommen op Java: Studiën over de staatkundige geschiedenis van de 15de en 16de eeuw* (The Hague: Martinus Nijhoff, 1974), 111.

7. Traces of Hindu-Javanese architecture are clearly visible to this day in the mosque and minaret of Kudus (see de Graaf and Pigeaud, *Eerste Moslimse vorstendommen*, 68–71). It was the same with their military organization: many of the elite regiments of the new north coast principalities had Majapahit precedents, with Islamic traditions now being more visible in the armed religious corps, such as the Suryagama and Suranatan, recruited from Islamic divines and students of religion, and in the style of urban fortifications.

8. Examples of this are the tales dealing with the exploits of the Prophet's uncle, or *Ménak Amir Hamza* cycle, and the very popular accounts of the Prophet Joseph's life, the *Serat Yusup*. See Th. G. Th. Pigeaud, *Literature of Java: Catalogue Raisonné of Javanese Manuscripts in the Library of the University of Leiden and Other Public Collections in The Netherlands* (The Hague: Martinus Nijhoff, 1967), 1: 212.

9. Renamed Batavia, this would serve as the Dutch headquarters until March 1942, when the Dutch were defeated by the Japanese.

10. The Hadhramaut (present-day South Yemen), particularly the town of Terim, was the area from which many of the well-born Arab settlers in Indonesia originated in the Dutch colonial period. Most emigrated to escape the poverty of their parched homeland and to enjoy the high status that was accorded them in the Muslim Malay world, where their position as descendants of the Prophet (*Sayyid*) was especially revered (see L. W. C. van den Berg, *Le Hadhramaut et les colonies arabes dans l'archipel indien* [Batavia: Landsdrukkerij, 1886]).

11. De Graaf and Pigeaud, *Eerste Moslimse vorstendommen*, 165–68.

12. For a discussion of the east Javanese "Damar Wulan" romances and Panji tales, see Th. G. Th. Pigeaud, *Javaanse volksvertoningen: Bijdrage tot de beschrijving van land en volk* (Batavia: Volkslectuur, 1938), 130, 403–9; De Graaf and Pigeaud, *Eerste Moslimse vorstendommen*, 165.

13. Among these craftsmen was a group of part-Balinese, part-east Javanese carpenters and metalworkers known as the *kalang*, who continue to maintain a separate identity in Kutha Gedhé and other south-central Javanese towns until this day (see Pigeaud, *Literature of Java* [The Hague: Martinus Nijhoff, 1970], 3: 267, s.v. "Kalang"; Thomas Stamford Raffles, *The History of Java* [London: Black, Parbury and Allen, and John Murray, 1817], 2: 327–29; and Mitsuo Nakamura, *The Crescent Arises over the Banyan Tree: A Study of the Muhammadiyah Movement in a Central Javanese Town* [Yogyakarta: Gadjah Mada University Press, 1984], ch. 2).

14. Soeripto, *De ontwikkelingsgang der vorstenlandsche wetboeken* (Leiden: Edward IJdo, 1929), 88, 268.

15. Ong Tae-hae, *The Chinaman Abroad, or a Desultory Account of the Malayan Archipelago, Particularly of Java*, ed. and trans. W. H. Medhurst (Shanghai: Mission Press, 1849), 24; Ong Tae-hae's account was originally published in Chinese in Fujian province in 1791.

16. M. C. Ricklefs, *A History of Modern Indonesia since c. 1300* (Basingstoke: Macmillan, 1993), 95.

17. P. B. R. Carey, "Aspects of Javanese History in the 19th Century," in Harry Aveling, ed., *The Development of Indonesian Society* (St. Lucia: University of Queensland Press, 1979), 49.

18. Jean Gelman Taylor, *The Social World of Batavia: European and Eurasian in Dutch Asia* (Madison: University of Wisconsin Press, 1983), 99.

19. Peter Carey, ed., *The British in Java, 1811–1816: A Javanese Account* (Oxford: Oxford University Press for the British Academy, 1992), 62 n. 135.

20. Ibid., 5–6.

21. These were the *pekojan* (literally, "the area of the Kojahs," from the Persian *chodjah* ["merchant"]).

22. Carey, "Aspects of Javanese History," 55–56.

23. Ibid., 59.

24. Peter Carey, "The Origins of the Java War (1825–30)," *English Historical Review* 91 (January 1976): 52.

25. P. J. F. Louw, *De Java-Oorlog van 1825–30* (Batavia: Landsdrukkerij; The Hague: [Martinus] Nijhoff, 1904), 3: chs. 6–9.

26. Ben White, *"Agricultural Involution" and Its Critics: Twenty Years after Clifford Geertz*, Working Paper series (The Hague: Institute of Social Studies, February 1983).

27. Irawan, "Het Vervoer via de Spoorlijn Semarang-Vorstenlanden als Welvaartsindicator voor de Bevolking in Java's Vorstenlanden (1874–1883)," in F. van Anrooij et al., eds., *Between People and Statistics: Essays in Modern Indonesian History Presented to P. Creutzberg* (The Hague: Martinus Nijhoff, 1979), 61. See also Djoko Suryo, "Social and Economic Life in Rural Semarang in the Later 19th Century" (Ph.D. diss., Monash University, 1982), ch. 3.

28. Suryo, "Social and Economic Life," 135.

THE HISTORICAL BACKGROUND OF BATIK ON JAVA

·

R ENS H ERINGA

The evolution of batik on Java has been a c

ies-long process in which designs and techniques from cultures far beyond the archipelago have blended with a basic Austronesian resist technique. The sophisticated central Javanese form of batik we know today—intricately hand-drawn with the help of a spouted brass wax container, the *canting*—may not have developed until the early seventeenth century.[1] Batik from the Javanese north coast, or Pasisir, the multicolored dress cloths that were commercially produced in workshops run by persons of mixed Indonesian-Chinese, Indonesian-European, or Indonesian-Arabian descent, form part of an even more recent development. This vivid style gradually evolved after the first quarter of the nineteenth century from the red and blue batik cloths tradition-ally made and worn along the Pasisir (FIGURE 14). The process catered mainly to the preferences of the middle and upper strata among a population of mixed ethnic origins.

Early Forms of Resist-Decorated Textiles

The decoration of textiles with a resist technique has probably existed in the archipelago since prehistoric times, although no examples predating the nine-teenth century survive. The origins of these early resist techniques are generally assumed to lie outside the archipelago. Though the suggestion of Chinese roots appears to be most acceptable, where and when the technique appeared in the archipelago remain largely a matter of speculation.[2] Several methods are known. A variety of materials or substances can either be applied to the unwoven yarn, as in *ikat*, or to a finished base cloth. The batik technique, in which vegetable paste or wax have been used as the

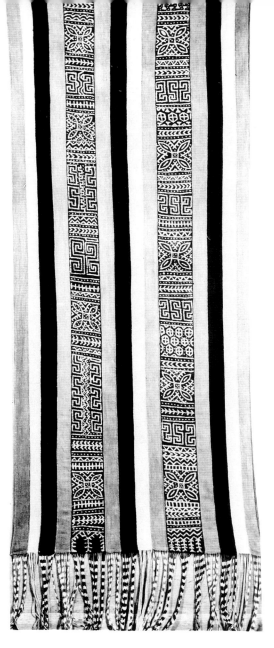

resist, belongs to the second type.[3] In earlier times fibers such as barkcloth and cloth woven out of hemp or abaca were decorated in this manner as were mats and pottery. Painted or printed, wax-resist-decorated nineteenth-century objects from all over the archipelago are present in museum collections.[4] Among these are long ceremonial banners from the island of Sulawesi (Celebes) (FIGURE 15).

Knowledge of the terms by which the technique was known on Java is equally limited. The Javanese term *bathik* was not encountered in written sources until the early seventeenth century.[5] It is, however, related to Old Javanese *thika*, which means writing, drawing, painting, and by inference, anything enhanced by writing, drawing, painting. The Old Javanese compound *tulis thika* stands for writings or drawings.[6] In modern Javanese the term *tulis*, or its verb form, *'nulis*, is used for writing and also for drawing or painting designs. Synonymous with *'mbathik*, the term also serves to denote the making of hand-drawn batik in Ngoko, the low level of spoken Javanese.[7] The proto-Austronesian lexeme *beCik*, which Robert Blust translates as "to tattoo," suggests a tantalizing link between body tattoo and batik.[8] The Indonesian tendency to relate two similar sounding terms in symbolic association may have been of influence in this respect. Whatever the case may be, a correspondence between the designs found in body decorations and textile patterns is a common feature of many Southeast Asian cultures.[9] Moreover, both types of decoration serve to denote a person's identity.

Several examples of the early techniques survive. Around 1900 Sundanese women still made a cere-monial cloth known as *kain simbut* (blanket or covering) in a technique referred to as *nulis*.[10] After undergoing an extensive preparatory process, a handwoven, white cotton cloth was dipped in a fixative and ornamented with a paste made of sticky rice and sugar water. This resist was either applied with a bamboo stick or merely drawn on with a finger. Subsequently, red or blue natural dyes were rubbed into the cloth. Upon removal of the resist, the simple motifs appeared off-white on a colored ground (FIGURE 16). The cloth formed part of a bride's dowry and played an important role during life-cycle ceremonies.[11] A present-day example that evolved as an intermediate form is the *batik-lurik* cloth from the Tuban area: waxed clusters of dots form small, geometrical units on the grid of a checked, handwoven cotton base cloth, or

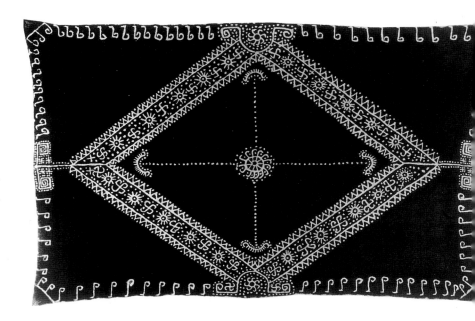

FIGURE 17
Waxing a *batik-lurik* cloth,
Tuban, 1978.
Photograph, Theo Vlaar

FIGURE 18
Hip wrapper, *kain panjang*
(detail) Java, Tuban, 1989
Hand-drawn wax resist on
handwoven cotton *lurik* base;
synthetic dyes
Koninklijk Instituut voor
Taal-, Land- en Volkenkunde

lurik. Although the motifs are executed with the *canting* (FIGURE 17), a bamboo stick would serve equally well.[12] The same holds for some of the motifs that are specific for the batik cloths from Jambi, on the east coast of Sumatra.[13]

The simple motifs that occur on the *kain simbut*, the *batik-lurik* cloths, and the batik cloths from Jambi are also encountered on a variety of objects that were made throughout South and Southeast Asia from neolithic times (FIGURE 18). Similar designs are found on the indigo-dyed stick batiks, called *laran*, made by many of the ethnic minorities of southwest China[14] as well as on batik clothing made by ethnic groups living in the mountainous areas of northern Thailand, Laos, and Burma.[15] While this type of motif has often been attributed to the Dongson art style, it may be more appropriately considered part of a cultural substratum common to the South Asian mainland and the archipelago.[16]

Mythical and Historical Origins

Little is known regarding the development of these ancient resist forms and their simple motifs into the elaborate Javanese batik technique with its complex flowing designs. Research on references to batik technique, motifs, or dress styles in the vast body of Javanese manuscripts has rarely been undertaken. According to Islamic precepts, knowledge regarding the deeper meaning of art is attributed to men and therefore inventing meaningful designs is their role. Moreover, according to Javanese concepts, the manufacture of textiles, a female task, was considered unworthy of description in written texts,

again, the province of men.[17] Nevertheless, an Islamic didactic treatise, probably written by a male author, does present the steps of weaving and the making of batik as a metaphor for the spiritual maturation of a woman.[18]

One Javanese myth dates the origin of batik on Java to the reign of the legendary Lembu Amiluhur, prince of the east coast region of Janggala, near Surabaya. His bride, a princess from the Coromandel coast of India, and her Hindu retinue are credited with teaching the arts of weaving, batik, and the dyeing of cloth to the Javanese. This reputedly occurred around A.D. 700 and continued during the reign of his son, Prince Panji Ima Kerta Pati.[19] The first dated source (A.D. 1518) possibly mentioning batik cloth is a pre-Islamic Sundanese manuscript from the polity of Galuh in northwest Java; it contains a short list of textile types, a few of which can be recognized

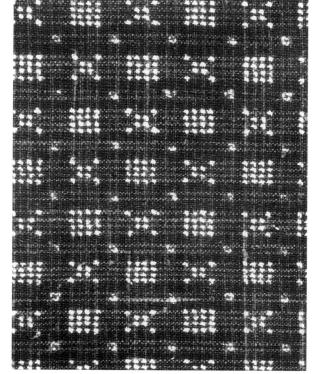

as present-day names of batik patterns.[20] Despite a gap of many centuries between the myth and the manuscript, both are related to the period prior to the establishment of Islam on Java and concern areas that are located near the Pasisir. The series of romances in which the wandering Prince Panji is the protagonist probably originated during the heyday of the Pasisir kingdoms.[21] During this period, between the twelfth and the mid-seventeenth centuries, Pasisir culture is known to have assimilated elements that were introduced by Indian, Persian, and Chinese immigrants. Wax-resist textiles imported from the Coromandel coast and possibly from Persia have much in common visually with traditional Pasisir cloths, in particular their size and format. Persian and Indian motifs, specifically those such as the carnation that suited Javanese symbolic

concepts, were incorporated into the design repertoire of Javanese textiles. There is, however, abundant proof that the imported cloths were *Indiennes de commande*, that is, the buyers indicated stringent preferences regarding size, format, color, and motif, without which the cloths could not be sold.[22] Moreover, the sizes and formats meant for export to the archipelago were never worn in India.[23] It seems logical that the imported piece goods followed the appearance of locally made Javanese textiles as closely as possible. The working methods of the Coromandel coast (in which the cloth is only patterned on one side; FIGURE 19) differs in too many details from the Javanese batik process to accept an Indian origin. The same principle holds for the Persian *kalamkari* block-printing process.[24]

Legends also recount the origins of specific motifs that in a later period came to be the prerogative of the rulers of the central Javanese Principalities. While an early legend ascribes the survival of Prince Panji to the protective power of the *parang*

rusak (jagged, rocky outcrop or broken dagger) motif, a later myth recounts how Sultan Agung, first Muslim ruler of Mataram (r. 1613–45), created the same design after contemplation of the jagged rocks of the south coast (FIGURE 20).[25] It was also Sultan Agung who, on his pilgrimage to Mecca, reputedly received the inspiration for the pattern *sembagen buk* (FIGURE 21); the *buk*, or Chinese mythical bird of good fortune, which descended from heaven contained in an egg, served as model for the motif drawn on the cloth in which the sultan kept his *jimat semail* (an amulet that often contained the Islamic profession of faith [*Sahadat*]).[26] Although confusing, the stories may reverberate faint echoes of the time and place of the origin of batik on Java. The somewhat incongruous *buk* in the central Javanese Islamic tale may refer to the role played by fifteenth-century Chinese settlers on the Pasisir in the dissemination of Islam. The possibility that the same immigrants from south China contributed to the development of the batik technique appears quite likely.[27] Women belonging to minority peo-

FIGURE 19
Tapih cinde
front and back (detail)
India, Coromandel coast,
late eighteenth-early
nineteenth century
Hand-drawn wax resist
on cotton; natural dyes
From G. P. Rouffaer
and H. H. Juynboll,
*De batik-kunst in Nederlandsch
Indië and haar geschiedenis*,
vol. 2
(Utrecht: A. Oosthoek,
1904).

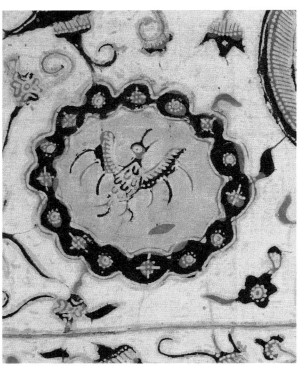

FIGURE 20
Hip wrapper (detail)
Java, Yogyakarta,
early twentieth century
Hand-drawn wax resist on
machine-woven cotton;
natural dyes
104.8 x 228.6 cm
(41 1/4 x 90 in.)
Los Angeles County
Museum of Art,
Costume Council and
Museum Associates purchase
M.77.110.2

FIGURE 21
Hip wrapper (detail)
Java, Lasem, c. 1880
Catalogue no. 8
Sembagen buk in Pasisir style.

ples in south and southwest China have decorated their hemp and cotton cloths with a wax-resist technique quite similar to the Javanese method from the Ming period to the present day.[28] Although some of the batik motifs of flowers and birds from these areas illustrated in blue and white in a recent Chinese source show an interesting similarity to traditional Pasisir patterns, further corroboration is needed.[29]

Colonial Influences

Documents of the United East India Company (VOC) dating to the seventeenth and eighteenth centuries give only sparse information on Javanese textiles. An early Dutch travel account dating to 1599 nevertheless presents a fairly balanced picture of the range of textiles traded in the market of the then important port of Tuban. Besides a variety of textiles from India and China, undefined types of locally made cloth are listed.[30] However, once the Dutch became actively involved in the trade during the seventeenth century, only imported textiles figure in the shipping documents. A variety of *custcleeden* (coastal cloths), woven, painted, and printed textiles from India, had functioned since at least the fifteenth century and possibly much earlier as the mainstay in the barter for spices from the Moluccas.[31] Three types that were traded throughout the archipelago are mentioned most often. First are the multicolored, painted or printed cotton cloths, the geometrically patterned *tapih cinde* (see FIGURE 58) and the flowered *tapih sarasa* from Coromandel (FIGURE 5).[32] Less frequently listed is the inspiration for their motifs, color, size, and format, the luxurious double-ikat silk cloth, the *patola*, from Gujarat. Cloth made on Java is not mentioned again until the middle of the eighteenth century, when the Javanese reacted to the

FIGURE 22
Hip wrapper (detail)
Java, Yogyakarta, 1930s
Hand-drawn wax resist
on machine-woven cotton;
natural dyes
105.1 x 276 cm
(41 3/8 x 108 3/8 in.)
Los Angeles County
Museum of Art,
gift of Sylvia, Nanies,
and Gordon Bishop,
M.77.97

inflated prices of imported fabrics with an increase in textile production of their own.[33] Information about the areas in which this development took place and whether batik formed part of it is not clearly given. Nevertheless, J. C. van Leur asserts that "the large local...weaving crafts supplying cloth for the weavers and their families...went on unchanged" during this period.[34]

After the demise of Indian imports at the end of the eighteenth century, colonial records at last pay attention to textiles manufactured in Java. Initially these continued to be considered primarily as commercial goods, in total disregard of their actual function. It is not until the last decades of the nineteenth century that European scholars and officials gave thought to the cultural role of batik and its possible origin. Excessive contemporary stress on a Hindu, and thus Indian, inspiration for everything Javanese gave rise to new distortions. "Batik art" was presented as having originated as an aristocratic pastime of the women at the central Javanese courts of Yogyakarta and Surakarta. The "native craft" made by village women elsewhere on Java had supposedly trickled down from the courts, to be produced merely for profit.[35] These views largely ignored the decisive influence of the Chinese and the role of local village women on the Pasisir.[36] In fact, the batik technique probably did not move inland until the mid-seventeenth century, with the adoption of Pasisir culture by the developing Mataram sultanate. Reputedly during the period when the court was established in the town of Kartasura (1680–1745), colors and motifs were modified gradually into the more subdued court style of central Java (FIGURE 22). Its descendants, the finely wrought batik cloths of Yogyakarta and particularly those of Surakarta, have been considered the pinnacle of artistic expression ever since, for a long time almost obscuring all other varieties.

Early Pasisir Traditions

Early Pasisir batik probably consisted of an amalgam of local and foreign elements, which gradually developed into the bright red and blue batiks that defined Pasisir dress in the early nineteenth century. A first, short description by Thomas Stamford Raffles of traditional Pasisir style of Javanese "batek or painted cloth" dates to 1817. He describes the cloth as having a red or blue-black ground with white motifs or a white ground with colored motifs. He also asserts that "men of all ranks are accustomed to pride themselves on the beauty of a cloth" made by their "wife, mistress or daughter".[37] A single contemporary example of the old method was encountered during fieldwork undertaken in an isolated group of villages near Tuban in 1977.[38] Three generations of women lived together in a compound, uniting in a communal effort to weave and decorate the cotton cloths used by their families. Each generation contributed to the work according to her stage in life. The initial sequence of tasks, such as spinning, warping, and weaving the plain base cloth, was executed by the oldest generation. "Bringing the cloths to life" by drawing the identifying motifs in hot wax was restricted to married women in their reproductive years (FIGURE 23). Young girls were slowly initiated into the various processes. The final procedure, applying color, was assigned to a family of female dyers, who guarded their hereditary, sacred knowledge of the use of natural-dye ingredients (FIGURE 24).

In this original division of labor the manufacture of batik is deeply embedded in the social structure of the community. A limited range of motifs and colors is directly related to a particular group of people who have the right to make and also wear them. Maker and wearer are linked through family relationships. Textiles that are made according to the traditional prescripts are rarely sold on the open market. In the course of the nineteenth century this limited method of production gradually changed all over Java into a commercial system. Waxing batik became a marketable skill, and the original family relationship between maker and wearer developed into a business connection.

FIGURE 23
A married village woman applying hot wax to cotton, drawing birds and flowers from memory,
Tuban, 1978.
Photograph, Theo Vlaar

FIGURE 24
The elder dyer in charge of the indigo vat, Tuban, 1978; of all the women in the village, only she is permitted to handle the sacred blue dye.
Photograph, Theo Vlaar

NOTES

1. Robyn Maxwell, *Textiles of Southeast Asia: Tradition, Trade and Transformation* (Canberra: Australian National Gallery; Oxford: Oxford University Press, 1990), 241.

2. On the basis of Japanese sources from the seventh and eight centuries, it is known that resist-decorated cloths, made by non-Chinese peoples at an unspecified location in China, were brought to Japan (Mattiebelle Gittinger, "Sier en symbool: De costuums van de ethnische minderheden in Zuid- en Zuidwest China," in *Indigo: Leven in een kleur,* ed., Loan Oei [Weesp: Fibula-van Dishoeck, 1985], 163).

3. Two other well-known resist techniques on ready-made cloth are *plangi,* a tie-and-dye technique, and *tritik,* where threads stitched into the fabric serve as the resist.

4. Maxwell, *Textiles of Southeast Asia,* 142, 345, 241; Bronwen Solyom and Garrett Solyom, *Fabric Traditions of Indonesia,* exh. cat. (Pullman, Washington: Museum of Art and Washington State University Press, 1984), 38, 39; Robert J. Holmgren and Anita E. Spertus, *Early Indonesian Textiles from Three Island Cultures: Sumba, Toraja, Lampung,* exh. cat. (New York: Metropolitan Museum of Art, 1989), 51, 52, 54; J. W. van Nouhuys, "Was batik in Midden-Celebes," *Nederlandsch- Indië Oud en Nieuw* 10 (1925–26).

5. G. P. Rouffaer and H. H. Juynboll, *De batik-kunst in Nederlandsch Indië and haar geschiedenis* (Utrecht: A. Oosthoek 1914), 427.

6. P. J. Zoetmulder and S. O. Robson, *Old Javanese-English Dictionary* (The Hague: Martinus Nijhoff, 1982), s.v. "tulis thika." Other explanations of the term have generally and mistakenly been based on the suggestion that the roots *thik* and *tik* are similar and that both translate as "dot(ting)" (G. P. Rouffaer, *Over Indische batikkunst, vooral die op Java* [Haarlem, 1900], 3). A linguistic connection between *thik* and *tik* must in any case be excluded. Moreover, Malay *titik* does indeed mean dot, drop, or point, but Javanese *titik* signifies sign or trace.

7. In *Krama,* the high level of Javanese, the term *serat* or *nyerat* is used.

8. Robert Blust, "Austronesian Culture History: Some Linguistic Inferences and Their Relations to the Archeological Record," in *Prehistoric Indonesia: A Reader,* ed., P. van de Velde (Dordrecht: Foris 1984), 220.

9. Maxwell, *Textiles of Southeast Asia,* 110.

10. Alit Veldhuisen-Djajasoebrata, *Bloemen van het heelal: De kleurrijke wereld van de textiel op Java* (Amsterdam: Sijthof; Rotterdam: Museum voor Volkenkunde, 1984), 51.

11. C. M. Pleyte, *De inlandsche nijverheid in West Java als sociaal-ethnologisch verschijnsel* (Batavia: Javasche boekhandel en drukkerij, 1912), 88–90.

12. Rens Heringa, "Textiles and the Social Fabric on Northeast Java," in *Indonesian Textiles: Symposium 1985,* eds., Gisela Völger and Karin von Welck, vol. 14 of *Ethnologica* (Cologne: Rautenstrauch-Joest Museum, 1991), 47–49.

13. Rens Heringa, *Een schitterende geschiedenis: Weefsels en batiks van Palembang en Djambi,* exh. cat. (The Hague: Museon, 1993), 25.

14. Gittinger, "Sier en symbool," 163–68.

15. Maxwell, *Textiles of Southeast Asia,* 240.

16. Ibid., 241. The Dongson style takes its name from archeological sites in northern Vietnam and dates to approximately the seventh century B.C.

17. Th. G. Th. Pigeaud, *Synopsis of Javanese Literature 900–1900 A.D.,* vol. 1 of *Literature of Java: Catalogue Raisonné of Javanese Manuscripts in the Library of the University of Leiden and Other Public Collections in The Netherlands* (The Hague: Martinus Nijhoff 1967), 290.

18. Astuti Darmosugito Hendrato, "Batik dalam kehidupan kita," in *Sekaring Jagad Ngayogyakarta Hadiningrat* (Jakarta: Wastraprema, Himpunan Pencinta Kain Batik dan Tenun, 1990), 21–30. The date of the manuscript, the *Suluk Pangolahing Sandhang Pangan,* is not mentioned.

19. J. V. J. Baak, "Nota van toelichting in zake verslag kunstnijverheid der Javaansche bevolking," *Tijdschrift voor Nijverheid en Landbouw van Nederlandsch Indië* 44 (1892): 2. The author does not mention the source of this tale.

20. G. P. Rouffaer, "Beeldende kunst in Nederlandsch Indië," *Bijdragen van het Koninklijk Instituut voor Taal-, Land- en Volkenkunde van Nederlandsch-Indië* 89 (1932): 639. As K. F. Holle ("Vlugtig Berigt omtrent eenige Lontar Handschriften, afkomstig uit de Soenda-Landen," *Tijdschrift voor Indische Taal-, Land- en Volkenkunde uitgegeven door het Koninklijk Bataviaasch Genootschap van Kunsten en Wetenschappen* 16 [1867]: 453–61) in his partial translation of the original palm leaf manuscript does not mention the terms used for batik or sorts of batik, Rouffaer's conclusion needs further research. The list may, in fact, contain various textile types decorated in resist techniques other than batik.

21. Denys Lombard, *Le Carrefour Javanais: Essai d'histoire globale* (Paris: Editions de l'Ecole des Hautes Etudes en Sciences Sociales, 1990), 2: 134.

22. Mattiebelle Gittinger, *Master Dyers to the World: Technique and Trade in Early Indian Dyed Cotton Textiles,* exh. cat. (Washington D.C.: Textile Museum, 1982), 137.

23. Heringa, *Een schitterende geschiedenis,* 14.

24. Rouffaer, *Over Indische batikkunst,* 2, 3. Nevertheless, the Indian import cloths have been denoted mistakenly as "batiks" for almost a century. See, for instance, B. Schrieke, *Indonesian Sociological Studies* (The Hague and Bandung: W. van Hoeve, 1966) 2: 22.

25. J. E. Jasper and Mas Pirngadie, *De batikkunst,* vol. 3 of *De inlandsche kunstnijverheid in Nederlandsch Indië* (The Hague: Mouton, 1916), 155.

26. The *jimat semail,* a special amulet, is in this case probably the *kalimat busada,* the text of the *Sahadat* written on a small piece of paper.

27. Lombard, *Le Carrefour Javanais,* 2: 271.

28. Gittinger, "Sier en symbool," 163.

29. Lu Pu, *Designs of Chinese Indigo Batik* (New York: Lee Publishing Group; Beijing: New World Press, 1981).

30. J. Keuning, *De tweede schipvaart der Nederlanders naar Oost-Indië onder Jacob Cornelisz van Neck en Wybrandt Warwijck 1598–1600* (The Hague: Linschoten Vereeniging, 1938–51) 42, no. 3: 34–40.

31. Dutch: *custcleeden,* textiles from the coasts of India.

32. Javanese: *tapi-tapih,* hip wrapper. Thus, the trade terms *tapih cinde,* hip wrapper with *cinde,* or geometrical, motifs; *tapih sarasa,* hip wrapper with floral motifs.

33. Schrieke, *Indonesian Sociological Studies,* 1: 235; M. C. Ricklefs, *A History of Modern Indonesia since c. 1300,* 2d rev. ed. (London: MacMillan, 1993), 81.

34. J. C. van Leur, *Indonesian Trade and Society: Essays in Asian Social and Economic History* (1955; reprint, Dordrecht: Foris Publications, 1983), 211, 379.

35. Dutch: *batik-kunst* (batik art) and *inlandsche kunstnijverheid* (native craft); note the titles of the two main publications of the period: *De batik-kunst in Nederlandsch Indië and haar geschiedenis* (The batik art in the Netherlands Indies and its history) and *De inlandsche kunstnijverheid in Nederlandsch Indië* (The native crafts in the Netherlands Indies).

36. This may have been due to the general bias regarding the Chinese contributions to Javanese culture after the mid-eighteenth-century Chinese revolt.

37. Thomas Stamford Raffles, *The History of Java* (1817; reprint, Kuala Lumpur: Oxford University Press, 1978), 1: 87, 168–69.

38. See Rens Heringa, "Dye Process and Life Sequence: The Coloring of Textiles in an East Javanese Village," in *To Speak with Cloth: Studies in Indonesian Textiles,* ed. Mattiebelle Gittinger (Los Angeles: Museum of Cultural History, University of California, Los Angeles, 1989), 107–30; idem., "Tilling the Cloth and Weaving the Land: Textiles, Land and Regeneration in an East Javanese Area," in *Weaving Patterns of Life: Indonesian Textile Symposium* (1991), eds., Marie-Louise Nabholz-Kartaschoff et al. (Basel: Museum of Ethnography, 1993), 155–76; idem., *Spiegels van ruimte en tijd,* exh. cat. (The Hague: Museon, 1994), for an extensive description and analysis.

FROM HOME CRAFT
TO BATIK INDUSTRY

·

Harmen C. Veldhuisen

By the end of the eighteenth century the exp

Translated by Rosemary Robson

painted and block-printed Indian textiles had declined
dramatically as a result of the rise of the competitive
European printed-textile industry. Hand-drawn
batik tulis from the north coast of Java gradually
replaced the coveted Indian imports throughout the
Indonesian archipelago. Peranakan Chinese traders
were the most active in organizing batik production
and sale. Even prior to 1800 their influence was
being felt on the economic organization of the villages of the north coast, where they had purchased
the right to collect taxes for the United East India
Company (VOC).[1] As traders in white cotton cloth
and the various components of batik making, they
established contacts in even the smallest and most
isolated villages, where they also fulfilled the role
of moneylenders.

Hip wrapper (detail)
Java, Lasem, Kudus, and
Surakarta, c. 1900–1910
Catalogue no. 13

The women who used to make batik at home
for family use began to produce for these traders.
As a result, the first batiks bought by traders were
those with patterns applied by the batik maker for
her own use. Soon, however, the traders ordered
motifs that met the desires of their customers. It is
therefore reasonable to conclude that the traders
were showing samples of desirable patterns and colors to the batik makers.

Traditionally making batik was seasonal work;
most women were also involved in sowing and har-
vesting as well as domestic chores. In order to meet
the rising demand for batiks, these traders introduced a system of advance payments to encourage
makers to increase the volume of their production.[2]
The advances carried with them stipulated deadlines,

and these transformed a home craft to a home industry, and for many women batik became a profession.

The Rise of the Entrepreneur

The first steps toward an entrepreneurial mode of production were taken when the Peranakan traders began to buy up fabrics drawn with wax, but not yet dyed (FIGURE 25). These were later dyed in the backyards of their own homes. From ancient times in Java dyeing had been women's work, and the wife of the trader had her own recipes for vegetable dyes.

the fact that very often her work was located quite a distance from her home, in many cases a walk of an hour and half each way.

The first centers of commercial batik developed in the vicinity of the three large port cities: Batavia (Jakarta), Semarang, and Surabaya. These cities possessed two essential factors necessary for the rise of the commercial batik industry: proximity to affluent consumers and harbors for exports to urban centers on Java and the islands beyond. In addition, clean, running water, indispensable to both the preparatory treatment of the cotton fabric and the use of vegetable dyes, was readily available in nearby rivers. Batik workshops, established subsequently in other cities, were also located close to rivers.

By 1850 Pekalongan, a small port city in central Java, was already an important batik center.[3] Besides Peranakan and Indo-Arabian workshops, around 1860 Indo-European women began establishing batik businesses there too. In many instances these were women who found themselves in financial difficulties. As the wives of low-ranking civil servants or young widows with numerous children,

FIGURE 25 (left) A trader (right) examines waxed but undyed *sarung*, Batavia (?), c. 1930. From P. de Kat Angelino, *Batikrapport* (Batavia: Landsdrukkerij, 1930–31).

During the first quarter of the nineteenth century she continued to prepare the dyes, but the arduous tasks of simultaneously dyeing a number of cloths was taken over by a hired dyer (FIGURE 26). By the second quarter of the century the entrepreneurial method of production was assumed by Indo-European women. (Indeed, along the Pasisir the Indo-European entrepreneurs were exclusively female.) The system of advances had shown that women were prepared to go to work for wages, especially when their families found themselves in dire straits as the result of crop failures. It was only such pressing needs that would force a woman to seek work outside her village community, which was rendered even more difficult by

they were able to maintain themselves within the European community with the money they made from their batik workshops. The alternative was a forced retreat to the *kampung* (native quarters). For

FIGURE 26 Batiks in large quantity are dyed in tanks by male workers, Batavia (?), c. 1930. From P. de Kat Angelino, *Batikrapport* (Batavia: Landsdrukkerij, 1930–31).

many Indo-Europeans who aspired to acceptance within the European community this was an ever-present concern.

Although commercial batik production was organized into workshops operated by both male and female entrepreneurs, work itself was divided by gender: men did the preparatory treatment of the white cotton cloth, while women, working from a range of patterns supplied by the entrepreneur, copied the patterns as precisely as possible in wax on cloth (FIGURE 27); men did the dyeing. The entrepreneur (FIGURE 28) designed the patterns; kept an eye on the rate of daily production, the consumption of wax, and the quality of the work, imposing fines for spilling wax or for irregularities in drawing; and was responsible for sales. In the larger workshops, which catered to a variety of clientele, batiks suitable for

Even during the time batiks were made at home, there was a division of labor among grand-mothers, mothers, and unmarried daughters.[4] In the batik workshops, however, the division of labor depended, not on social position, but on skill. The most experienced women were given the task of applying the main design. Others were entrusted with the tiny filler motifs, and those with the least experience waxed the areas of the cloth that were not to be exposed to dye. Casual labor was taken on during peak periods such as the celebration of the rice harvest or the end of Ramadan, the principal occasions when people bought new batiks. This casual labor was also assigned tasks according to their skills.

Because of their constant supervision and specialization the Indo-European entrepreneurs

FIGURE 27 (above)
Women using the *canting* wax the same design on numerous batiks, Pasisir, c. 1915. From J. D. Daubanton, *Beknopte beschrijving van de batik-industrie of Java* (Rotterdam: Internationale crediet- en handels-vereeniging Rotterdam, 1922).

FIGURE 28
Batik entrepreneur Tee Boen Kee and his work-shop, Batavia, c. 1930. From P. de Kat Angelino, *Batikrapport* (Batavia: Landsdrukkerij, 1930–31).

different ethnic groups could be worked on simulta-neously. Because of the handwork involved in the production process, the *batik tulis* industry was never one of mass production. Women who made batik for their private use repeated traditional local patterns. By contrast, the entrepreneurs were sensitive to their clients' desires for new designs. They even initiated changes for the purpose of enticing new orders. Entrepreneurs who wanted to expand their share of the market were the trendsetters in altering layouts, patterns, and color ranges. Success was measured largely by the speed with which rivals adopted popu-lar changes. Over time this resulted in entirely new batik creations.

were able to produce work of the highest quality at the lowest cost. Their example was followed by the Peranakan and Indo-Arabian entrepreneurs. It was the Peranakan entrepreneurs in the north coast towns of Lasem and Rembang, however, who introduced a change in working relationships. By manipulating the system of advances, they constrained their workers not only to work but also to live in their compounds in order to augment pro-duction. In many cases this led to a state of chronic indebtedness.[5]

Peranakan traders and batik entrepreneurs formed a widespread network of family and commer-cial relations, which put them a unique position to judge the quality and compare the cost of waxing and dyeing in various batik centers. They often acted as middlemen as well for batiks made elsewhere by relatives. They exchanged textiles in order to offer a wider variety of merchandise. About the middle of last century Peranakan traders in central Java began to buy up *kain panjang* (long cloths) drawn with wax but as yet undyed in the cheapest production centers for shipment to other locations where dyeing was similarly economical. Should the desired color scheme be blue and brown, for example, they transported the waxed batiks twice, first to a place where they could be dyed blue and next to another where they could be dyed brown.[6] In this way they succeeded in bringing a relatively inexpensive product to the market.

This system was used in the production of *sarung* known as *kain dua negeri*, cloth dyed in two different batik centers. Red would be applied to the *kepala* (head panel) and borders on the north coast (frequently in Semarang during the second half of the nineteenth century, then in Pekalongan at the beginning of this century, after the railway had been built and *batik Pekalongan* had gained in popularity). The red pattern having been protected with a second coating of wax, the *badan* (main field) was given its pattern of blue and brown in the Principalities.

Kain tiga negeri (chapter frontispiece) was made in three different production centers and was, by contrast with *kain dua negeri*, a relatively expensive product. It was likewise the outcome of reciprocal Peranakan contacts. The entrepreneur who started the batik was the owner of the cloth and often applied his or her name stamp. In this case the emphasis was not on saving money but on utilizing the very best craftsmanship available in the batik centers on the north coast and in the Principalities. The main pattern was applied in red in Lasem. Parts of this and the background were provided with congruent filler motifs in blue in either Kudus or Demak. Finally the remaining parts of the main pattern along with the background were dyed in *soga* brown, a vegetable dye commonly used in Yogyakarta and Surakarta.

The Introduction of the Copper Stamp

From the inception of commercial batik production the rising demand for *batik tulis* could not be met. Consequently, in the first half of the nineteenth century a growing market developed for imitation batiks, which were printed in Europe. This stimulated a search for new techniques to speed up the waxing process.[7] After a great deal of experimentation, for example, stamps were made of sweet potato, into which patterns were etched. In a subsequent development a stamp of iron pins set into a wooden base was used to transfer a waxed pattern to the cloth. Finally the copper stamp, or *cap*, was developed, probably in the Principalities, around 1840–50 (FIGURE 29).[8] Various data support this. When interviews were conducted in the Principalities in 1927, informants seemed to know about the precursors of the *cap*, a knowledge handed down by tradition.[9] The middle of the nineteenth century was a period in which a great deal of *batik tulis* was produced in the Principalities for export via Semarang and Surabaya and for the batik market in Bandung in west Java. The *kain panjang* of the Principalities were patterned with an all-over repeat. The *cap* was excellently suited to printing such repetitive patterns in wax directly onto cloth, reducing the time required for this process from several weeks to several hours. All that was needed were two such stamps (mirror images of each other): one for the front and one for the back. A great many more stamps were required to make a *sarung* than a *kain panjang*; in addition to stamps for the *badan*, various others were needed for the *kepala* and borders. As their manufacture was labor intensive, stamps made by Peranakan stamp makers represented a significant cost factor; therefore, they were only economically viable if a large number of *sarung* was to be produced at one time. This number could not exceed about two hundred, however, because of wear and tear on the stamp.

There is a reference to the *cap* in use in Pekalongan in 1859.[10] There, just as in the Principalities, batik production existed on a large scale, thus making Pekalongan a logical place for the use of stamps to occur shortly after being developed in central Java. In all cases stamping was carried out by men as seasonal work (see Appendix 3).

FIGURE 29
Stamp makers, Batavia (?),
c. 1930.
From P. de Kat Angelino,
Batikrapport (Batavia:
Landsdrukkerij, 1930–31).

Cotton

The determining cost in the batik industry was that of machine-woven, white cotton cloth. At the beginning of the nineteenth century such yardage had been imported from England, but by about 1840 the best-quality cloth came directly from the Netherlands, where the cotton industry, in part due to the intervention of King William I, had commenced production,[11] using raw cotton imported from North America. When the supply was interrupted by the outbreak of the American Civil War (1861–65) and the North's blockade of the South, prices for cotton cloth soared. To cash in on the rising prices, the producers of *batik cap* increased their production, exhausting their stocks of fabric. Unfortunately, in their haste they saturated the market, and many of the smaller entrepreneurs were forced into bankruptcy. (The bigger entrepreneurs continued to exist on other sources of income, such as money lending and trade.) When the import of cotton cloth resumed after 1865, the prices of batiks plummeted, and once again many entrepreneurs, now including the makers of *batik tulis* who were forced to sell finished wares at less than the price they'd paid for cotton, suffered financial disaster.[12]

The Golden Age of Batik Pasisir

The commercial batik industry experienced its greatest success between 1890 and 1910. Between 1860 and 1890 a number of changes occurred in Java which led to this renaissance. With improvements in health care the population of Java and the other islands of the Indonesian archipelago rose. Simultaneous growth of trade and industry gave all people increased purchasing power. After the opening of the Suez Canal in 1869, an event that was contemporaneous with the development of steamships, the number of Europeans who settled in the Indies, among them a large contingent of women, swelled. The introduction of steamships also meant that exports to the other islands, as well as to Burma, Cambodia, Malaysia, Singapore, and Thailand, grew apace. In Java itself the building of the rail network during the final three decades of the nineteenth century meant that commercial batik could be introduced into hitherto isolated areas.[13] Finally, the idea of fashion, which in the West had encouraged consumers to cast off wearable items, was introduced into Java by European women at the end of the nineteenth century.

One city in particular was especially influential in the spread of batik designs during this period. Bandung, the capital of the Sunda region in the southwestern portion of the island, acquired a reputation as the Paris of Java. The coffee and tea plantations there made Sunda relatively well-to-do, and Sundanese women were prepared to spend lavishly on their clothing. When rail links were established in 1894, Bandung became the center of the batik trade, the place where fashions were introduced. The large-scale traders from outside Java naturally maintained agents in the important batik centers along the north coast and the Principalities, but it was Bandung that offered an overview of batik output. Up to about the turn of the century the batiks traded there came mainly from the Principalities, but after about 1900 *batik Pekalongan* (batik made in Pekalongan for Java and export) grew in favor.[14]

Designs that were in demand in Bandung were copied in other batik centers along the Pasisir. This was not particularly easy to accomplish, especially in the matter of the small filler motifs, as every center had its own style. This difficulty spurred entrepreneurs to adopt another strategy: "poaching" batik makers from trendsetting centers. For example, at the beginning of this century there was widespread demand in Bandung for Indo-European–style batik from Banyumas, in central Java. Sundanese batik entrepreneurs from Ciamis and Tasikmalaya enticed batik makers from Banyumas away from their employers by offering them higher wages and then paying off their advances.[15]

World War I had an enormous influence on the batik industry. The import of white cotton cloth from the Netherlands was interrupted, and the price of batiks began to climb. Once again this led to a cycle of overproduction followed by bankruptcies. The import of cotton cloth resumed after the armistice in 1918, but the recovery in the batik industry was only temporary. Following a brief revival, the *batik cap* industry suffered a severe relapse induced by the Depression. The wearing of *batik tulis* had become the exception rather than the rule among the European section of the population, and only those entrepreneurs whose batiks catered to the taste of wealthy Peranakan consumers survived.

After World War I the batik industry was caught in a downward spiral,[16] and after 1925 even the market for imitation batik *sarung* and *kain panjang* printed in the Netherlands, disappeared (the demand for head cloths lingered until 1933).[17] This decline unleashed rigorous competition in the labor market. Many batik workers found themselves without employment. Thanks to rail links along the north coast, women who were prepared to work for lower wages than local batik makers were brought in from other locations.

Deprived of their incomes, some of the younger batik makers turned to prostitution. Even among those who had been hired elsewhere, prostitution became a supplement for the pittance they were paid. This exacerbated the rivalry between locals and out-of-towners.[18] A further result of this mingling of batik makers was the mingling of characteristics of local batik styles along the north coast, a trend toward standardization that had actually begun toward the end of the nineteenth century with the emergence of Bandung as a fashion center.

The batiks made during the Japanese occupation (1942–45) were given the name *Djawa Hokokai*, derived from the name of the Javanese Service Association, a propaganda tool of the army of occupation. These batiks were made by the Indo-European, Peranakan, and Indo-Arabian entrepreneurs who were obliged to work for the Japanese because of the highly esteemed quality of their craftsmanship. The cotton cloth was provided from supplies requisitioned by the occupiers.

The *kain panjang* from this period display a crowded floral background. This new style, previously believed to have been introduced by and for the Japanese, in fact, had appeared a few years earlier. A group of batiks was made by two Peranakan batik workshops in Kudus and Solo working in cooperation about 1940.[19] These also feature the repeated bouquet against an extremely crowded background and were known as *buketan Semarangan*, intended for sale to well-to-do Peranakan women in Semarang.

After independence in 1945 the batik industry struggled slowly to its feet, but it never again reached the production levels it had enjoyed during its heyday. *Batik tulis* remains the privilege of the happy few in Indonesia.

NOTES

1. D. H. Burger, *De ontsluiting van Java's binnenland voor het wereldverkeer* (Wageningen: H. Veenman & Zonen, 1939), 15–20.

2. D. H. Burger, *Sociologische-economische geschiedenis van Indonesia* (Amsterdam: Koninklijk Instituut voor de Tropen, 1975) 1: 4, 60, 83, 131.

3. P. de Kat Angelino, *Batikrapport* (Batavia: Landsdrukkerij, 1930–31), 2: 211.

4. Rens Heringa, "Tilling the Cloth and Weaving the Land," in *Weaving Patterns of Life: Indonesian Textile Symposium* (1991), eds., Marie-Louise Nabholz-Kartaschoff et al. (Basel: Museum of Ethnography, 1993), 162–64.

5. Burger, *De ontsluiting van Java's binnenland*, 23–25.

6. On the Pasisir waxing was done prior to the application of each color; after a color was applied, the wax was boiled away. In the midlands of central Java the wax was not boiled away if additional colors were to be applied. Instead, the areas to be exposed for each successive color were scratched out of the wax layer, with wax added to cover up areas already dyed.

7. Rens Heringa, "Javaanse katoentjes," in *Katoendruk in Nederland*, exh. cat., ed., Bea Brommer (Tilburg: Nederlandsch Textielmuseum; and Helmond: Gemeentemuseum, 1989), 142.

8. R. M. P. Soerachman, *Het batikbedrijf in de vorstenlanden* (Weltevreden: Landsdrukkerij, 1927), 7–8.

9. Ibid.

10. Kat Angelino, *Batikrapport*, 3: 160.

11. *Gedenkboek der Nederlandsche Handel-Maatschappij 1824–1924* (Amsterdam: Nederlandsche Handel-Maatschappij, 1924), 53–58.

12. J. Thomas Lindblad, "De handel in katoentjes op Nederlands-Indië, 1824–1939," *Textielhistorische Bijdragen* 34 (1994): 101; Kat Angelino, *Batikrapport*, 1: 189.

13. Kat Angelino, *Batikrapport*, 1: 187.

14. Ibid., 1: 97–99.

15. Ibid., 2: 5.

16. Ibid., 2: 221.

17. G. H. Rodenburg and G. W. Bijisma, *Van Vlissingen & Co's Gedenkboek 1846–1946* (Helmond: Van Vlissingen, 1948), 44.

18. Kat Angelino, *Batikrapport*, 2: 231.

19. An example is in a private collection in the Netherlands.

BATIK PASISIR
AS MESTIZO COSTUME

•

Rens Heringa

The sight, the fragrant scent, and the evocati

Her costume was specifically Indisch.[1]

She was usually dressed in a long kebaya with lacy borders and a colorful sarong.

Her jet-black hair was rubbed with coconut oil and pinned

at the back of her head into a smooth, brilliant coil, that was encircled by jeweled pins,

while a wreath of kemuning and melati flowers spread an intoxicating fragrance.

In her ears and on her large bosom diamonds sparkled like suns, while heavy gold bracelets

enclosed her wrists. Her left hand held a large white handkerchief, the right a fan,

and high-heeled Chinese slippers completed the elegant and practical outfit.[2]

Hip wrapper (detail)
Java, Pekalongan, c. 1900
Catalogue no. 31

FIGURE 30
Woman of mixed descent on her way to the Dutch Reformed Church, Batavia, c. 1810, accompanied by a male slave and female servant, carrying her prayerbook, betel box, and spittoon.
Koninklijk Instituut voor de Tropen, Amsterdam

he sound announcing a mestizo lady's appearance (FIGURE 30) were caught admirably in this portrait of an early nineteenth-century governor general's Padang-born wife. Its author, Victor van de Wall, Eurasian himself, gave quite a flattering picture. A newly arrived Dutch visitor described the same lady in a much more critical manner: "[I] found the lady of the house in sarong and kebaya with her hair hanging down, sitting on a mat on the floor, ringed by a number of woman slaves . . . while cleaning vegetables. Close by her ladyship stood a great silver cuspidor, into which she spat whole streams of blood-red spittle every now and then."3 Such contradictory opinions regarding the originally indigenous costume, which was widely adopted by all groups of mixed descent in the archipelago and from the mid-seventeenth century by many European settlers as well, abound in the literature. The negative views, generally those of the Dutch-born, came to prevail during the final decades of the nineteenth century, with the expansion of the Dutch colonial state and a gradual increase in officially promulgated racial distinctions. Few European sources have therefore noted details of the colorful *sarung*, which day and night functioned as the principal item of dress for many.

Batik Pasisir: A Lingua Franca?

Throughout Indonesia decorated textiles are known to convey a variety of nonverbal messages. Through its dress each ethnic group emphasizes specific messages that are linked to local cultural norms and values. One type of garment, however, may have served as a kind of common language throughout the archipelago. This type is generally called *batik Pasisir* (batik from the north coastal area). Over time it came to include a wide range of styles that were worn primarily by the Asian-born wives, concubines, and daughters of Chinese, Arabian, or European settlers and their descendants (FIGURE 31). By the early nineteenth century *batik Pasisir* made up part of men's and women's costume for an extensive range of creole and mestizo groups. While the textiles were worn mainly on the north coast of Java, they also functioned in regional dress practically everywhere else in the archipelago. Sumatra was most important, but the populations of Bali, Kalimantan, and the Northern Moluccas also incorporated *batik Pasisir* into their daily and in some cases into their ritual attire (FIGURE 32). Export of these textiles moreover spread beyond the archipelago to Singapore, the coasts of Malaysia, Cambodia, Thailand, the Philippines, and even the West Indies.[4]

Many questions regarding the different styles and possible reasons for the wide dispersion of *batik Pasisir* remain to be answered.[5] What was its meaning to the respective groups of wearers? Did it indeed contain a common message, universally understood by all users, or might the same cloth have a specific meaning for each group of wearers? Some of the answers are gleaned from the cloth itself; others, from various literary sources. During the nineteenth and early twentieth centuries dress styles fulfilled an increasingly important function in colonial Java,

identifying each group of mixed descent as traditional Javanese costume was gradually transmuted into distinctive mestizo styles. Particular fabrics were thought to be suitable for personal or public occasions. Various formats and developments in regional and ethnic color schemes and motifs were adopted to express the mixed cultural backgrounds of each particular group.

Dress in Java

In Java a strong awareness of the relative position of each group and member of the community is one of the most pervasive aspects of culture. Younger and older generations, people of higher or lower status, men and women address each other in a specific manner through the use of different levels of the Javanese language. Moreover, in multiethnic contacts these speech levels are expressed in a mixture of dialects and languages. In a similar manner, an appropriate mixture of dress elements and styles is required to convey a suitable range of meanings for each person and each occasion. Batik cloth is the main dress compo-

FIGURE 33
A Peranakan woman
in a costume indicating her
dual Chinese-Javanese
heritage: her *sarung* has a
central Javanese motif
with a Pasisir *kepala*.
The carnations in the lower
border are typically Chinese
as are her shoes,
Probolinggo, 1918.
Koninklijk Instituut voor
de Tropen, Amsterdam

FIGURE 34A
The headman of the Arab
community in Tegal and his
sons all wear the white
trousers, long, open coat, and
turban prescribed for wear by
Indo-Arabians on official
occasions, c. 1890.
Koninklijk Instituut voor
de Tropen, Amsterdam

FIGURE 34B
The same man in the local
dress typical of Javanese
Muslim men: a batik shoulder
cloth in Pasisir style and a
prayer cloth slung
over his right shoulder,
a checked *sarung*, and black
velvet *kupiah*, c. 1890.
The short batik hip wrapper
and head cloth worn by the
sunshade carrier are typical
Javanese men's wear.
Koninklijk Instituut voor
de Tropen, Amsterdam

nent carrying these messages, though other parts of each costume play a role as well. As elsewhere in the archipelago, the combination of colors and formats does encode the age, gender, social group, and place of residence of the wearer. The choices made by persons of mixed backgrounds are even more complex, as a mixture of styles may be called for. Each specific choice should clearly establish the ethnic affiliation of the wearer (FIGURE 33). By dextrous negotiation of the various possibilities, however, the impression a person makes can be manipulated.

Obviously in a stratified colonial society that dictated a constant awareness of hierarchical and racial differences, the choices were not based on mere cultural prescripts, let alone individual preference. Dress regulations were used universally by those in power to delineate mandated status differences or political divisions. In a series of decrees that date from the middle of the eighteenth century particular *larangan* (forbidden) batik patterns were repeatedly specified as restricted to the rulers of the central Javanese Principalities of Yogyakarta and Surakarta and their close relatives.[6] While these particular prescripts had little impact among the majority of the population elsewhere in Java, this does not imply the absence of order or regulations, as has been asserted.[7] Although, to my knowledge, rules of dress for nonaristocratic wearers were never put into writing, batik cloth, as an indispensable element in Javanese costume, undeniably functioned as an emblem of the user and the occasion. The ensuing precepts may have been far more intricate than the narrow concept of particular patterns restricted to an elite. This is clearly demonstrated by the specific dress rules for the various social groups in villages near Tuban.[8] Similar systems spelling out social divisions in the community were probably in existence all over Java.[9]

The Javanese preoccupation with position was soon emulated by the Dutch. Around 1680, a little over half a century after the settlement of Batavia (Jakarta), only the highest officials of the VOC in the city and their families were allowed to display wealth by decorating their costumes with pearls and gold and silver trimmings. In 1754 the Measures for Curbing Pomp and Circumstance, proclaimed by Governor-General Jacob Mossel, obtained for all

the residents of a much wider Dutch-held territory, including, apart from Europeans, "the Native, Chinese and Mohammedan inhabitants." Implicitly the code presented a society with a typically Asian propensity for status display. Detailed rules were stipulated for Batavia residents regarding the type of costly jewels to be worn, the number of slaves to follow their masters, and the right to have an umbrella carried over one's head. Explicit stipulations on the choice between European and Indonesian costume were included in the regulations meant for the so-called Outer Offices, the Dutch-controlled regions beyond Java.[10] There all European and Indo-European employees of the VOC and their wives were allowed to dress "according to native custom." Western costume was, however, prescribed for public appearances during visits to Batavia. The preference for an Asian mode of living is evident, and apparently during this period race could still be overlooked in favor of rank and wealth. A little over a century later the need was felt to impose more stringent racial and religious divisions. In 1872 the colonial government made an attempt to keep the different racial and religious groups in their "places" by imposing a prohibition against anyone's appearing in public dressed in anything but their own "national" costume (FIGURES 34A–B). The various groups were specifically listed: "those who have legal rights equal

A

B

to the Europeans; Chinese, including those who have become Muslims; Foreign Orientals such as Arabs and Chinese[;] and lastly Natives, including those who have equal legal rights with the Europeans." Deviations that are pronounced acceptable are listed in an appendix. Some native women—who are not defined in more detail but who probably had some link with the Dutch community—were allowed to wear the white, flounced *kabaya* (loose garment) favored by Europeans and Indo-Europeans, while Christianized natives were entitled to wear European dress in those areas "where it had become customary" (FIGURE 35).[11] These few examples clearly bring out the sometimes perplexing choices open to those who had crossed the narrow "national" borders. Strangely none of the regulations specifically alluded to batik cloth as a key component or a major part of these national costumes. It may well be that the rules were intended primarily to prevent the unauthorized use of European clothing.

Textiles as Women's Property

For most women, in addition to indicating their group affiliations, batik cloth and jewelry have been the traditional means of accruing property. Javanese women have always been accorded certain proprietary rights by customary law, even as these are delimited to a certain extent by Islamic tenets.

Though women of Arabian descent have often been presented as similar to the natives, their rights were much more restricted than those of local women. If a woman of Arabian descent had any

property, it was administered by her father, husband, or failing these, by the Council of Religious Scholars.[12] As a wife she could easily be divorced. Only the gifts of cloth and jewelry received from the groom's family at the wedding were hers to use as she pleased.

More or less comparable circumstances obtained for Chinese Peranakan women. Especially in well-to-do families extensive amounts of batik cloth formed part of a bride's dowry and also of the gift that was offered to the bride's mother in exchange for her daughter. The mother-in-law had first choice; the rest fell to the future wife, who also could inherit textiles that were left by her mother, grandmother, or great-aunts.[13] Women were excluded by the patrilineal Chinese system from a share in the inheritance of both their fathers and husbands. Moreover, many Chinese men had secondary wives, who were even lower in status than the first wife. Therefore, clothing and jewelry were a Peranakan woman's only private property.

Women categorized as European were quite diverse in background; creoles, mestizos, recognized illegitimate children, and Asian wives were all officially identified as Dutch,[14] although socially there might remain huge distances. According to Dutch law, a woman could be named sole heir of a man's property.[15] Therefore, the legal wives and daughters of old creole and mestizo families who belonged to the elite generally had recourse to resources other than clothing. Nevertheless, their Asian backgrounds made the display of expensive cloth and especially jewelry of the greatest importance to express status. At least, clear and specific rules obtained for all groups of well-to-do women. Throughout the nineteenth and early twentieth centuries the rights of many of the women associated with the lower echelons of Europeans were not so clear. Most Europeans never considered legalizing their partnerships with their local-born *nyai*, or housekeepers. She herself, generally of lowly background and deficient education, was in no position to insist upon legal marriage, although this would immediately have made the "native party" eligible to be declared equal before the Dutch law.[16] The principal obstacle was her illiteracy, which hampered adoption of the Christian faith, part and parcel of legal marriage. The children born

FIGURE 35 (left)
In this wedding portrait of a Chiristian couple the groom wears Western attire, while the bride and her attendant have donned an Indo-European–style *sarung* and white *kabaya*, Celebes, c. 1900. Koninklijk Instituut voor de Tropen, Amsterdam

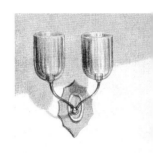

FIGURE 36 (below)
The colored rather than
white *kabaya* worn by these
nyai, c. 1850, indicate that
they probably belonged to a
Chinese household. The
woman lounging wears her
lace handkerchief (*toka*) with
keys to the storage rooms
knotted to one corner;
the other is polishing
a silver belt (*pending*).
Koninklijk Instituut voor
de Tropen, Amsterdam

FIGURE 37 (right)
A *klontong* and *nyai* transact
business, c. 1850. The *nyai*
probably belongs to a
Chinese household or is of
Chinese descent, as she wears
a long, flowered *kabaya* and
Chinese mules.
Koninklijk Instituut voor
de Tropen, Amsterdam

out of these alliances were in many cases not officially recognized. If they were recognized, the sons
might be sent to Holland to get an education, while
the daughters were married off when barely in their
teens. The possession of a hoard of batik cloth and
jewelry, easy to pawn or pack, was therefore insur-
ance against times of need for most women of mixed
backgrounds, including those officially belonging to
the European group (FIGURE 36).

How Batik Cloth Was Obtained

As late as the end of the eighteenth and up to the
mid-nineteenth century well-to-do European and
Indo-European women spent their lives in semi-
segregation among the women of their extended
families.[17] Brought up and waited on hand and foot
by Asian servants from birth, they rarely left the
compound and never by themselves. Indo-Arabian
women were held in isolation in the women's quarters of their homes, while Peranakan women were
supposed to spend their time inside the compound,
learning the arts of cooking and embroidery.[18] How
then did these women come by their precious textiles? A network of Javanese female batik traders,
the *tiyang wadé*, would circulate among the homes
of affluent customers. Arriving with their bundles
during the afternoon siesta, they would spread out
their wares to be chosen from, and bargained for, at
leisure by the ladies of the house. Outright payment
in cash was rare; as a rule purchases would be made
on monthly installments with a choice of larger or
smaller payments with interest applied to the debt.
Thus the retailer, who generally obtained the textiles on credit herself, could accumulate huge profits.
As an added service, textiles with particular designs
or colors could be ordered with an advance payment.
Servants often acted as go-betweens with male itinerant traders: the *koja*, or Arabian trader of imported
cloth, and the *klontong*, or Chinese peddler, who
carried material for *kabaya*, needles, and thread as
well (FIGURE 37). All three groups of retail traders
formed the end of a long chain of commercial links,
which often bridged long distances and a series of
intermediate buyers and sellers.

During the last quarter of the nineteenth century the city of Bandung in West Java became known
as the main fashion center where male batik traders

from all over the archipelago could buy in bulk from
the abundant choice in the market. A second well-
known wholesale market was the Tanah Abang
market in Batavia. These developments were probably due to the fact that both Bandung and Batavia
had limited batik production themselves. In batik-
producing towns elsewhere in Java, cloth could be
obtained directly from the workshops.[19] Therefore,
Sumatran, Chinese, and Arabian batik dealers settled
in many of the Pasisir towns to trade directly with
the batik entrepreneurs.[20]

By the turn of the century Dutch-born immigrant women, the so-called *totok*, enjoyed more
freedom. In *De Echo: Weekblad voor dames in Indië*
(The echo: weekly magazine for ladies in the Indies),
which appeared in both the Indies and The Hague,
ladies preparing to come out to the archipelago for
the first time were advised in 1900 not to buy any
batik textiles before their departure. They were
warned that the cheap, low-quality, imitation batik
available in Holland was suitable only for sleepwear.
A much better deal could be made with the help of
more experienced guests after arrival at the hotel in
Batavia. A crowd of batik traders would show up
daily with a wide choice of varying quality. With
prices ranging between 2.5 guilders for good quality
Dutch imitations to 25 or even 40 guilders for a gen-
uine hand-waxed cloth, a dozen cloths should be
acquired for a start, with at least three dozen *kabaya*.
In the end, with a change of dress three times a day,

a collection of twelve dozen *kabaya* for different occasions, was not considered excessive. As the latter could quickly be made to order, it was not advisable to turn one's hand to the endeavor oneself, in order not to appear as the typical *"baar,"* or newcomer. European—or probably Indo-European—girls at one of the two sewing schools in the city knew exactly how to provide the latest local styles and make the newcomers look instantly like a seasoned inhabitant of the Indies. The need to adjust as soon as possible was obviously felt to be of high priority.[21] During the 1920s and 1930s women were free to go out shopping by themselves. The *toko Bombay*, shops run by Indian owners, provided an abundant choice of lace, muslin, and other yard goods for *kabaya*. Batik cloths of medium and lower quality could be bought in the special section of the large textile markets that had been erected by the colonial government in all towns and cities. The finest-quality batik was always obtained directly from the workshop, in many cases through the agency of the traditional female cloth trader.

Mestizo Adaptations to Javanese Dress

In pre-Islamic times Javanese costume consisted of a single garment, the long skirt cloth that served as both male and female dress. The cloth was wrapped or bound around the hips or directly under the armpits in typical Southeast Asian fashion, while the size of the cloth was adapted to the manner of wrapping. The open, rectangular, and loosely wrapped *kain panjang* (long cloth) was the oldest version. Present-day Javanese costume consists of a hip wrapper, a blouse or jacket, and a shoulder cloth for women and for men a pair of trousers, a hip wrapper, and a head cloth. These dress forms, which have long been denoted as traditionally Javanese, probably developed around the fifteenth century, largely as a result of Islamic tenets of propriety, which entailed the covering of the body. It is possible that at the same time, in addition to the *kain panjang*, the more modest tubular *sarung* came into fashion combined with a blouse or jacket for women. Men also covered their upper bodies and, under the *sarung*, started wearing rather loose, knee-length pants, with a wide inset in the crotch. Both men and women added a second cloth to cover the head and upper body.[22] The men covered their heads with an *iket kepala*, a square cloth tied in a variety of local styles. A narrow, rectangular cloth, when worn on ritual occasions by women as a breast covering, was known as a *kemben*; when it functioned in daily life as a sling to carry children or market items, it was known as a *gendongan* or a *selendang*, respectively (FIGURE 38). A large shawl, the *kudbung*, was worn by Muslim women over head and shoulders when they appeared in public (FIGURE 39). All these cloths were decorated with batik, most commonly on a base of imported cotton. The *baju* (jacket, tunic) and *kabaya*, which were worn by both men and women, never consisted of batik material, however, but of Indian flowered chintz, fine, imported cotton, or velvet. The use of imported materials and foreign terminology indicate that the tailored garments were later additions. It has been suggested that the *ka(m)baya* style was imported from the port town of Cambay in India.[23] However, Cambay may just as well have been the port of origin of the material used for the long-sleeved, open blouse. Although the term *kabaya* is derived from the Persian word for this type of garment, *cabay*, fifteenth-century Muslim Chinese immigrants may well have been instrumental in introducing the garment to the north coast. The form of the wide, long-sleeved robe with an open front meeting edge to edge, is quite similar to that of the Chinese *bei-zi*, which functioned as

FIGURE 38
The seated woman wears her *selendang* thrown back over her shoulders; the woman in the background uses her *selendang* as a carrier c. 1895. From E. Nijland, *Handleiding voor de Kennis van het Volksleven der Bewoners van Nederlandsch Oost Indië* (Leiden: E. J Brill; Utrecht: C. H. E. Breijer, 1897). Koninklijk Instituut voor de Tropen, Amsterdam

FIGURE 39
Nyai wearing a *kudbung*, c. 1840.
From *Java: Tooneelen uit het leven, karakterschetsen en Kleederdragten van Java's Bewoners* (The Hague, 1853–55). Koninklijk Instituut voor de Tropen, Amsterdam

FIGURE 40
Shoulder cloth
Java, Juana or Rembang,
c. 1900
Catalogue no. 72

FIGURE 41
Europeans who were
longtime residents of the
Indies adopted the
sarung and long *kabaya*
for informal dress.
This was said to be the
favorite costume of Governor-
General H. W. Daendels,
who wore it not only
in private but in
the office as well.
From *Jaarboekje Warnasarie*
(1854).
Koninklijk Instituut voor
de Tropen, Amsterdam

ceremonial dress for lower-class women during the Ming period.[24] Thus, foreign elements from India, Persia, and China all contributed to the dress styles that were adopted primarily by the immigrants' local-born wives. Although the costumes were eventually worn by all north coast inhabitants, they may be considered the first mestizo style.

Each new group of wearers developed adaptations of its own. Neither *iket kepala* nor *kudhung* were ever a part of non-Muslim costume. Shoulder cloths for women came to be fashioned out of silk (*selendang lok can*) as a sign of leisure and status (FIGURE 40). By the late eighteenth century the skirt cloth was again the main batik constituent of non-Muslim costume, serving for both men and women as informal attire. The model of the upper garment expressed gradations of mixed blood. A mestizo woman wore a "chemise called *baju*,"[25] a collarless tunic with an opening at the neck, which she put on over her head. Over the left shoulder she draped a *toka*, a square cloth decorated with silver or gold embroidery, to which her keys, a housewife's badge of office, were attached. Those who were categorized as Dutch or European wore an ankle-length *kabaya* with an *ang kin*, or tasseled sash, often made of red silk, around the waist.[26] Women wore the same combination when going on formal calls. A *kabaya* shorter by a few inches was allowed during the late eighteenth century for informal visits or in meeting with persons of lower rank.[27] At home men wore the *sarung* in combination with a knee-length *kabaya* (FIGURE 41). "Old hands" among the European group adopted the costume even to receive visitors.

For formal occasions many of the early nineteenth-century descriptions still mention the *saya*, a pleated or gathered skirt in white cotton or flowered Indian chintz, which was combined with a

kabaya of thin, white cotton, which fell open from the waist and reached just below the calf.[28] This style was originally introduced during the VOC period by Portuguese-speaking mestizo women from Goa and Dutch settlements on the Indian coasts, many of whom came to Java as wives of VOC officials. Therefore, the use of the *saya* may have been restricted to this elite group, possibly with the inclusion of other Portuguese-speaking Asian Christians.[29] After the British interregnum "Dutch" ladies were ideally supposed to change into Western fashions for the evening. In practice many of them appeared for a short while at evening parties and balls "laced up and penned" into corsets and European gowns, only to disappear and change for the rest of the evening into the more comfortable *sarung* costume.[30] Peranakan women also kept to their silk embroidered Chinese coats and skirts for occasions related to their ancestors, such as praying at the family altar, part of the wedding ritual and funerals.[31] High-quality *sarung* were, however, worn during the Javanese parts of Peranakan wedding rituals, such as the ceremonial meeting of bride and groom and their sitting in state, or while mourning. Outside the home men of most groups generally wore their "national" dress.

After the mid-nineteenth century the distinction between male and female costume became ever more marked. Henceforth batik trousers supplanted the *sarung* for men, while the short *baju Cina*, a sort of pajama jacket without a collar, took the place of the *kabaya*.[32] Peranakan men had always kept to the *seluar*, long, rather wide pants that originally overlapped and were knotted or tucked in at the waist. During this period, however, they were held up by a drawstring. Indo-European and European men chose slightly longer and narrower batik trousers,

also with a drawstring, called *celana* (FIGURE 42). Although older women of the Peranakan community kept to the rectangular open cloth until the end of the nineteenth century, the whole group eventually preferred the more convenient tubular *sarung* style. This choice was followed by Indo-European and European women. Although both Chinese and European women wore a *kabaya* with lace borders, each group had its specific style. The Dutch preferred a simple, white jacket with lace borders. The Peranakan women chose *kabaya* in pastel colors, often with patterns of small flowers and long, extended points in front. The costume was not complete without the appropriate accessories. Besides the *ang kin*, on special occasions the *pending*, an intricately worked gold or silver belt, might be used to keep the *sarung* in place.[33] Men used flat leather sandals, while women wore elegant silk or velvet slippers embroidered with colored beads or gold thread and sometimes fitted with gold-painted, high wooden heels. Only married women were allowed to wear fragrant flowers in their *kondé*, the hair coil. A matching set of necklace, rings, earrings, bracelets, and not least the *kroncong*, three pins on a chain to keep the front of the *kabaya* together, completed the costume. The amount of jewelry and the size of the precious stones indicated the lady's affluence and status. Last but not least, an elegant parasol was carried in the open air, also when riding in a carriage, to protect the skin from the dreaded effects of the sun.

FIGURE 42
Trousers
Java, Pekalongan, c. 1920–3●
Stamped wax resist on machine-woven cotton; synthetic dyes
Length: 88.5 cm (34⅞ in.)
Los Angeles County Museum of Art,
Inger McCabe Elliott Collection,
M.91.184.494

Changing Times

During the last decades of the nineteenth century, in the period that often is described as the last years of "*tempo dulu*" (the good, old days),[34] easier transportation brought more Dutch-born women to the colonies. Some were quite emancipated and held paid jobs as governesses or music teachers. As a result, racial differences became more pronounced and

Batik Pasisir

"going native" was frowned upon. This development had its particular impact on dress styles for European women. Western gowns were now considered the only decorous attire, with a Japanese kimono or a loose, white smock (*bébé*) becoming fashionable as housewear. The *sarung* and *kabaya* came to be looked down upon as indigenous women's wear by many who wanted to present themselves as European in an effort to distinguish clearly between a proper Dutch lady and the *nyai* she despised. The costume was, however, still acceptable for an early morning walk in the garden or near the house, with the husband in sleeping pants and *baju Cina*. However, even in Batavia, one might wear the denigrated *sarung* under the cover of darkness, while sitting in one's carriage and listening to a band concert presented at the military club. This pastime, called *nonton*, made it possible to look on, without having to dress up, but still be in the know.[35] Outside Java, on the mail boats that sailed regularly between the islands and in the outer provinces, the old, easy-going atmosphere continued into the twentieth century. Travel outside the bigger towns remained difficult, with practically no hotels and primitive means of transportation. Comfortable clothing was therefore important. On some of these occasions a *sarung* might also be put to other uses. Spread on the floor by a servant, to wrap the first change of clothing needed quickly after one of the many transfers, it might serve as a convenient substitute for a suitcase.[36]

With the arrival of the twentieth century class distinctions kept increasing along racial lines among the European community. Due to the ever more Europeanized lifestyle, women had become more active both socially and in their households. An easier *kabaya* style came into fashion; its length decreased, first, to just below the knee, later, merely covering the upper part of the leg (FIGURE 43). Indo-Europeans who kept to the local costume outside their homes were generally of less-elevated status. In 1905 a noncommissioned officer was buried in a clean *kabaya* and batik sleeping trousers,[37] whereas his superiors would be clothed in their Western uniforms

for this purpose. Several manuals appeared in which Dutch-born women were given advice on how to manage the life of a housewife in the Indies. All of them explain how to wear the "sarong and *kebaya*," and one of these publications, by the hand of a well-known Indo-European lady, even includes a pattern.[38] With increasing numbers of newly arrived young Dutch families living on plantations in the outer islands, such guidelines were probably badly needed. In Java, however, those who insisted on dressing in the casual style could only do so under the pretext of not feeling well. It was even considered bad manners to show oneself thus attired on the front porch.[39] Nevertheless, by 1927 the Dutch-born Mrs. Rutten-Pekelharing in her manual, *What Should I Remember, What Should I Do?"* bemoans the gradual disappearance of the convenient, cool, and easy-to-wear attire that needed no corsets, only a thin bodice, the *kutang*, underneath.[40] In the end Western cultural dictates determined life for the European group, and by the 1930s Western fashions had taken over. Even most of the Indo-European women involved in producing batik cloth would never appear in public in it. To them it was merely a way of making a living.[41]

The other groups of mixed descent were directly influenced by these developments. Both men and women belonging to the leading classes among the Peranakan Chinese adopted European dress for certain public occasions, especially after 1920, when they had been *gelijkgesteld*, or declared equal to the Dutch before the law (FIGURE 44). Nevertheless, Pasisir-style batik remained the Peranakan dress for private and family occasions. Thus, each carefully considered choice came to express a momentary

FIGURE 43 (below)
In this morning scene a woman wears the short *kabaya* of the early twentieth century, decorated with a wide lace border.
The man wears the *jas tutup* of the Dutch civil service.
Koninklijk Instituut voor de Tropen, Amsterdam

FIGURE 44 (right)
A Chinese foreman at a Dutch-owned tin company and his family in front of their house in the Riouw archipelago, c. 1920.
He wears the *jas tutup*; his wife wears an Indo-European batik with a wide bow border and Chinese slippers.
Koninklijk Instituut voor de Tropen, Amsterdam

alignment, while the traditional but hybridized local costume, with its European-derived motifs and Chinese choice of color, effectively expressed the Peranakan position in the middle, as the liaison between the Dutch and the locally born population. Similar choices obtained among Indo-Arabian women. The elite among both groups came to distinguish themselves by spending increasing sums on various new, almost baroque styles that primarily expressed class and status. Among the affluent Peranakan the *kabaya* was often elaborately and colorfully embroidered to form a set with the luxurious hip wrapper. The preoccupation with Dutch superiority continued to influence most of the designs until the outbreak of the Pacific War.

In spite of the sudden break caused by the Japanese occupation (1942–45), the prewar developments in dress styles show a certain continuity into the 1950s and 1960s. After the Dutch had been removed from their leading position by the Japanese invasion and once Indonesia had become an independent republic, one after the other, those in power to a certain extent put their stamp on designs and dress styles. The colonial state was replaced by a democracy with feudal characteristics, in which a preoccupation with position remained of continuing importance.

Appearance and Meaning of
Batik Pasisir

Each hand-drawn batik cloth is to a certain extent a unique piece. In a concerted effort the creativity of the designer, the fluid movement of the woman who guides the *canting* across the cloth, and the art of the dyer produced—and still produce—these works of art. Nevertheless, all three are bound to certain fixed precepts. The four main design components to give expression to these rules are the size, format, color, and motifs of a cloth. Each aspect can be related to the principle that guides all decisions: the needs and preferences of the various groups that wear the cloths.[42]

A

Size, Format, and Function

All commercial batik cloths are made of specially woven cotton material approximately 105 centimeters (41 3/8 in.) wide. Square or rectangular pieces of this fabric form the base for the batiks, of which most are not meant to be sewn but wrapped or bound directly around the body. The size of a cloth determines on which part of the body and in what manner it will be worn. The smallest cloth (FIGURE 45A) was a rectangle averaging one square meter. It served as an *iket kepala* for Muslim men or a handkerchief or key holder for housewives. Women used the medium size (FIGURE 45B) as a breast or shoulder cloth. It measures half the width of the woven cloth, approximately 50 centimeters by 2 to 3 meters. Muslim women modestly cover head and shoulders with a somewhat wider version (FIGURE 45C). The hip wrapper for both men and women is the largest cloth (FIGURE 45D), with a width of approximately 105 centimeters (which forms the vertical dimension when wrapped) and a length two to two and a half times as great.

Each of these cloths is divided into a main field (*badan*) and various types of surrounding borders (see Appendix 1). The cloths in traditional Pasisir style show a two- or threefold border. The *badan* of most cloths is set off against one or more sections (*kepala* and borders) that are decorated with contrasting motifs and/or colors. The design aspects of these *kepala* and borders determine one of several ways in which a cloth is named. The two main formats of the hip wrapper are the *kain panjang* and the *sarung*.

FIGURE 45A
Head cloth
Java, Lasem, c. 1880
Catalogue no. 74

FIGURE 45B
Breast cloth
Java, Lasem, c. 1910
Catalogue no. 68

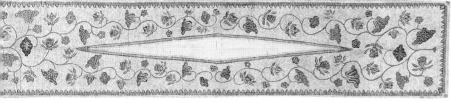

B

C

D

FIGURE 45C
Head cloth, *kudhung*
Java, Lasem, c. 1910
Hand-drawn and stamped
wax resist on machine-woven
cotton; synthetic dyes
89.5 x 218.3 cm
(35¼ x 86 in.)
Los Angeles County Museum
of Art, Inger McCabe
Elliott Collection,
M.91.184.21

FIGURE 45D
Hip wrapper
Java, Lasem, c. 1900
Catalogue no. 1

FIGURE 46 (right)
Hip wrapper
Java, Pekalongan, c. 1910
Catalogue no. 4

Kain Panjang

The oldest type of Pasisir cloth is the *kain panjang*, which has a format similar to the layout of the cloths imported into the archipelago from India (see FIGURE 1). It is divided into a *badan* (body) and series of surrounding borders, the *pinggir*, which in some areas are called *sikilan* (resembling extremities). The two end sections are called *kepala* (heads). In older cloths each end section shows a vertical row of isosceles triangles set on a rectangular base, the *papan* (board). Though these triangles are often denoted as *tumpal*, this term may be a recent (and, moreover, European) invention (to my knowledge it has never been used by the general public in Java or elsewhere in the archipelago). In earlier times on the north coast a wide range of somewhat more expressive regional terms, such as *telacap* or *cacap* (cape), *sorotan* (rays of light), *pasung* (root of the nose), or *pucuk rebung* (young bamboo shoot), was known. These terms all connote ideas of outwardly expanding movement. Some of the terms used for the sections of the overall design, such as *badan*, *kepala*, and *sikilan*, present an anthropomorphic metaphor, which finds further expression in the various design possibilities that are linked with the marital status of the wearer. When the two *kepala* are similar in color, symbolizing two human beings fused together, the cloth is meant to be worn by a married woman. When, however, the *kepala* and borders differ in pattern or color or both, the cloth is denoted *kain panjang sisiban* (long cloth with dissimilar halves; FIGURE 46). Originally this type was meant to be worn by bridal couples just before the wedding, while they were still separate.[43] When one end section is predominantly red and the other shows a contrasting blue or black, the cloth may be worn in two manners. Young women will wrap the cloth so the light section is visible, while older women keep the dark end on the outside. The third traditional type of *kain panjang* known on the north coast shows a *badan* merely enclosed by a small white edge, or *seret*, while the *kepala* sections are absent. This type is denoted as *buntungan*, which means "without issue." It was originally meant to be worn by postmenopausal women, who had left their reproductive years behind. Later the same format was adopted as the specific dress of the central Javanese Principalities, where it was denoted as *kain seret* (cloth with a plain border). There, instead of being wrapped in a circular movement, it formed a spiral that tapered toward the ankles in a more elegant manner. As a result, after functioning as the cloth type for "the elders," the *kain panjang* with the

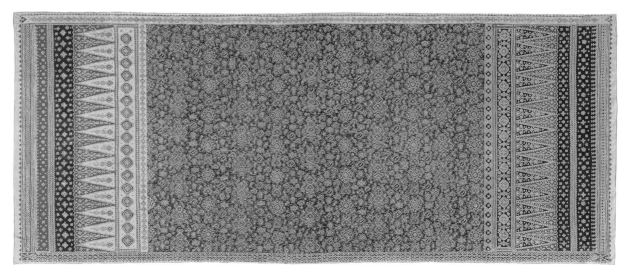

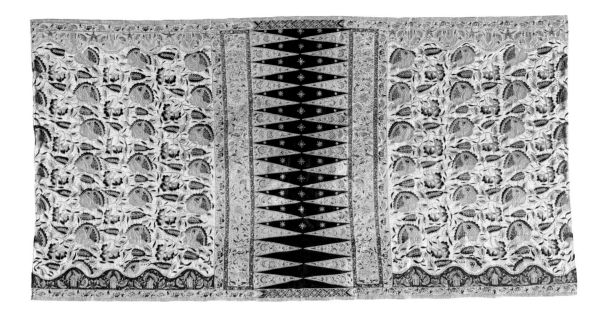

FIGURE 47A (left)
Hip wrapper
Java, Indramayu, c. 1910
Catalogue no. 7

FIGURE 47B
Hip wrapper
Java, Cirebon, c. 1910–20
Catalogue no. 14

plain borders of the Pasisir came to be linked with high status. After the traditional *kain panjang* went out of fashion during the first quarter of the twentieth century, the central Javanese *kain seret* influenced north coast dress in its turn as it gradually developed into the costume for the elite (catalogue no. 53). These examples elucidate the manner in which the meaning of design elements followed changing cultural and political values.

Sarung

The tubular *sarung*, the second main format, was known by the early nineteenth century as the style for women of mixed racial backgrounds. It is noteworthy that until the abolishment of slavery in 1860 the tubular skirt was worn by slave women, while only free women were allowed to wear the *kain panjang*.[44]

Again, various design formats can be distinguished. In the oldest version the *kepala* bisects the *badan* (FIGURE 47A); in the later form it is encountered at one end of the cloth (FIGURE 47B). When sewn into a tube, each of them was meant to be worn in a particular manner (see Appendix 2). Young village women and the lower classes wore the classical type, with its double row of triangles at the back and superfluous material folded in front to hide the seam. The second form was considered more formal. It was wrapped with the *kepala* in front, folded left over right toward the right leg, with one half of the *tumpal* rows visible. The new style thus almost

resembled the *kain panjang*, worn by free women. It may well be that slaves and other women of lowly origin who needed an emblem after rising in status by becoming the concubines of European and Chinese men were the originators of this fashion. Men wrapped their *sarung* the other way around, right over left.

Peranakan women developed their own manner of folding the *sarung*. Their *kepala gigi balang*, in which the space between the rows of triangles is filled in with a row of diamonds (FIGURE 48), was worn almost completely visible in front. This custom and the heavily decorated style may be related to the Chinese silk bridal skirt with its wide, flat panel in front (FIGURE 49).[45] Sometimes in an intermediate form the traditional and the Peranakan *kepala* types were positioned at either end of a single

kain panjang, possibly to denote the wearer's mixed background.[46] In the Indo-European *kepala* style the rows of triangles were also gradually supplanted, in this case by floral designs (see Appendix 1). These cloths were worn with more than half the floral panel showing as well (FIGURE 50).[47] For the purpose of tucking the seam neatly under the fold, the *kepala* of the Indo-European cloths was moved in approximately one hand's width from the end of the cloth (see catalogue no. 22). It should be noted that the European way of folding the *sarung* was precisely opposite the Asian manner. In 1888 Mrs. Forbes mentioned that the *kepala* should be folded straight along the left leg, as did Mrs. Kloppenburg-Versteegh in 1913.[48] This mode of closing a woman's garment right over left is typically European. Figure 11 confirms that the European custom is also followed for men's wear, as the fold of the gentleman's *sarung* falls clearly left over right.

Regional and Ethnic Color Styles

A second approach to categorizing batik is by color. The various brightly colored styles of *batik Pasisir* that immediately strike the eye remain through time the first characteristic that indicates a person's background. While differences in color type have been related to geographical location in the standard approach to Javanese batik styles,[49] a consideration of the many different and changing population groups who chose color as an expression of their ethnic and social affiliations offers a more definitive understanding. Until the end of the nineteenth century only natural dyes and mordants were available.[50] Specialized, often Peranakan, dyers were praised early on for the quality of their work.[51] The original Pasisir colors consisted of gradations of blue in combination with shades of bright red to reddish-brown. Each town or region had slowly perfected its own recipes, which resulted in specific shades for motifs and backgrounds. Differences were partially due to the local properties of water and soil. The high salinity and iron content of the water in the eastern part of the Pasisir resulted in a bright red hue of *mengkudu* dye, which came to be known as Lasem red (see catalogue no. 12). In the east this red contrasts with a clear, creamy white base, but the backgrounds of the cloths made in the western areas around Cirebon show rich cream, almost yellow tones, with motifs in a deep orange-red (see catalogue no. 14). This was the result of repeatedly kneading the base cloth with oil, alternated with rinsing baths in the river. The cloths from Indramayu were well known for an intense shade of blackish blue, for which the cloths were steeped in a bath of mud mixed with leaves and unripe fruit (see catalogue no. 7).[52] In general it can be said that the cloths from the eastern regions give a much brighter impression than those made in western areas. Nineteenth-century cloths from Pekalongan and

FIGURE 49
A Peranakan bride in traditional Chinese wedding attire, Java. Koninklijk Instituut voor de Tropen, Amsterdam

FIGURE 50
The Indo-European *kepala buketan* flanked by floral borders replaced the *kepala tumpal* with its rows of triangles, Java, c. 1910. Koninklijk Instituut voor Taal-, Land- en Volkenkunde, Leiden

FIGURE 51
Hip wrapper (detail)
Java, Pekalongan,
c. 1900–1910
Catalogue no. 30

Semarang, towns located approximately in the center of the Pasisir, show shades that are midway between the extremes (see catalogue no. 10). It may well be that this gradual change from clear to deep tones is not fortuitous. A comparable system still exists on a smaller scale in villages near Tuban. There bright tones are considered suitable for those living in the eastern part of the area, where the sun rises, while those in the western part, where the sun sets, prefer darker shades. Moreover, the lightest color, especially bright red, is meant for young, marriageable women, while the darkest shades are worn by those who have come to the end of life.[53] It appears that a similar division was found in other areas on the Pasisir, for instance, in Tegal.[54]

Thus, originally color would express the residential area or age group of the wearer. With the development of the colonial infrastructure around the middle of the nineteenth century the various color styles started to be more widely distributed and worn. Personal preference guided by aesthetic appreciation now entered into the decision. The occasion for which the cloth was chosen presented yet another option. Moreover, choices made by Peranakan and European or Indo-European women were based on divergent symbolic meanings that had a clear ethnic base. A cloth in soft blue and white, a light version of the color combination called *kelengan*, was worn by a Indo-European bride on her wedding night as an expression of virginity and purity (FIGURE 51). After the wedding the cloth was carefully washed and stored to be used at her funeral, when it stood once more for purity. A Peranakan bride wore bright red, the Chinese color of happiness and prosperity, when she was received in her husband's home. Parts of the cloth were often richly decorated with *prada* (gold leaf; FIGURE 52). In this case too the wedding cloth was usually kept for burial, thus procuring prosperity for her descendants.[55] To the Peranakan Chinese, however, blue-and-white cloths served as mourning apparel;[56] the closer the relative, the deeper the shade of blue. (After the passage of time or for distant kin, a lighter blue-and-white cloth with accents of green, might serve.) The blue-black and cream *kelengan* batiks from Indramayu were especially in demand for this purpose among affluent Peranakan all over Java.[57] For some who belonged

FIGURE 52
Hip wrapper
Java, Semarang, c. 1850
Catalogue no. 17

to both groups, the choice between the opposing prescripts might lead to confusion. A Dutch lady, who had been widowed early in her marriage to a much older Peranakan husband insisted on a blue-and-white cloth to be buried in. This choice understandably confounded her Peranakan relatives. They offered several explanations; in one of them, fitting the Chinese system, it was pointed out that the old lady had never remarried. Thus, by choosing blue and white, she purportedly indicated that she had never given up mourning for her late husband. A second explanation, more in line with her Dutch background, may have been her wish to be buried in the European bridal and funerary cloth.[58]

After the turn of the century natural dyes were gradually replaced by synthetic dyestuffs imported from Europe. Soon a wide range of shades became available all over Java, and multicolored cloths were generally affordable. Sometimes a combination of natural and synthetic dyes was used. By the 1920s the old regional color styles could be imitated anywhere (see catalogue no. 3). The most famous among them were, however, denoted by the expression *tiron* (imitation of), followed by the name of their original place of production.[59]

The huge variety of modern shades also made new choices possible. Relative age could now be more subtly expressed through a multitude of graded shades: soft pink for young girls; a stronger red, with increasing accents of blue or green, for maturing women; and gray, mauve, or purple for those of middle age. Nevertheless, ethnic preference dictated specific combinations. While the European and Indo-European wearers preferred clear shades of pink and red combined with a variety of blues (FIGURE 53A),

the Peranakan Chinese developed a predilection for mixed tints; the orangy pink, yellow-green, and lilac and their graded shades are reminiscent of the colors of Chinese silk embroidery (FIGURE 53B). Women of Indo-Arabian descent chose strong shades of deep red, green, and blue (FIGURE 53C). Color now could express ethnicity in a varied manner, with the new choices also adapted to denote racial divisions.

Daily and Ceremonial Motifs

Each section of a cloth is decorated with specific motifs, which in their totality express most clearly its symbolic meaning. All of the motifs depict more or less stylized forms and are often taken from nature. Characteristic combinations of motifs will be designated here as motif types. Two main categories of traditional motif types can be distinguished. The geometric or abstract style consists of a single pattern uniformly repeated over the whole field, thus forming a grid of diagonal bands, squares, or diamonds (see catalogue no. 5). In the free style, though a certain regularity is maintained and the motifs are repeated, an impression of greater freedom is achieved.[60]

Until the mid-nineteenth century each of these types was meant for a particular occasion, a custom that was adhered to by all wearers, whether Pasisir Javanese, Peranakan, or even Sumatrans. The early, free-form motifs are mostly made up of floral creepers, birds, fruits, and insects in a two-dimensional representation that was primarily deemed suitable for informal occasions and daily wear. The geometric motif type can be seen as an abstracted and, therefore, more symbolic image of predominantly floral motifs. This made them suitable for formal and ritual dress. On the cloths worn by the Dutch-affiliated groups a gradual change took place in which the highly valued abstracted forms were relegated to the second plane as a backdrop for the large floral elements that came to typify the Indo-European cloths (see catalogue no. 33). It is doubtful whether at that point the original symbolic meaning was still understood. Instead, they may have considered the motifs as pleasing, purely decorative elements. Indo-Arabian and devout Muslim women, however, always insisted on motifs with a great degree of abstraction, in accordance with the Islamic discouragement of the depiction of living creatures.

FIGURE 54A
Hip wrapper (detail)
Java, Lasem, c. 1870
Catalogue no. 5

Borders: Snakes and Laces

The motifs used in the borders of traditional cloths generally reflect a notion of containment or enclosure and at the same time the exclusion of outside influences. Originally the outer edge consisted of a *seret*, a single row of tiny, vertical stripes or triangles (said to depict a fence or row of arrowheads) that runs along both selvages of the cloth. These triangles are comparable to those in the *kepala* and on the north coast are often denoted as *gigi walang* (cricket's teeth) or as *gigi balang* (edge that throws [something] out). The motifs are said to provide protection from untoward influences to those who wear the cloth. The second, inner border is a wider band decorated with a floral vine, which completely surrounds the central field (FIGURE 54A). The symbolism encoded in this design has Islamic overtones. The garden of paradise, to which the *badan* is often compared, is said to be protected on all sides by impenetrable creepers that are intended to keep out intruders.[61] The two borders thus provide double protection.

Over time the motifs in the borders of both the *kain panjang* and the *sarung* underwent changes along ethnic lines. In many elaborate Peranakan cloths a third border, consisting of an undulating line, was added along the lower edge of the cloth. It represents a snake or dragon, mythical animals that, according to both Javanese and Chinese symbolism, are related to rain and nourishing water, both metaphors for abundance.[62] This addition was used specifically on dowry cloths to express wishes for

prosperity and numerous offspring (FIGURE 54B). On cloths for Indo-European women the deeply symbolic traditional borders were modified into a series of fashionable designs, that mostly expressed status. The traditional snake border developed around the mid-nineteenth century into a pattern resembling lace scallops, to form a rich and pleasing

FIGURE 54B
Hip wrapper (detail)
Java, Cirebon, c. 1910–20
Catalogue no. 14

combination with the lace border of the *kabaya*[63] (FIGURE 54c). By 1900 the lace patterns had gradually grown into an even wider wavy pattern, which was called the *boob* (bow). By this point the second border, or *pinggir*, had disappeared.[64] Only the small, outer edge of vertical stripes remained, now often denoted as "imitation fringe," an explanation that is not based on any symbolism.[65] The upper borders were unchanged at this point, still consisting of a

FIGURE 54C
Hip wrapper (detail)
Java, Semarang, c. 1860–70
Catalogue no. 18

FIGURE 54D
Hip wrapper (detail)
Java, Banyumas, c. 1890
Catalogue no. 21

pinggir with varied forms of small creepers or gar-lands (FIGURE 54D). In place of the more elaborate snake or lace border, these could be worn at the lower end for less formal occasions. It was not until the second decade of the twentieth century that the borders became symmetrical, which made choices less complicated but also less eloquent.

At the outer edges of traditional cloths, on the *kepala* section, a different design is encountered, a design also familiar from Indian import cloths

(FIGURE 54E). Javanese women on the north coast call this section *gandawari*, which means sweetly wafting scent. The heavily stylized motifs are said to represent the flowering stalks of rice plants, a female symbol, while the small tufts at the end refer to the bushy flower of maize, a male symbol. The third element is the fragrant *melati* flower, which is used to adorn bridal couples. Together the three symbolize a marriage.[66] On cloths worn by Indo-Europeans, the floral borders are not interrupted and also enclose the *kepala* (see catalogue no. 18).

The Badan: Creepers and Bouquets

The *badan* forms the center of attention in each batik cloth, with motifs and colors expressing the essence of its message. As the only nineteenth-century source, Mrs. Forbes lists the most important of contemporary motifs: "floral patterns, all kinds of strange motifs, crawling animals, a village with houses and scenes from daily life."[67] Floral motifs,

FIGURE 54E
Hip wrapper (detail)
Java, Semarang, c. 1910
Catalogue no. 9

FIGURE 55
Hip wrapper (detail)
Java, Semarang, c. 1880
Catalogue no. 16

first on this short list, do indeed form the main theme (FIGURE 55). A variety of birds, though not named, form a second significant theme.

Again, each ethnic group had its particular choice of styles and species. Notably the floral motifs invariably consist of cultivated species, planted and raised in gardens and ponds. The center field of a cloth is thus presented as a metaphor for a secluded garden, a concept expressed in various ways among Muslim people in India, China, and Indonesia. According to Islamic images, this garden is the heavenly garden of paradise, where superlative bliss and sensual satisfaction reign.[68] The abstracted floral motifs worn by Muslim women are therefore often denoted as *bintang* (stars). The Chinese conceive of the ideal garden as a retreat from the world of affairs, a timeless paradise set up as a microcosm of the universe.[69] Flowers and fruits are also symbolically related to women, the progenitors who flower and bear fruit for the continuation of the race.[70] Javanese and Chinese women's names are frequently floral. As flowers are indispensable for ritual and medicinal uses, each domestic compound on Java is planted

with fragrant flowers in the ritually meaningful colors white, red, and yellow. Some poisonous species that may serve medicinal purposes grant protective power when used as a decorative motif. The white *melati* and *kemuning* worn in the hair of the governor-general's lady in Victor van de Wall's description are also used for many other purposes. They may serve as offerings to the ancestors, together with the red Javanese rose. At funerals hundreds of these flowers are strung into long garlands to cover the bier. The fragrant *melati* or jasmine, symbol of innocence and modesty, is strewn on the wedding bed. As in the rest of Asia only the blossoms are used. All these species are also encountered as batik motifs (FIGURES 56A–E).

Until approximately 1830 the preferences regarding motifs chosen for the *badan* by the Peranakan accorded closely with north coast Javanese choices. By comparison with central Javanese batik, the filler motifs on traditional Pasisir cloths are generally bolder and less detailed. Both the *lung-lungan*, the flowering vine that winds its way across the garden, and the blossoms strewn in

A

FIGURE 56A
Lotus
Hip wrapper (detail)
Java, Lasem, c. 1910
Catalogue no. 11

FIGURE 56B
Chrysanthemum
Hip wrapper (detail)
Java, Pekalongan, c. 1890
Catalogue no. 24

FIGURE 56C
Poppy
Hip wrapper (detail)
Java, Pekalongan,
c. 1900–1910
Catalogue no. 33

B

ritual come to life on the precommercial north coast cloths. Many are related to water, fertility, and growth. Fruits like the *buah delima* (passion fruit) are depicted with a profusion of seeds, which to the Chinese alluded to the birth of sons.[71] Plants symbolically linked with water abound, among others the *ganggeng*, the trailing water weed that covers inundated rice paddies, and the *cempaka mulya* (blossom of the tulip tree). Their inspiration is the *teratai* (lotus) that springs forth from the primeval waters. Moreover, the light base of the cloth is in some regions covered with multiple small dots, the *cocohan*, or rice seedlings, which make the cloth a metaphor for the paddy.[72]

Similar series of interrelated motifs give rise to a variety of meanings. Medicinal or alimentary uses of plants offer further associations. Another deeply meaningful motif is the *pohon hayat* (tree of life), which is also encountered on the large *palempore* covers imported into the archipelago from India. Often depicted growing on top of a small mountain, with birds fluttering between its flowering branches, the tree is a cosmic symbol, the axis between the upper and the underworld. It is one of the most enduring examples of the manner in which motifs of Indian, Chinese, and Muslim origin were fused with Javanese concepts (see catalogue nos. 10, 12, 17, and 23).[73]

C

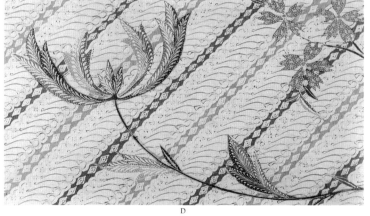

D

FIGURE 56D
Cempaka mulya
Hip wrapper (detail)
Java, Pekalongan, c. 1930
Catalogue no. 50

FIGURE 56E
Iris and starflower
Hip wrapper (detail)
Java, Kedungwuni, 1982
Catalogue no. 67

E

The Peranakan also used floral motifs of their own which have their source in Taoist and Confucianist philosophy and are often encountered in similar forms on wood carvings, porcelains, and embroidered objects. To the Chinese the peony, lotus, chrysanthemum, and prunus stand for spring, summer, autumn, and winter.[74] Though the tropical climate of Indonesia doesn't experience seasonal change, Peranakan women still use comparable flowers to represent the stages of life.

The same philosophical background is the origin of a second motif found on Peranakan cloths, a variety of birds and mythical animals. In Chinese symbolism the phoenix with its long tail feathers is considered female, while the dragon is male. In Indonesian classification, however, the Chinese symbols are reversed, with birds seen as heavenly male creatures and dragons and snakes considered chthonic and female.

The European use of flowers differs from the Asian. Stemmed flowers are bound together into nosegays or bouquets to be given as presents and displayed in baskets or vases. These are also some of the ways in which floral motifs came to be represented on Indo-European cloths. By the eighteenth century a profusion of imported European floral species "were continually blooming throughout the year in the gardens of Batavia."[75] The suggestion that European herbals may have served as the design source of the floral motifs, therefore, seems unnecessary.[76] Like the Peranakan women, the Indo-European wearers also chose their own distinctive European flowers that bloom in spring, summer, or autumn to suit their stage of life. The color of the flowers was important as well. White was for a first communion or a bride, blue for virgins, and red for ardent love and therefore married women. Violet stood for modesty and was appropriate for widows.[77] Love and marriage form a second theme that is expressed by such typical European motifs as cupids, lovebirds, and courting peacocks (see catalogue nos. 23, 29, 45).

Fairy tales symbolic of the milestones in a woman's life also provide thematic subjects. Though not universally understood, Little Red Riding Hood, wandering through the forest and threatened by the Wolf, is associated with the difficult period of maturation. Prince Charming is associated with courtship and marriage.

After 1870 fashionable trends dictated increasingly intricate designs, culminating in the *tiga negeri* style that incorporated on a single cloth the filler motifs and color styles of three different regions (see catalogue no. 13). In a way the combination of motifs from the Pasisir and central Java present the wearer as well connected or related to groups in both regions. To some elite Peranakan women, for example, these batiks may indeed have been an expression of their widely dispersed family links. At a later stage the display of affluence through the use of the expensive cloth was probably as important.[78] These developments proliferated into the twentieth century. Around 1900 large floral bouquets, surrounded by butterflies and birds and often depicted on plain grounds, increasingly took center stage as fashion for Europeans and Indo-Europeans. To this day this so-called *buketan* style is considered by many typical of *batik Pasisir*. Originally intended as a mark of high quality, the signature of the batik entrepreneur, who also devised the designs, continued to distinguish the best among these cloths.[79] Soon the *buketan* style was adopted by Peranakan Chinese in an effort to express their position as legally equal to the Dutch. European flowers were depicted in an elaborately layered, albeit often almost unrecognizable and decorative manner (FIGURE 57). By the 1930s the symbolic meanings of the motifs had lost their intricate variety. Still many of the later cloths show remnants of earlier meanings, even when purely European design sources and styles are used. It should be remembered how, after the first decade of the twentieth century, conscious feelings of racism increased among the European group, a development that also had its impact upon the rest of society. Although the Europeans themselves only wore batik as housewear, to Peranakan women batik cloth not only served to express class and status but also underlined the need to link oneself with the dominant Europeans, thereby to a large extent pushing aside the original theme of regional identity.

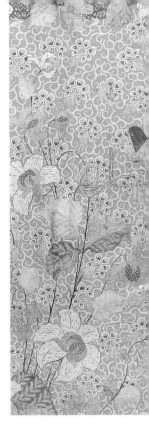

FIGURE 57
Hip wrapper (detail)
Java, Pekalongan, 1937–42
Catalogue no. 51

The Past Fifty Years

Throughout the twentieth century Pasisir styles for the urban elite of mixed descent have continued to show increasing levels of elaboration. Interestingly this trend appears almost impervious to the shattering political changes that affected the archipelago after the early 1940s. The expression of ethnic identity and status, which for the mixed groups was generally linked with economic prominence, continued to take precedence throughout the last fifty years.[80] The *kain panjang*, worn in the more elegant central Javanese style, gained popularity. Its designs, however, changed and became a fusion of the Europeanized florals with the intricate backgrounds and specific color combinations that were consistent with Peranakan or Indo-Arabian tastes.

The most complex and vibrant examples of these elaborate styles are the cloths designated *Djawa Hokokai*, an organization established by the Japanese as a tool for indoctrinating every Indonesian over fourteen years of age; it ultimately became the cradle of the nationalist movement.[81] Almost no information is available regarding the wearers of *Hokokai* batiks. No examples seem to have been recovered in Japan, though initially the style incorporated Japanese design elements and was made for the officers of the army of occupation, who were the only customers able to afford these costly pieces.

After Indonesia became independent in 1945, a similarly complex style was found to satisfy the needs of the two remaining groups of mixed descent, the Peranakan and the Indo-Arabians. Both continued to choose their own specific colors. The taste of the Peranakan ran to shimmering pastels, while women of Arabian descent preferred a deeper and often more subdued range of color. Remarkably during the late 1950s the latter for a short period came to be worn by many modern Indonesian women, who were part of the elite in and around the new capital, Jakarta. This may indicate that the distance between these two groups was subsiding rapidly.[82] The postwar styles were often denoted as *Djawa baroe* (New Java),[83] a term that to this group of wearers may well have been charged with aspirations for unity.[84] A separate batik style denoted as *batik nasional* (see FIGURE 64) was created during the 1950s and early 1960s, when President Sukarno promoted efforts by various designers of both Indonesian and mixed backgrounds to fuse central Javanese motifs and Pasisir colors. This style was meant to serve as true national dress. Similar hybrid designs have continued to decorate most of the cloths in Pasisir colors until the present day.

Retracing our steps to the initial question, whether *batik Pasisir* served as a lingua franca across the archipelago, the following conclusions can be offered. It has been revealed how initially a limited range of colors and motifs on various styles of locally made cloths combined into a closed system of meanings for Javanese or locally born Peranakan wearers. While, in the course of the nineteenth century, the same range of colors and motifs came to serve as emblems of gradually widening regional and ethnic identities, each new group of wearers in Java, Sumatra, and possibly Bali made their own choices from the existing designs to accord with their particular preferences and fit them into their local concepts. After the mid-nineteenth century, however, the gradual development of a pluralistic colonial society went hand in hand with an expanding range of designs that included specific Europeanized and Chinese motifs and colors and served to distinguish between the various racial groups. By 1870 the increasingly hierarchical and racial divisions necessitated cloths that gave expression to changed priorities of identity, particularly for the Peranakan. They employed the local dress, adorned with hybrid Europeanized designs and Chinese colors, to express their intermediate position between the colonial establishment and the local population. After 1945 and Indonesian independence *batik Pasisir* continued to serve mainly to distinguish between different groups. Instead of serving as lingua franca, it consisted of a series of different dialects and creole languages based on the same roots.

NOTES

1. *Indisch* is the Dutch term for persons with a Dutch or Indo-European father and an Indo-European or native mother.

2. V. I. van de Wall, *Vrouwen uit den Compagnies Tijd* (Weltevreden: Visser, 1923), 247; translation by the author.

3. Jean Gelman Taylor, *The Social World of Batavia: European and Eurasian in Dutch Asia* (Madison: University of Wisconsin Press, 1983), 116, citing Q. M. R. Ver Huell, *Herinneringen van eene reis naar de Oost-Indiën*, 2 vols. (Amsterdam: Zweesaardt, 1835).

4. P. de Kat Angelino, *Batikrapport* (Weltevreden: Landsdrukkerij, 1930–31), 1: 86, 95; 2: 22; and Robyn Maxwell, *Textiles of Southeast Asia: Tradition, Trade and Transformation* (Canberra: Australian National Gallery; Oxford: Oxford University Press, 1990), 414.

5. An initial attempt is made in Danielle C. Geirnaert and Rens Heringa, *The A.E.D.T.A. Batik Collection* (Paris: Association pour l'Etude et la Documentation des Textiles d'Asie, 1989).

6. G. P. Rouffaer, *Over Indische batikkunst, vooral die op Java* (Haarlem, 1900), 15; idem., "Beeldende Kunst in Nederlandsch Indië," *Bijdragen van het Koninklijk Instituut voor Taal- Land- en Volkenkunde van Nederlandsch-Indië* (hereafter *BKI*) 89 (1932): 645; and Alit Veldhuisen-Djajasoebrata, "On the Origin and Nature of Larangan: Forbidden Batik Patterns from the Central Javanese Principalities," in *Indonesian Textiles*, 1979 Roundtable on Museum Textiles, ed., Mattiebelle Gittinger (Washington D.C.: Textile Museum, 1980), 210–22.

7. J. E. Jasper, "Javaansche batikmotieven," in *Het Daghet* (Bandung: Kolff, 1905–6), 1: 335–36.

8. See Rens Heringa, *Spiegels van ruimte en tijd*, exh. cat. (The Hague: Museon 1994).

9. J. W. van Dapperen, "Tegalsche klederdrachten in de achttiende en negentiende eeuw," *Djawa* 13 (1933): 191–98.

10. Gelman Taylor, *Social World of Batavia*, 66–68.

11. *Staatsblad*, nos. 110–11 (1872), cited in *Tijdschrift voor Nederlandsch Indië* 2 (1882): 399–400.

12. *Encyclopaedie van Nederlandsch Indië* (The Hague: Martinus Nijhoff; Leiden: E. J. Brill, 1919), 2: 171; and L. W. C. van den Berg, "De Afwijkingen van het Mohammedaansche familie- en erfrecht op Java en Madoera," *BKI* 41 (1892): 456.

13. Aquasi Boachi, "Mededelingen over de Chineezen op het eiland Java," *BKI* 4 (1856): 288–91; Harmen C. Veldhuisen, *Batik Belanda 1840–1940* (Jakarta: Gaya Favorit, 1993), 62.

14. Gelman Taylor, *Social World of Batavia*, 127. Creoles are descendants of European settlers; mestizos, persons of mixed racial ancestry.

15. Ibid., 72.

16. Berg, "Afwijkingen van het Mohammedaansche, 464.

17. Gelman Taylor, *Social World of Batavia*, 73.

18. Tan Chee Beng, *The Baba of Melaka: Culture and Identity of a Chinese Peranakan Community in Malaysia* (Kuala Lumpur: Pelanduk Publications, 1988), 105.

19. Kat Angelino, *Batikrapport*, 1: 86, 95; and J. J. B. Ostmeijer, *Handleiding bij het schatten samengesteld ten behoeve van het personeel van den pandhuisdienst* (Batavia: Albrecht, n.d.), 256.

20. Kat Angelino, *Batikrapport*, 1: 22; 3: 23.

21. *De Echo: Weekblad voor dames in Indië* (hereinafter *De Echo*) (1900–1901): 101.

22. Maxwell, *Textiles of Southeast Asia*, 306.

23. G. P. Rouffaer and H. H. Juynboll, *De batik-kunst in Nederlandsch Indië and haar geschiedenis* (Utrecht: A. Oosthoek, 1914), 171.

24. Valery M. Garrett, *Chinese Clothing: An Illustrated Guide* (Hong Kong: Oxford University Press, 1994), 22.

25. F. de Haan, *Oud Batavia: Gedenkboek* (Batavia: Kolff, 1922), 1: 148–49.

26. Ibid., 1: 149; Myra Sidharta to the author, Jakarta, June 1995.

27. Gelman Taylor, *Social World of Batavia*, 66; Haan, *Oud Batavia*, 1: 147. Besides the *kabaya*, other types of open jackets were worn over time, some of them known by somewhat confusing names, such as the *kebayak Javanese*), a short jacket open at the front and tied at the wrists worn by Javanese women.

28. Haan, *Oud Batavia*, 1: 49; Harmen C. Veldhuisen, *Batik Belanda*, 26.

29. See Gelman Taylor, *Social World of Batavia*, 46–49.

30. Ibid., 100; Haan, *Oud Batavia*, 1: 147.

31. Ate Tan-Loa, oral communication, Jakarta, December 1994.

32. Haan, *Oud Batavia*, 141.

33. Mevrouw A. Forbes, *Het verre oosten: Reisindrukken van Mevr. Henry Forbes. Vertaling A. M. van Deventer-usken Huët* (Amsterdam: van Kampen & Zoon, 1888), 41.

34. "Vrouwenmode in Indië nu voor vijftig jaar," in *Gedenkboek 10 Jaar van de Huisvrouw in Indië* (Batavia: Vereeniging van Huisvrouwen, 1941), 470.

35. Ibid., 467.

36. Ibid., 479.

37. *De Echo* (1905–6): 357.

38. J. Kloppenburg-Versteegh, *Het leven van de europeesche vrouw in Indië* (Deventer: Charles Dixon, 1913), 12–13.

39. J. M. J. Catenius-van der Meijden, *Ons huis in Indië* (Semarang: Masman & Stroink, 1908), 73.

40. C. J. Rutten-kelharing, *Waaraan moet ik denken? Wat moet ik doen? Denken voor het Hollandsche meisje dat als huisvrouw naar Indië gaat* (Gorinchem: Noorduyn & Zoon, 1927), 6.

41. Harmen C. Veldhuisen, oral communication, Rotterdam, 1994.

42. Part of the following material was used by the author in a different form in Geirnaert and Heringa, *A.E.D.T.A. Batik Collection*.

43. See Heringa, *Spiegels van ruimte en tijd*, for an extensive analysis of this concept as it operates in Tuban.

44. Text of unnumbered plate, "Eene pseudo slavin…," in A. van Pers, *Nederlandsche Oost-Indische typen* (The Hague: C. W. Mieling, 1856).

45. J. J. M. de Groot, "The Wedding Garments of a Chinese Woman," *Internationales Archiv für Ethnologie* 4 (1891): 182–84, pl. xvi.

46. Geirnaert and Heringa, *A.E.D.T.A. Batik Collection*, 15, ill. xxvii.

47. Veldhuisen, *Batik Belanda*, 64.

48. Forbes, *Het verre oosten*, 41; Kloppenburg-Versteegh, *Het leven van de Europeesche vrouw*, 14.

49. Rouffaer, *Over Indische batikkunst*, 10.

50. Extensive information on the use of color on Java can be found in Rens Heringa, "Dye Process and Life Sequence: The Coloring of Textiles in an East Javanese Village," in *To Speak with Cloth: Studies in Indonesian Textiles*, ed. Mattiebelle Gittinger (Los Angeles: Museum of Cultural History, University of California, Los Angeles, 1989), 107–30.

51. Traditionally only postmenopausal women were allowed to handle the natural dyes; in the batik industry paid male laborers executed the heavy dye work under the supervision of the owner.

52. Kat Angelino, *Batikrapport*, 1: 193.

53. See Heringa, *Spiegels van ruimte en tijd*, 17–18, for a detailed analysis of these divisions.

54. Dapperen, "Tegalsche klederdrachten," 191–98.

55. J. J. M. de Groot, *The Religious System of China: Its Ancient Forms, Evolution, History and Present Aspect, Manners, and Customs and Social Institutions Connected Therewith* (Leiden: E. J. Brill, 1892), 21.

56. M. J. de Raadt-Apell, *De batikkerij Van Zuylen te Pekalongan* (Zutphen: Terra, 1980), 17; Harmen C. Veldhuisen, "Ontwikkelingen in de Batik van Java," in *Handwerken zonder Grenzen* (Utrecht: Kluwer, 1983–84), 125–27.

57. Kat Angelino, *Batikrapport*, 1: 194; Myra Sidharta, oral communication, Jakarta, December 1994.

58. Ate Tan-Loa, oral communication.

59. Ostmeijer, *Handleiding bij het schatten*, 261. In the catalogue section of the present volume this development is indicated by naming the actual place of production with "in the style of" for the origin of the color style.

60. The two motif types may be compared with those on imported textiles from India, the geometric *cinde* and the freeform *sembagi* or *sarasa*.

61. Schuyler V. R. Cammann, "Symbolic Meanings in Oriental Rug Patterns," *Textile Museum Journal* 3, no. 3 (1972): 15.

62. Groot, *Religious System of China*, 24; C. A. S. Williams, *Outlines of Chinese Symbolism and Art Motives*, 3d ed. (New York: Dover, 1976), 132.

63. Veldhuisen, *Batik Belanda*, 45.

64. Ibid., 64.

65. Ibid., 19; Veldhuisen, oral communication.

66. Rens Heringa, "Tilling the Cloth and Weaving the Land: Textiles, Land and Regeneration in an East Javanese Area," in *Weaving Patterns of Life: Indonesian Textile Symposium* (1991), eds., Marie-Louise Nabholz-Kartaschoff et al. (Basel: Museum of Ethnography, 1993), 158.

67. Forbes, *Het verre oosten*, 7.

68. Barbara Leigh, "The Theme of the Heavenly Garden: Gold Thread Embroidery in Aceh" in *Weaving Patterns of Life*, 181.

69. Jack Goody, *The Culture of Flowers* (Cambridge: Cambridge University Press, 1994), 347.

70. See Rens Heringa, *Een schitterende geschiedenis: Weefsels en batiks van Palembang en Djambi*, exh. cat. (The Hague: Museon, 1993), 8.

71. Goody, *Culture of Flowers*, 370.

72. Heringa, "Tilling the Cloth," 157.

73. Robyn Maxwell, "The Tree of Life in Indonesian Textiles: Ancient Iconography or Imported Chinoiserie?" in *Indonesian Textiles: Symposium 1985*, eds., Gisela Völger and Karin von Welck, vol. 14 of *Ethnologica* (Cologne: Rautenstrauch-Joest Museum, 1991), 110.

74. Williams, *Outlines*, 192.

75. Ong Tae-hae, *The Chinaman Abroad, or a Desultory Account of the Malayan Archipelago, Particularly of Java*, ed. and trans. W. H. Medhurst (Shanghai: Mission Press, 1849), 69.

76. Mary Hunt Kahlenberg, "The Influence of the European Herbal on Indonesian Batik," in *Indonesian Textiles*, 1979 Roundtable on Museum Textiles, ed., Mattiebelle Gittinger (Washington D.C.: Textile Museum, 1980), 243–45.

77. Goody, *Culture of Flowers*, 241–46.

78. Veldhuisen, *Batik Belanda*, 87.

79. This practice had actually started several decades earlier. See ibid., 62.

80. At present most autochthonous Indonesians prefer central Javanese styles for official wear.

81. M. C. Ricklefs, *A History of Modern Indonesia since c. 1300*, 2d rev. ed. (London: MacMillan, 1993), 206–9.

82. Hamid Algadri, *Dutch Policy against Islam and Indonesians of Arab Descent in Indonesia* (Jakarta: Pustaka LP3ES Indonesia, 1994), 24: 139.

83. Alit Veldhuisen-Djajasoebrata, *Batik op Java* (Lochem: De Tijdstroom, 1973), 41.

84. More research is needed regarding the relations among Muslim groups of different backgrounds.

THE ROLE OF ENTREPRENEURS
IN THE STYLISTIC DEVELOPMENT OF *Batik Pasisir*

•

HARMEN C. VELDHUISEN

Indo-European, Peranakan, Javanese, and I.

Translated by Rosemary Robson

NOTE

1. Inger McCabe Elliott, *Batik: Fabled Cloth of Java* (New York: Clarkson N. Potter, 1984); M. J. de Raadt-Apell, *De batikkerij Van Zuylen te Pekalongan: Midden-Java 1890–1946* (Zutphen: Terra, 1980); Pepin van Roojen, *Batik Design*, 2d ed. (Amsterdam: Pepin, 1994); and H. C. Veldhuisen, *Batik Belanda 1840–1940* (Jakarta: Gaya Favorit, 1993).

abian entrepreneurs were active along the north coast of Java. Little information about many of these men and women and their workshops was recorded. Recent publications have shed light on the lives of Indo-European entrepreneurs, always women on the Pasisir, and to a lesser extent Peranakan entrepreneurs,[1] but our knowledge of Javanese and Indo-Arabian entrepreneurs, with a few notable exceptions, remains scanty.

Carolina Josephina von Franquemont
(Java, 1817–67)
Catalogue nos. 17–18

Carolina von Franquemont's grandfather, Philip August David von Franquemont joined the Netherlands East Indies Army at the end of the eighteenth century, arriving at Batavia (Jakarta) as an officer in 1791. His brother Carl, also an officer, arrived in 1794. Both married Indo-European women shortly after their arrival. In 1815 Carolina's father, Mattheys von Franquemont, married his sixteen-year-old cousin Charlotte Elisabeth. Carolina was born in Batavia March 25 1817. Her grandfather moved to Surabaya after her birth, where he was registered as a merchant. In 1835 her father also moved there as a merchant.

Carolina von Franquemont never married and in 1840, at age twenty-three, started a batik workshop. Indeed, she is the earliest female Indo-European batik entrepreneur known to us today. She moved her workshop in 1845 to the slopes of volcanic Mount Ungaran near the Ungaran River in Semarang, where she had relatives. There she had at her disposal not only clean water for the preparation of white cotton and the dye process but also trained batik makers and only a short distance away a well-to-do clientele. G. P. Rouffaer writes that she "made sarung almost exclusively, all expressly for sale to half or wholly European ladies and Chinese women—the latter, as everybody knows, always of mixed blood in our colonies, originally the children of Chinese immigrants by Javanese women, they later married within their own group."[1]

Demand for her batiks was bolstered by their technical perfection.[2] Using vegetable dyes, Von Franquemont succeeded in imitating the rich color scheme of Indian chintz. In addition to red, blue, ocher, and brown, she developed a

A. J. F. Jans née Veenstra
(Java, c. 1850–c. 1920)
Catalogue no. 22

A. J. F. Jans was well known as the only Dutch batik entrepreneur in Pekalongan. She was born in Java of Dutch parents. Before her marriage Jans had started a batik workshop, and she always wore sarung and kabaya, even when attending celebrations at the local Dutch club.

At an early age she married Theodor J. Jans, a young solicitor who had come out from the Netherlands. They settled in a large house on the Heerenstraat, the main street of Pekalongan. Through her marriage she became a member of the European upper crust, even though she ran a batik workshop, which was not done in those circles.

After the death of her husband around 1885, Jans signed her batiks "Wed. J. Jans" (wed. is the abbreviation for the Dutch weduwe [widow]). This is noteworthy for dating her batiks. Around 1900 she resumed signing J. (possibly for Johanna)[1] Jans; the design of these batiks distinguishes them from those made before 1885.

colorfast green, which, given the Malay pronunciation of her surname, came to be known as Prankemon green.

A Von Franquemont batik is recognizable by its color range, the perfection of its drawing, and the design. Von Franquemont was a trendsetter, but the limited production of her workshop meant that her finished batiks were fairly exclusive items. Her designs were sought after, however, and quickly imitated by other entrepreneurs. Von Franquemont herself copied designs from colleagues and borrowed European motifs from the Dutch women's journal *Aglaia*. Rouffaer states that she had the exclusive right to copy these.[3] This says a great deal about the prestige Von Franquemont enjoyed. She probably also copied Chinese designs from Peranakan entrepreneurs. This deduction is validated by the fact that there is a mythological story illustrated on a batik from a Peranakan workshop which is virtually identical to a Von Franquemont batik (as well as to one by another Indo-European entrepreneur, Catharina van Oosterom).[4] Von Franquemont also made use of traditional north coast designs as well as some from the Principalities.

In 1867 Mount Ungaran erupted and swept Von Franquemont and her workshop away. Contemporary entrepreneurs had succeeded in imitating her green dye, but their styles differed from the real *batik Prankemon*.

NOTES

1. G. P. Rouffaer and H. H. Juynboll, *De batik-kunst in Nederlandsch Indië en haar geschiedenis* (Utrecht: A. Oosthoek, 1914), p. 138.

2. G. P. Rouffaer, "De voornaamste industriën der inlandsche bevolking van Java en Madoera," in *Koloniaal Economische Bijdragen*, ed. C. Th. van Deventer (The Hague: Martinus Nijhoff, 1904), p. 24.

3. Ibid.

4. H. C. Veldhuisen, *Batik Belanda 1840–1940* (Jakarta: Gaya Favorit, 1993), no. 13.

Being a widow with small children but no pension, she could not survive on the earnings of her workshop and so took in lodgers and developed her hobby, growing roses and orchids, into a business. In 1893 she was named chairwoman of a local committee charged with preparing an official gift for the newly crowned Dutch queen, Wilhelmina: ten dolls representing the diverse trades of Pekalongan. The dolls included five batik makers and a cotton spinner.

In 1909 Jans had approximately sixty batik makers in her service, making her workshop one of the biggest in the town. Sometime between 1911 and 1915, she sold the workshop to a Mrs. Wiler, who in turn sold it to Jacqueline van Ardenne. The new owners in succession paid the employees' advances and purchased Jans's color recipes and the rights to copy her designs and signature. The style of these later "Jans" batiks differs from that of the originals and the signature is larger.[2]

NOTES

1. H. C. Veldhuisen, interview with Annie Tussenbroek, Meppel, 1992; Tussenbroek thought she recalled mention of the name Johanna.

2. H. C. Veldhuisen, *Batik Belanda 1840–1940* (Jakarta: Gaya Favorit, 1993), no. 76.

Lien Metzelaar née de Stoop
(Java, c. 1855–1930)
Catalogue no. 24

Lien de Stoop was Indo-European, though nothing more is known about her parents. Her husband, H. C. Metzelaar, worked for the forestry service. They lived in an old colonial house on the Heerenstraat in Pekalongan. At that time A. J. F. Jans lived at the far end of the street, and from 1904 the Jan van Zuylen family lived just three houses away. In 1880, after her husband's death, she started her batik workshop and ran it until 1918. It was she who introduced the greatest number of innovations reflective of European taste into *batik Pekalongan*.

H. C. Metzelaar died young, leaving his widow with four children and a very small pension. Like Jans, she took in lodgers and sold floral arrangements, but her main work consisted of batik design, the actual textiles made by women working in their own homes. An Indo-Arabian arts and crafts dealer from Batavia, named Baoudjir, eventually became an admirer of her work and lent her the money to set up a workshop. Baoudjir's customers were willing to pay a premium for *batik Metzelaar*, or *batik Metz*, as it came to be known.

Perhaps it was through her association with Baoudjir that Metzelaar began producing her most striking contribution to the Indo-European *sarung*, her *nitik* design, which resembled woven textiles. Alternating horizontal bands of such patterns and tiny flowers were introduced into the *kepala*. The lower border,

THE SISTERS VAN ZUYLEN NÉE NIESSEN

Christina ("Tina") and Eliza ("Lies") Niessen and their brother, Mathieu, were the children of a Dutch soldier in the Netherlands East Indies Army and his Indo-European wife, whose last name was Achterbeek. After Mathieu's birth in 1864, Niessen was seriously wounded and sent back to the Netherlands to recuperate. His wife did not feel at home with her Dutch in-laws or in the Roman Catholic area where they lived and so returned with her children to Batavia, though she had no source of income there. With a common-law husband, a petty bureaucrat, she moved to Gang Klinci (Rabbit Alley), said to have been named for the swarms of children who lived there. Mrs. Niessen had four more children while living there. Tina and Lies earned money selling homemade pastries to passersby. Later the sisters married two brothers, Jan and Alphons van Zuylen, who also lived on the alley.

Christina ("Tina") van Zuylen
(Java, 1861–1930)
Catalogue no. 25

Around 1885 Jan van Zuylen was transferred to the customs service at Pekalongan. The couple settled on Bugisan, a peninsula where many Indo-European batik entrepreneurs lived. To earn extra income Mr. Van Zuylen sold school supplies in a little shop he rented, while his wife sold floral arrangements to private clients and bouquets for Sunday services at the Protestant church. Their family grew steadily; every year there was another child. Mrs. Van Zuylen started to order batiks to sell. Home-, not workshop-made, these were the then fashionable tablecloths, tea cozies, handkerchiefs, and other relatively small and inexpensive items. When this turned out to be a success, she commissioned *sarung*, which required a larger outlay. Because she did not have resources to pay advances for batik makers of her own, her friend, Lien Metzelaar, lent her three of her trained workers. This was the beginning of Tina van Zuylen's workshop.

or both upper and lower borders, also imitated woven patterns. The *badan* of these batiks display such European symbols as the cross, anchor, and heart (for faith, hope, and charity) or a horseshoe depicted on a cream ground.[1] The application of the *nitik* pattern required a special *canting* and long training. In Pekalongan Indo-European entrepreneurs delegated this specialized work to Indo-Arabian entrepreneurs, who for many years had dedicated themselves to the reproduction of imitation-weave patterns on batik for Muslim customers.

Early in her career Metzelaar signed her batiks "L Metzelaar Pekalongan," but after she had established her reputation, around 1890, she signed them "L Metz Pek." This is useful not only for dating her batiks but also for dating those of entrepreneurs who copied her trendsetting designs.

With a portion of a substantial legacy left by her father, the twenty-eight-year-old Jacqueline van Ardenne purchased Metzelaar's workshop and house in 1918. Metzelaar then bought a house in Bandung, but after the marriage of her son, Kees, in 1920, she lived most of the time with the young couple in Pekalongan, then Yogyakarta, and finally Surakarta. She died there in 1930 but was buried, according to her wish, in the graveyard in Pekalongan, where other batik entrepreneurs had been laid to rest.

NOTE

1. H. C. Veldhuisen, *Batik Belanda 1840–1940* (Jakarta: Gaya Favorit, 1993), nos. 47–48.

Jan van Zuylen died around 1905, leaving his widow to raise eleven children: eight boys and three girls. She took in lodgers and gave private lessons in Dutch to young Indo-Chinese boys who needed to speak it well in order to be accepted at the Dutch government school, a prerequisite for higher education in Java.

Around 1920 the batik *canting* industry collapsed, and Van Zuylen was one of many entrepreneurs forced to close her workshop. She had not been an innovator in design and had no specific clientele of her own. She moved to Batavia with her youngest son and took in lodgers. Her five oldest sons contributed to her support. Though a Protestant, she lived in a Roman Catholic district, where her friendly and helpful character contributed to her popularity. When she died, her grave was carpeted with flowers from those who cherished her.

Eliza Charlotte ("Lies") van Zuylen
(Java, 1863–1947)
Catalogue nos. 26, 30–34, 53–54

*Indo-Europeans usually fol-
lowed Dutch custom with
regard to the use of personal
names. Accordingly, Eliza
van Zuylen was always
addressed by the diminutive
"Lies." "E" or "Eliza" was
for formal use only, for
example, the actual signing
of batiks.

In 1888 Alphons van Zuylen was appointed inspector of the government orphan-
age in Pekalongan. He supplemented this sinecure with work at the government
pawnshop. The couple settled in Bugisan near Jan and Tina. Lies van Zuylen
was very industrious and helped out in her sister's workshop. Descendants state
that her husband was displeased with the amount of time she spent there and
gave her the advance money for three batik makers and a workshop of her own.
She ran the shop in a businesslike manner, assisted by her husband with its growing administration.

By 1904 the Van Zuylen family and workshop had outgrown the compound
at Bugisan, and their prosperity made a move to the Heerenstraat possible.
Their house was renovated, and in the backyard two work spaces were erected
for the batik makers. Sleeping quarters were built for those who worked into
the evening. When Mr. Van Zuylen died in 1918, his widow owned the largest
Indo-European batik workshop in Java.

Lies van Zuylen copied the designs of the other batik businesswomen but
produced her own creations as well. Art nouveau patterns of wading birds combined with an asymmetrical tree appeared in the *badan*, and after this achieved
some success, it evolved into an asymmetrical wisteria tree under which two
peacocks shelter. She then repeated the pattern from the *badan* on the *kepala*.
Around 1910 this in turn became a bouquet of assorted flowers. Van Zuylen's
bouquet became the trademark of *batik Pekalongan* and was copied along the
entire north coast.

Due to her personal popularity and the fact that she catered to the only clientele, the Peranakan, still able to afford expensive batiks, Van Zuylen was the sole
Indo-European batik entrepreneur to survive the economic crisis of 1935, the
worst year of the Depression in Java. The Peranakan preferred the bright colors
obtained from synthetic dyes, which forced Van Zuylen to abandon vegetable
dyes for synthetics. Her purple was a water-soluble aniline mixture; the bright red
on some of her earlier batiks is synthetic as well.[1] In 1935 her son George,
a chemist, assumed supervision of the dyeing process, using synthetics.

Mrs. Simonet née Tan Ien Nio
(Java, c. 1865–1937)
Catalogue no. 27

Tan Ien Nio was the daughter of a Peranakan business acquaintance of Jacobus
Constantijn Simonet, an Indo-European born in Java in 1836. When Simonet's
Indo-European wife died after childbirth, Tan Ien Nio's father proposed that
Simonet take his daughter as a housekeeper *(nyai)*. Simonet lived on the
Residentsweg, a road that lies behind the Heerenstraat; his backyard bordered
Lien Metzelaar's. The wives of his neighbors were also batik entrepreneurs.
Simonet and Tan Ien Nio had four daughters and a son. Their first daughter,
Jacqueline Charlotte, was born in 1890, the year they were married. It was she
who bought Metzelaar's workshop in 1918.

Although she could neither read nor write, at an early age Tan Ien Nio
learned batiking from her mother. When she started a small workshop with three

Van Zuylen signed her batiks, "E v Zuylen." Many were stamped "Batikkerij [batik workshop] / Mevr. E. van Zuylen / Pekalongan." Since many of her batik makers worked in their own homes, especially during peak periods, this oval ink stamp represented a security measure, effectively preventing the sale of unfinished batiks to third parties. Today the stamp proves a batik is an original Van Zuylen despite the often badly drawn signatures and work less perfect than that usually associated with her shop. Poor workmanship typifies peak-season batiks that were not made under her personal supervision. She herself was a noted perfectionist.

From 1937 on, assigned pattern numbers were applied directly with the *canting* to each batik to facilitate reordering by customers. (Formerly paper labels had been used.) After 1940 Van Zuylen's signature was eliminated when she had problems drawing with pencil on fabric. Her signature was being faked by other entrepreneurs in any case, and her devoted clients could recognize a real Van Zuylen even without the signature.

During the Japanese occupation of Java Van Zuylen's batik *obi* for Japanese women and *kain panjang pagi sore* were ordered by high-ranking Japanese military personnel. These differed from those she had made previously, having far more crowded backgrounds and many tiny motifs in the patterns. The result is so overcrowded that the bouquets are difficult to discern.

The Van Zuylens were interned by the Indonesians after the capitulation of Japan. Suffering from diabetes, Van Zuylen died in the Franciscan convent in Pekalongan in January 1947 and was buried in the graveyard there. The batik workshop was plundered, but Oei Khing Liem, a Peranakan entrepreneur, offered Van Zuylen's heirs a very large sum of money (an amount of 60,000 guilders was mentioned by her son Willem Alphons)[2] for the right to her signature—a handsome figure given that the batik industry seemed moribund—but the offer was declined.

NOTES
1. H. C. Veldhuisen, *Batik Belanda 1840–1940* (Jakarta: Gaya Favorit, 1993), no. 70.
2. M. J. de Raadt-Apell, *De batikkerij Van Zuylen te Pekalongan: Midden-Java 1890–1946* (Zutphen: Terra, 1980), 57.

batik makers, her husband taught her to write her signature with the *canting*. Her designs are in the European manner and display a strong, original style. When she closed her workshop in 1930, she still had only a few batik makers in service, and these were taken over by her daughter Jacqueline (Mrs. Arthur van Ardenne), who continued to produce batik, despite the Depression, until 1935. Mrs. Simonet's house was sold to the Ursuline Sisters, who built a girls' school on the property, while she herself moved to Bendan Street in the southern part of Pekalongan and died there in 1937.

The Role of Entrepreneurs

Maria Paulina Carp née Rapilla
(Java, 1860–1916)
Figure 63

In service to Pangeran Ario Tjondronegoro, the regent of Demak, Maria Paulina Rapilla's mother had a son and three daughters by her employer, whom she left, according to descendants, when the regent announced that he had chosen his "first wife." Rapilla, who had learned batik as a child at court, settled with her children in Banyumas, where she converted to Protestantism. Her conversion permits us to deduce that she had entered the service of Catharina van Oosterom, who welcomed experienced batik makers into her flourishing workshop. It is known that Van Oosterom placed enormous pressure on her personnel to become Protestants.

Maria was born in 1860 and learned batik from her mother. It is probable that she and her two sisters also worked for Van Oosterom. Through a Dutch Protestant family in Semarang, Maria came in contact with W. E. Th. Carp. Carp was born in the Netherlands in 1841. At an early age he immigrated to Java in the service of a Dutch plantation company. Lower-level employees came to such companies unmarried and were not allowed to marry on Java until they had reached positions with incomes adequate to sustain a "proper" marriage. Therefore, most had illegitimate children by their housekeepers. By the time he met Maria, Carp's

Susannah Elisabeth Bouwer née Ferns
(Java, 1880–1944)
Catalogue no. 28

FRONT ROW LEFT

Susannah Ferns's parents, Susannah Weston Gregory and William Ferns, were married in the Roman Catholic church in Liverpool in 1867. He was an engineer who worked on a oceangoing steamboat. Their first three offspring died in childhood, and the couple decided to move to Java. In 1875 they settled in Surabaya and some years later in Pekalongan, where William got a job in a sugar factory. They lived on the Residentsweg, next to the Simonets. The Ferns had three more children, two daughters and one son. Susannah, the eldest, was born in 1880. Mrs. Ferns had brought her sewing machine with her from England and earned money by sewing dresses for the wives of prominent citizens. She also took batik makers in service, who made *sarung* to her designs. Susannah and her sister, Emma, learned the business in their mother's workshop.

In 1910 Susannah married Bastiaan Bouwer, a garden supervisor on a sugar plantation near Pekalongan. He was Indo-European, and for that reason Susannah's brother broke off relations with the newlyweds. The couple took the house next to her parents, and Susannah started a batik workshop of her own. When it proved successful, the pair leased a parcel of land from a neighbor in

The Role of Entrepreneurs

Javanese housekeeper and mother of his four children had died, and Carp wanted a wife and mother for the children. When Carp married Maria, he had attained the position of administrator of a large plantation in West Java. He had a large estate of his own, kept Australian horses, and ran a fashionable carriage. When he died in 1897, however, he left his wife and their ten children with more debts than assets. Financial backing from her oldest stepson enabled her to open a batik workshop in 1900 in Pekalongan.

Grandchildren describe Maria Carp as a haughty woman who had no innate talent for business. She never found it easy to be a Javanese entrepreneur among the established Indo-Europeans, to which group she belonged by marriage and by membership in the Dutch Protestant church. In addition, she had been deprived of the luxury she had once enjoyed. To add to her troubles, the Javanese batik makers in her employ felt demeaned by working for another Javanese.

The six signed batiks that have so far come to light do not reveal a personal style. Clearly she imitated the batiks of her Indo-European colleagues to perfection. No documentation indicates how long she continued her workshop.

order to build a more spacious workplace. In 1918 Bouwer died, leaving his widow with four children, the youngest a baby. His employment entitled her to a fairly generous pension, but, like other entrepreneurs she took in lodgers and arranged flowers on commission.

In 1920 Susannah Bouwer had forty batik makers in permanent service. She did not have her own draftsman, however, and ordered designs from a man who worked for other shops as well. Without the capital to invest in a large stock of batiks, the bulk of her production was sent by train cash-on-delivery to Batavia in packets of twenty *sarung*. Other *sarung* were made to order or sold by middlemen. By 1935 the few batik makers who continued to work for her did so at home. Only the dyeing was still done at her compound.

Interned by the Japanese in October 1943, Bouwer died the following year. Among the few belongings she took to the internment camp were drawings of her batik designs. These she entrusted to her daughter, who carried them with her when she was repatriated to the Netherlands. She lost them while moving from one boardinghouse to another.

The Tie Siet
(Java, d. before 1981)
Catalogue nos. 52, 65

PHOTOGRAPH, ALIT VELDHUISEN-DJAJASOEBRATA

One of the most important Peranakan batik entrepreneurs in Pekalongan was The Tie Siet. He ran his business from about 1920 until the 1950s. Around 1930 he introduced various extremely crowded backgrounds, composed of such motifs as ferns, on *batik Pekalongan* with repeated bouquets. This background was featured in either the *kepala* or *badan*. On *kain panjang pagi sore*, divided equally into different patterns and color ranges, the dense ground was applied to one of the halves. Crowded backgrounds were not a new phenomenon on north coast batiks, but in most instances these were purely repetitive. The's freely drawn style had been a feature of commercial Lasem batiks but was then unknown in Pekalongan. In the wake of his initiative, there was an increasing use of such backgrounds on textiles produced in Peranakan workshops.

Oey Soen Khing
(Java, 1861–1942)

Mrs. Oey Kok Sing née Kho Tjing Nio
(Java, d. 1966)
Catalogue no. 51

Oey Djien Nio
(pseud.: Jane Hendromartono;
Java, 1924–86)

Kho Tjing Nio's mother-in-law, Oey Soen Khing, was born in 1861. She ran a batik workshop in Pekalongan but never signed her batiks. She died in 1942. Kho Tjing Nio's husband, Oey Kok Sing, was born about 1896 and assisted his mother in her workshop. He married Kho Tjing Nio, who was born in Solo (Surakarta) and not accustomed to batik production. After their marriage she learned the profession from her mother-in-law and husband. She signed her designs "Nj. (abbreviation for the Malay *njonja* [Mrs.]) Oeij[1] Kok Sing" and used her husband's name stamp. She died in 1966.

Oei Khing Liem
(Java, fl. c. 1910–60)
Catalogue nos. 46–49

The earliest batiks of Oei Khing Liem can be dated around 1910. His house and workshop were on the Residentsweg in Pekalongan, and his backyard bordered on Lies van Zuylen's. One of her daughters remembers that her mother and Oei used to converse in Dutch over the hedge early in the morning when she inspected her compound.

Oey Soe Tjoen
(Java, 1901–75)

and Kwee Tjoen Giok
(Java, b. 1905)
Catalogue nos. 56, 67

PHOTOGRAPH, BRIAN BRAKE

Oey Soe Tjoen's parents ran a workshop for stamped batiks in Kedungwuni. In 1925 he married Kwee Tjoen Giok, a schoolteacher, whose parents also owned a workshop for stamped batiks, in nearby Batang. (Kwee assumed a European-style name, Nettie Kwee.) Oey and Kwee started a workshop for hand-drawn batiks, for which both created designs and color schemes, though they signed their designs individually: he as Oey Soe Tjoen Kedoengwoeni (Kedungwuni) and she as Kwee Nettie Kedoengwoeni, inverting her name in the Chinese manner.

Kwee told me that in the beginning she and her husband used vegetable dyes but no example is known. When they determined that his batiks sold far better than hers, she decided to stop designing and devote herself to assisting him by assuming supervision of production. There is some doubt about this information because the batiks signed by Oey later on have far more in common with his wife's designs and the quality of her work than with earlier batiks signed by him. The result of their collaboration was the best Peranakan-made batiks. While Oey started by imitating Lies van Zuylen's bouquets, he is the one who created a unique three-dimensional effect, which was perfectly copied by other Peranakan

For many years before The's death, his son and daughter-in-law assisted him, gradually assuming responsibility for the business. When he died, they inherited the workshop and continued to sign their product with his name. The present production is hand-waxed, but the dyeing is mainly *colet* (painted with a brush). In addition to *sarung* and *kain panjang*, readymade skirts and T-shirts are decorated in large quantities for tourists and for export, especially to Thailand. The Tie Siet's grandchildren have attended university and have no wish to become batik entrepreneurs.

Her daughter Oey Djien Nio was born in 1924 and became a third-generation batik entrepreneur in Pekalongan. She married Liem Siek Hien and signed her batiks with her husband's name. After 1965 she used the new Indonesian family name—Hendromartono—adopted by her husband.[2] She combined this with the name people used to address her, Jane. She died in 1986.[3]

NOTES

1. Oeij rather than Oey in conformance with the Dutch spelling.

2. Peranakan citizens were advised by the government to adopt Indonesian names to demonstrate their loyalty.

3. Inger McCabe Elliott, *Batik: Fabled Cloth of Java* (New York: Clarkson N. Potter, 1984), 122–26; Rens Heringa, interview with Mrs. Liem Giok Hwa, Jakarata, 1995.

Oei learned to draw through a Dutch correspondence course. The dyes he used were synthetic. During World War II he made batiks for the Japanese. It was Oei who, after Lies van Zuylen's death offered her heirs a large sum to license her signature. There appears to be no record of when he stopped working or what happened to his workshop.

entrepreneurs. Even with a bouquet designed by Van Zuylen and copied, the batik is unmistakably a Oey Soe Tjoen based on this effect, obtained with rows of dots as filler motifs in the flowers and the diverse shades of each color within a flower, as well as color scheme. Van Zuylen herself tried to imitate the effect after 1935 for a Peranakan customer but did not succeed. The batiks produced in both workshops in that period were of top quality, and both were highly successful. Oey is said to have employed 150 workers, possibly more than Van Zuylen.

During the Japanese occupation the couple made *obi*, material for kimonos, and *kain panjang pagi sore* for the Japanese. According to Kwee, these batiks were not signed, but there is a *batik pagi sore* in the *Djawa Hokokai* style with the signature O. S. T. Pek. The quality of the work is superb, though not typical of the style of Oey; rather it looks like his interpretation of the Japanese taste. No batik entrepreneur from Pekalongan with the initials O. S. T. is known. Probably Oey mentioned "Pek" (Pekalongan) because it was better known than Kedungwuni.

After Oey died in 1975, his son, Muljadi Widjaya, and daughter-in-law, styandi Setiono, ran the shop with Kwee, signing their work with Oey's name.

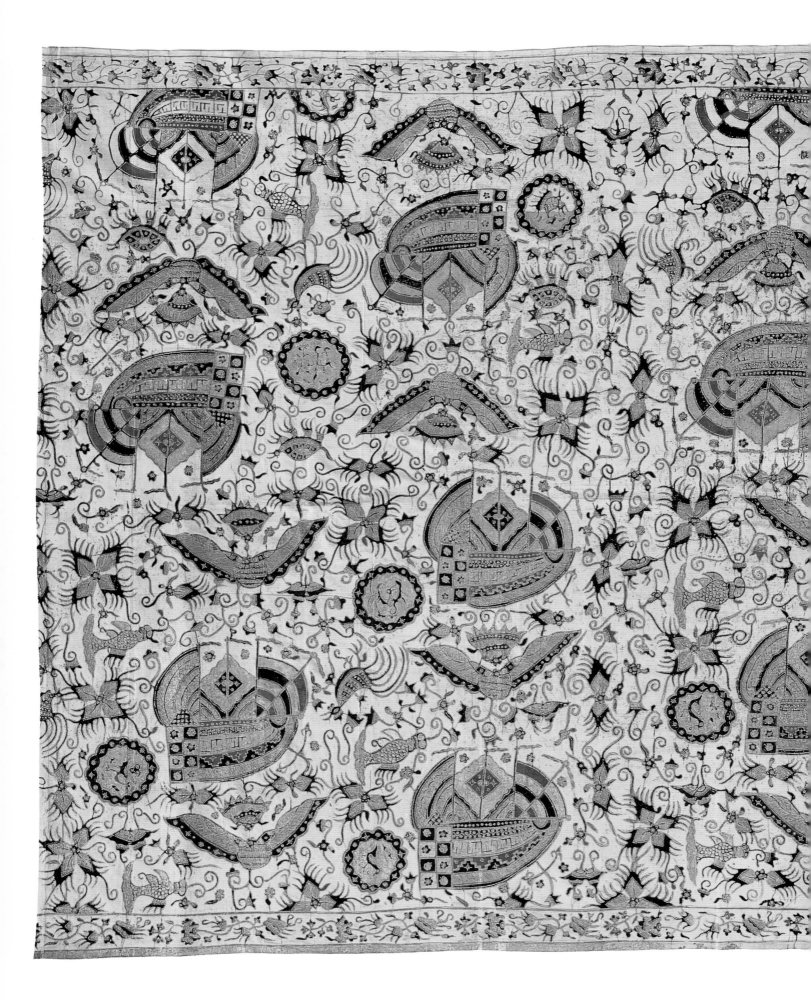

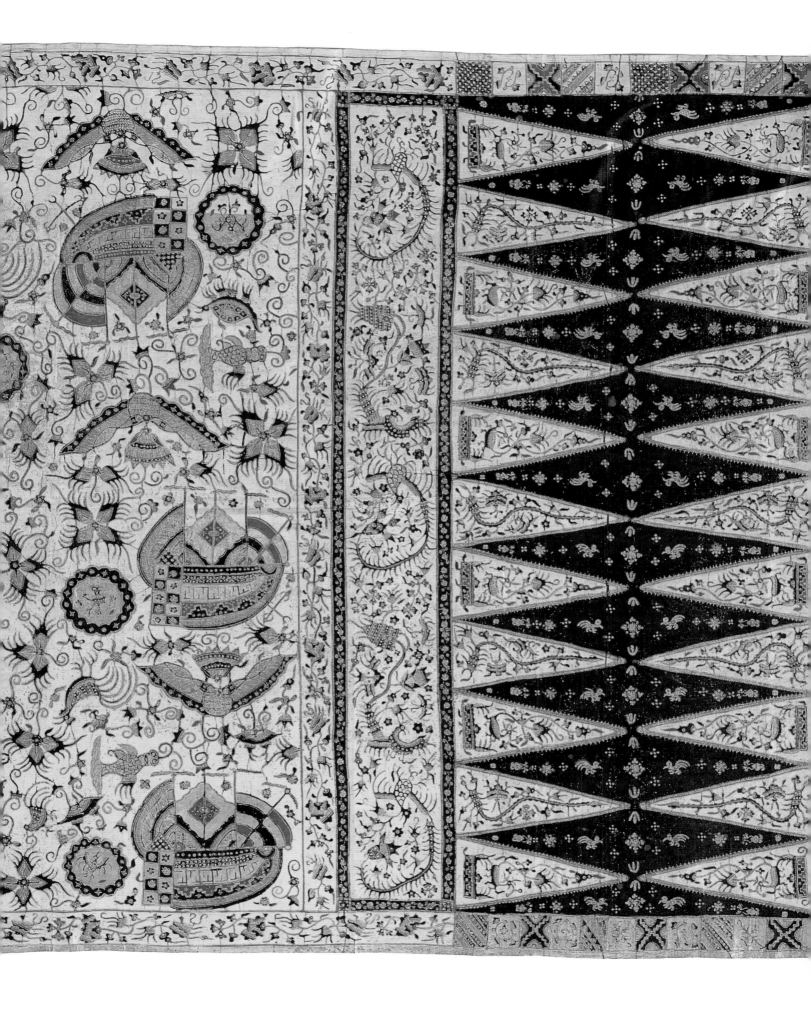

CATALOGUE
•
RENS HERINGA
•
HARMEN C. VELDHUISEN

Hip wrapper
Java, Lasem, c. 1880
Catalogue no. 8
(left and preceding pages)

Sources of Inspiration

The development of Pasisir batik in its historical and socioeconomic contexts was presented in the preceding chapters. The entries in this partial catalogue of the museum's collection, however, do not follow a chronological sequence. As none of the ever-growing variety of styles was ever limited to a clearly delineated period, a chronological approach is impractical at best and possibly misleading. Therefore, the various batik formats constitute the organizing principles here. This facilitates the "reading" of batiks, which at first glance may seem to comprise a welter of motifs and colors. By looking at a group of related items, the profusion of detail can be disentangled step by step.

Despite a degree of similarity, each group of formats presents its own noteworthy aspects. In particular, the *sarung*, which became widespread as dress for women of mixed descent, reveals distinctive styles associated at different times with different ethnic groups.

Three other resist-dyed textile types are directly related to the commercially produced nineteenth-century Pasisir batik. Its "ancient" predecessors, the Indian *kain sembagi* and the traditional handwoven village batik of the Javanese north coast, each contributed to its appearance. The central Javanese *kain panjang*, developed subsequently, owes in its turn a debt to the traditional Pasisir style. A comparison of the ways in which the three are similar to and different from a Pasisir cloth is instructive.

The principal similarity among the *kain sembagi* (FIGURE 58), the village *kain panjang* (FIGURE 59), and the traditional Pasisir *kain panjang* (FIGURE 60) is their format: a *badan* surrounded by borders and a *kepala tumpal* at both ends (see Appendix 1). The *kain sembagi (kalamkari)* differs, however, in several respects from the Javanese batik; notably in the Indian *kalamkari* technique the resist was applied to only one side of the fabric, whereas in almost all Javanese batiks the pattern on the front was repeated on the back, making both sides identical. Javanese batik could therefore be worn on either side. Second, *kalamkari* designs are often outlined in black or white. Black outlines never occur in Javanese batik; white outlines generally occur only on early *batik Pasisir* together with other kalamkari-inspired elements.

Most resist-dyed Indian cloths display a variety of bright colors, while early north coast batik depends on shades of blue and red, which combine for black. Green does not occur in the classical style. Although central Javanese colors are more muted than those of the Pasisir, they too are basically combinations of a brownish red and blue.

Most hand-drawn batik cloths are unique pieces,[1] yet certain precepts of size, format, motif, and color were—and still are—followed. First, a batik design consists of superimposed layers;[2] illusions of depth are expressed through the scale of motifs, contrasting color, or degree of abstraction. The upper, or first, layer forms the principal theme of the batik. Smaller motifs form the second layer, which often resembles the upper layer and is, therefore, difficult to distinguish. These smaller motifs often add details that strengthen the main theme. A third layer of small and regularly repeated motifs completely fills the background of the cloth to form the base. Some of these motifs are associated with particular regions, but all of them originally expressed the concept of abundant growth.

Two general categories of motifs occur on the *badan* of all four textile types—the *kain sembagi*, the village batik, the traditional Pasisir batik, and its central Javanese counterpart (FIGURE 61). First is a free-flowing style by which, despite a certain regularity, the (generally) floral and faunal elements achieve an impression of freedom. Second is a more formal, stylized, or abstracted floral design consisting of a single pattern uniformly repeated over the whole field, resulting in a grid of squares and/or diagonal lines.

NOTES
1. The exception being the precise imitation of signed designs by Indo-European entrepreneurs at a later time.
2. Analogous to the "layers" in a highly stratified society, such as that of Java.

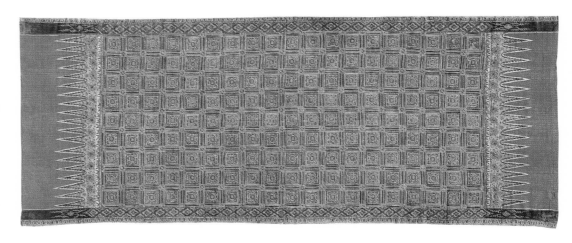

FIGURE 58
Hip wrapper,
kain sembagi, tapih cinde
India, Coromandel
coast,
nineteenth century
Hand-drawn and
stamped mordants and
wax resist on
handwoven cotton
(worked on one side);
natural dyes
107.2 x 266 cm
(42¼ x 104¾ in.)Los
Angeles County
Museum of Art,
Inger McCabe Elliott
Collection,
M.91.184.650

Indian export textiles were made to order under the supervision of VOC officials either by Indian craftsmen in their villages or in trading enclaves, the so-called factories, of the VOC on the east coast of the subcontinent. The rainbow colors link the *sembagi* (*kalamkari*) to the world of ancestors and gods, resulting in its ritual use. This cloth was acquired in south Sumatra, where it would have been used as a hip wrapper or shoulder cloth at weddings. As a family heirloom, it could also have functioned as a shroud or ceremonial wall hanging.

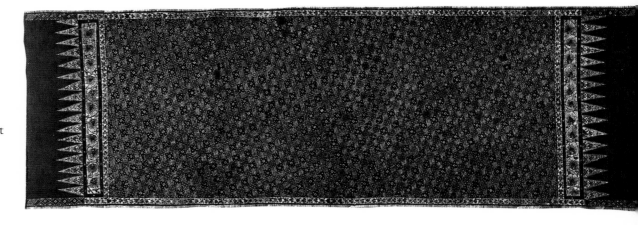

FIGURE 59
Hip wrapper
kain panjang kepala tumpal, jarit irengan
Java, Kerek (near
Tuban), 1983
Hand-drawn wax resist
on handspun,
handwoven cotton;
natural dyes
90.5 x 263 cm
(35 ⅝ x 103½ in.)
Los Angeles County
Museum of Art,
Inger McCabe Elliott
Collection,
M.91.184.303

Village women in the Tuban area still manufacture such cloths communally for family use and as gifts during ceremonial exchanges. The format of this *jarit* (woman's hip wrapper) is similar to that of the *kain sembagi*, with a *badan* surrounded by a border and small edge along the selvages. Each end shows a row of elongated triangles. This cloth was acquired in 1983 in the village where it was made.

FIGURE 60
Hip wrapper (detail),
*kain panjang kepala
tumpal, kain kelengan*
Java, Indramayu,
c. 1900
Hand-drawn wax resist
on machine-woven
cotton; natural dyes
105.4 x 256 cm
(41 1/2 x 100 3/4 in.)
Los Angeles County
Museum of Art,
Inger McCabe Elliott
Collection,
M.91.184.401

The format of this traditional Pasisir cloth is similar to that of both the *sembagi* and village batiks. The small, blue dots *(cocoban)* in the background are exclusive to batik from Indramayu and Lasem. The *kelengan* color scheme of deep blue-black on creamy beige is also characteristic of Indramayu, where Peranakan mourners attribute apotropaic properties to it. The blue-black suggests that the wearer is close to the world of death while firmly grounded in the world of life (beige).

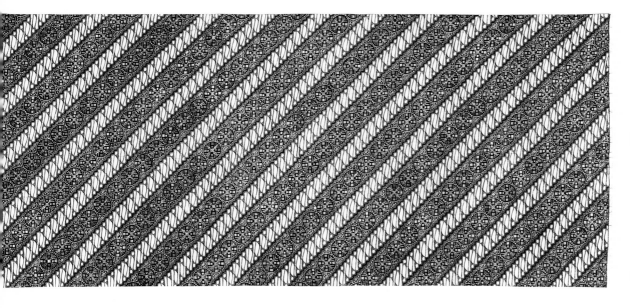

FIGURE 61
Hip wrapper,
kain panjang,
parang seling nitik
Java, Yogyakarta,
first half 20th century
Hand-drawn wax resist
on machine-woven
cotton; natural dyes
103.5 x 228.6 cm
(40 3/4 x 90 3/4 in.)
Los Angeles County
Museum of Art,
Costume Council Fund
M.73.73.17

A typical example of a central Javanese *kain panjang* with undyed borders on the narrow ends only. It was this type of cloth in indigo blue, reddish-brown *soga*, and cream that colonial Dutch and central Javanese authors considered the "true" batik, of which the north coast product was thought to be a "degenerate" form.

Traditional Pasisir Style: Batik in Red and Blue

Even after commercial production began, the traditional Pasisir style continued to be worn primarily by the ethnic groups who produced them. The designs and colors continued to express values associated with particular localities. Much of their original significance was unappreciated, however, when the batiks were exported to Sumatra, Bali, and other islands in the archipelago, where their designs were given new interpretations. Thus, through export the limited range of traditional designs came to express a wider spectrum of meanings. Therefore, it should be stressed that in most cases more than one explanation is possible. Even within a single ethnic group it has invariably been a matter of associative thinking and a propensity to link one metaphor with another that has determined local meaning.

Hip wrappers come in two main formats, the rectangular *kain panjang* and the tubular *sarung*[1] (see Appendix 2). Several distinctions and developments require a word of introduction. The traditional *kain panjang kepala tumpal* remained in use throughout the nineteenth and first quarter of the twentieth century. Each of its various design formats communicated the wearer's marital status. The *kain sisihan*, for example, was initially meant for couples soon to be wed. At each end it shows a *kepala* and borders whose colors and motifs contrast with each other (catalogue nos. 1–2). At the wedding and for some time afterward the red, or bright, half would be worn on the outside, while the black, or dark, half served later in life. Women with children also might wear a symmetrical *kain panjang* or, more often, a *sarung* in which the two rows of triangles in the *kepala* form a single unit. The original tubular *sarung* format had the *kepala*, the so-called *kepala pasung*, in the middle, thus bisecting the *badan*. It was worn at the back. In the later form the double *kepala* was moved to the end of the cloth and worn, folded in half, in front. In both cases the seam was invisible under the fold.

About the middle of the nineteenth century the designs in the *kepala* underwent the first in a long series of changes. The area enclosed by rows of opposing triangles, which in the classic cloths (and incidentally in the *kain sembagi*) remained undecorated, often showed rows of small starflowers. On Sumatra the starflowers were in some cases added in gold. More complex embellishments and a trend to stress the center of the *kepala* of the *sarung* developed almost simultaneously.

The lay-out of motifs on the *badan* also evolved gradually. The size of designs varied according to the batik center where the cloths were waxed. Around the 1870s, however, the principal motifs began to grow in relation to the subsidiary ones. Moreover, these sizable designs obtained a directional focus and unlike earlier cloths could only be worn one way. Subsequently motifs came to be mirrored along a vertical line through the middle of the *badan*, which again provided a choice. In a further development the *badan* was also divided along an imaginary horizontal line with two sets of motifs mirroring each other and oriented toward the long borders of the cloth. The latter, originally rather simple and symmetrical, also became more complex.

The addition of a third border initiated a new asymmetrical style. The *gandawari*, adjacent to the *tumpal*, also saw many changes, probably due to a decline in understanding of its original meaning.

The limited color range of the classic cloths and their function as an indicator of age persisted in the wider market context without change. With the availability of synthetic dyes around the turn of the century imitations of famous regional color combinations could be tried. That the best results were still bound to a specific location was fully realized in the *kain tiga negeri*, which exploited the interregional contacts that existed among Peranakan entrepreneurs. On Sumatra particularly many cloths intended for ceremonial use were decorated with gold leaf. This material and its yellow color were restricted to the use of the elite. The disproportionate representation of this sumptuous type in the collection is understandable but may overshadow the intricacies of the other cloths.

NOTE

1. The seams of many of the *sarung* in the museum's collection have been opened.

Catalogue no. 1
Hip wrapper,
*kain panjang kepala
tumpal, kain sisihan,
kain prada*
Java, Lasem, c. 1900
Hand-drawn wax resist
on machine-woven
cotton; natural dyes
and applied gold leaf
102.5 x 259 cm
(40 3/8 x 102 in.)
Los Angeles County
Museum of Art,
Inger McCabe Elliott
Collection,
M.91.184.339

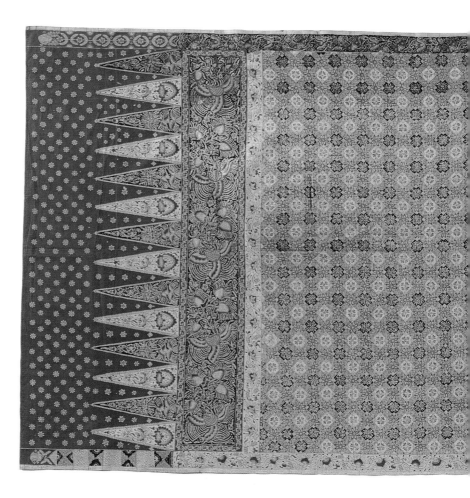

In the *badan* of this asymmetrical cloth three types of heavily stylized, blue, cream, and black rosettes are arranged in diagonal bands on a red ground with *banji* (swastika) motifs. Until the 1870s such petite designs were the fashion. In Sumatra, however, this early style persisted into the twentieth century. The colors and motifs in each section of the *kepala* and the borders divide the cloth into two sections, characteristic of a *kain sisihan*. This particular color combination is named *bang biru*: one end section has a red ground; the other, blue-black. Centipedes and jellyfish wind their way among floral elements on a white-based *papan*. At the other end abstracted birds nip at clustered flowers, set off by feathery, white accents that add a vibrant effect against the bright blue ground. The same feature occurs in one of the borders. Rows of small, white starflowers fill the end sections of the *kepala*, running into the spaces between the triangles.

MAKER

This type of *kain panjang kepala tumpal* was originally produced on the north coast for local consumption. During the nineteenth century an increasing quantity of these cloths was made for export to Sumatra. One of the most important centers for making *kain panjang kepala tumpal* for the Sumatran market was Lasem. Part of this cloth was decorated in Sumatra with gold leaf following the batik pattern.

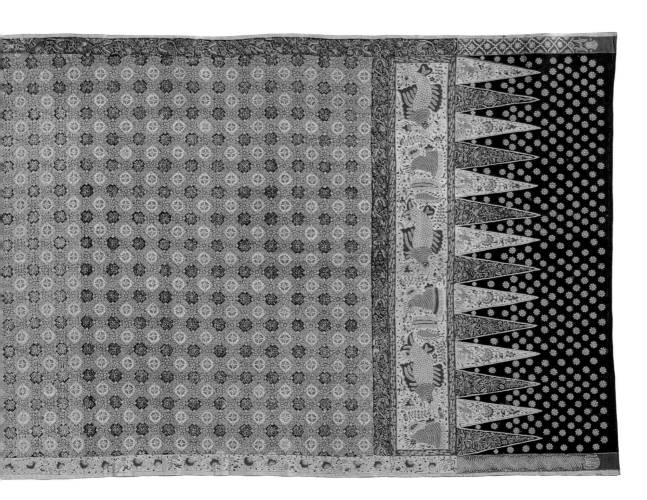

NOTE
1. H. C. Veldhuisen,
interview with Adrian Idris,
Jakarta, 1979.

In one corner are remnants of the number 16, embroidered in chain stitch with a tambour needle (see Appendix 3). In Indian and Dutch textile mills this was done to indicate that the length of the bolt of cotton was sixteen yards. This information was important to the batik entrepreneur who had to decide the size and number of *kain panjang* or *sarung* to be cut from the bolt.

The end borders are hand-hemmed, the custom in Java, but not Sumatra. Most likely an antique dealer in Jakarta bought this batik in Sumatra and had the end borders hemmed; the more refined the stitching of the hem, the more valuable the batik to dealers and contemporary collectors.[1]

WEARER

Highly abstracted rosettes were suitable for Muslim Sumatrans, who used cloths such as this as part of the bridal gift or ceremonial dress. The venomous centipedes provide protection during momentous changes in life. On the north coast the *banji* motif had similar apotropaic functions and was found carved on doorposts. In this case it forms a protective barrier for the bride's lower body. According to Chinese belief, it also functioned as a harbinger of prosperity and progeny. Birds, creatures of the sky, in one end section contrast with jellyfish, creatures of the sea, in the other. Thus placed, they symbolize the groom and bride, who are as yet separate. These symbolic concepts were probably largely unfamiliar to Sumatrans. To them the golden embellishment was the most important aspect of the cloth, an indication of its use by the *ratu sehari*, the bride who was "queen for a day."

Catalogue no. 2
Hip wrapper,
*kain panjang kepala
tumpal, kain sisiban,
kain prada*
Java, Lasem,
c. 1900–1910
Hand-drawn wax resist
on machine-woven
cotton; natural dyes
and applied gold leaf
107.2 x 261.5 cm
(42 ¼ x 103 in.)
Los Angeles County
Museum of Art,
Inger McCabe Elliott
Collection,
M.91.184.326

This intricate cloth, even more clearly than the last, shows a division in halves, which is effected through the contrasting colors of the bisected borders and the end sections of the *kepala*. Three flowering trees of life grow out of mountain-shaped roots on a plain background, mirroring each other vertically on the two halves of the cloth. A single species of flower blooms among the leaves, and small birds flutter among the branches. The trees fill the space in an organized manner, though each is different. Together they give the impression of a traditional, free-flowing floral creeper. The background is sprinkled with a profusion of small *kembang jeruk* (orange blossoms). The *kepala* is filled with starflowers, butterflies, and other small insects on the black end section, while the red section is orna-mented with starflowers alone; the triangles are alternately blue and cream. As in the previous batik, the motifs and colors of the *papan* also form a contrast: birds and flowers on cream at one end, flowers on blue at the other. All borders follow the same division, even those along the *kepala* section. The end borders are unhemmed.

MAKER

This batik was made in a Peranakan workshop and exported to Sumatra, where the *prada* was applied.

WEARER

Batiks such as this sumptuous *kain sisiban* were used at Javanese and Peranakan weddings as part of the dowry or as a gift from the groom's family. As the end borders remain unhemmed and the *prada* is characteristically Sumatran, this par-ticular cloth was probably worn by a Sumatran bride. The rich detail of filler motifs, the vibrant and contrasting use of red, blue, and cream, together with the evocation of the fragrance of orange blossoms and shimmering layer of gold make this cloth fit for a queen. Some of the leaves suggest the symbolically protective centipede, which occurs undisguised in the *papan*. The myriad fauna that can be glimpsed among the profuse growth are a north coast interpretation of a tradi-tional pattern that forms part of the central Javanese design vocabulary under the name of *alas-alasan*. Combining all flying, walking, and creeping creatures in nature, it has cosmological overtones.

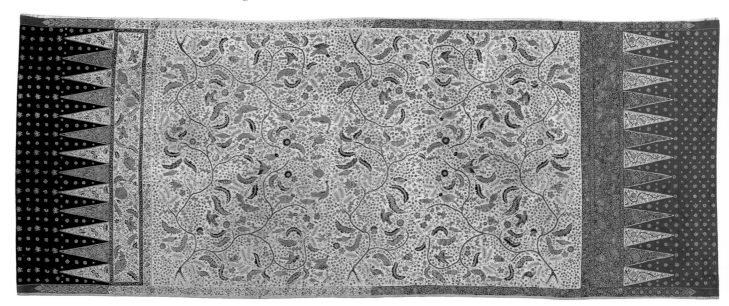

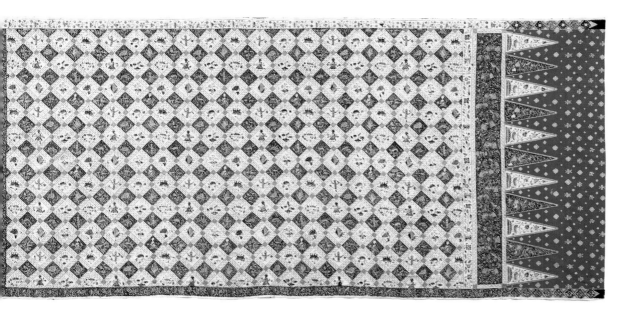

Catalogue no. 3
Hip wrapper,
*kain panjang kepala
tumpal, kain sisiban*
Java, Cirebon,
c. 1910–20
Hand-drawn wax resist
on machine-woven
cotton; natural and
synthetic dyes
108 x 271.6 cm
(42½ x 107 in.)
Los Angeles County
Museum of Art,
Inger McCabe Elliott
Collection,
M.91.184.54

NOTES
1. J. J. B. Ostmeijer,
*Handleiding bij het schatten:
Samengesteld t.b.v. het personeel
ij den pandhuisdienst* (Batavia:
Albrecht, n.d.), 1: 261.
2. H. C. Veldhuisen, *Batik
Belanda 1840–1940* (Jakarta:
Gaya Favorit, 1993), nos. 12,
14–15.
3. C. A. S. Williams,
*Outlines of Chinese Symbolism
and Art Motives*, 3d ed. (New
York: Dover, 1976), 404.

A very late example of the traditional asymmetrical Pasisir format, this cloth shows the motif *kotak seribu* (one thousand pigeonholes), exclusive to Cirebon. Connected through *banji* motifs, the blue lozenges alternate with white ones, which are adorned with yet another version of *alas-alasan*: scorpions, turtles, cattle, flowers, birds, and butterflies follow each other in neat rows. An unusual feature are the small human figures that alternate in contrasting colors: blue on white and white on blue. One of the *papan* shows only flowers. The fish that swim among the usual birds, insects, and flowers on the other end are often seen in batik from the fishing port of Cirebon. A portion of the border motifs above the *kepala* resembles motifs encountered on *kain sembagi*. They consist of diamonds crossed on the diagonal with a figure eight or large S form. The color is denoted as *bang biru tiron Lasem* (imitation of Lasem-style red and blue).[1] Due to the availability of synthetic dyes the Lasem-style colors could easily appear on this batik typical of Cirebon production.

MAKER

This batik comes from a Peranakan workshop. A similar S-form motif was employed by Carolina von Franquemont[2] and is also depicted on Indian *sembagi*. Lies van Zuylen used the motif around 1900 on *kain panjang* executed in the traditional Pasisir style.

WEARER

This particular bridal cloth was worn in Cirebon, but it would also have been acceptable to Muslim Sumatrans because of its abstracted style. In Java the human figures with their contrasting colors may have represented bride and groom. The cosmological associations of the sea, land, and sky creatures would have made it a perfect gift for a bride at a time when she was considered the center of the universe. Wishes for marital happiness were expressed by the flowers, birds, and butterflies. The turtle, apart from having medicinal and therefore protective properties, is, according to the Chinese, an emblem of spiritually endowed creatures who attained a great age.[3] The S figures are reminiscent of the Chinese ying-yang symbol, which expresses the balance between male and female properties, similar to the meaning of the traditional *gandawari* border.

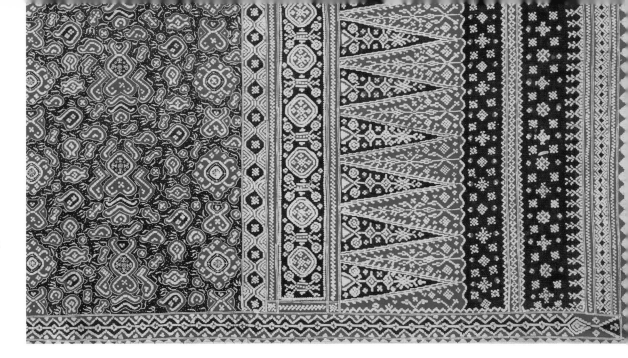

Catalogue no. 4
Hip wrapper,
*kain panjang kepala
tumpal, kain sisihan*
Java, Pekalongan,
c. 1910
Hand-drawn wax resist
on machine-woven
cotton; natural and
synthetic dyes
106.6 x 248 cm
(42 x 97 5/8 in.)
Los Angeles County
Museum of Art,
Inger McCabe Elliott
Collection,
M.91.184.345
See FIGURE 46

This cloth is an unusual variant of the asymmetrical *kain sisihan*. The stylized, bright red floral motifs show a strong *cinde* inspiration. The neat rows of larger florals contrast with the white *wos utah* (scattered rice) on a *wungon* (purplish) ground. The end sections, which are usually of a single, contrasting color without decoration are here densely covered with a series of vertical bands, in which the contrasting reds reappear in combination with black. Gold-decorated cloths woven in silk in Sumatra or Bali come to the mind. Both the triangles and their negatives are filled with motifs, which gives the effect of a double *tumpal* row. The triangles and their intermediate spaces are alternately decorated with small trees and a motif that may represent a crayfish. The latter resembles a motif that is found on Indian cloth for the Thai market. The selvage borders, consisting of a geometric decoration and a row of small triangles, *gigi walang* (cricket's teeth), continue till the corner of the cloth. The bright red and purple on this heavily pre-oiled piece combine natural *mengkudu* dye and purple aniline dye, one of the first synthetic dyes to come on the market around the turn of the century. As these early synthetic dyes were not colorfast, the purple is somewhat faded.

MAKER

Indo-Arabians in Pekalongan specialized in creating batiks with *nitik* motifs, a design greatly appreciated by their Muslim customers. Around 1890 Indo-European batik entrepreneurs in Pekalongan also started to include such designs in the *kepala* and borders. The work, however, was generally sent out to Indo-Arabian workshops.

WEARER

This is a rare example of the strongly stylized motifs and deep colors that were predominantly worn by Indo-Arabian women on Java but also by a widely dispersed clientele of devout Muslim women throughout the archipelago and possibly mainland Southeast Asia. This partially explains the varied design influences that can be noticed in this cloth. The stylized floral motifs may represent stars in the sky (*bintang*) or flowers in the Muslim garden of paradise. The same style was exported to Sumatra, where it was also used as a head covering (*kudhung*).

NOTES

1. H. C. Veldhuisen, field notes, Lasem, 1979.

2. Linda Hanssen, "Ceremoniële doeken van de Minangkabau: Textiel als metafoor voor sociale ordening," master's thesis, Utrecht University, 1995.

This *sarung*, with its original hand-sewn double seam, is an example of the earliest north coast format, with two rows of triangles in its *kepala* lined up in the middle of the cloth. The *badan* is solidly covered with a diagonal grid enclosing alternating rows of small clustered stars, flowers, and birds. Following a trend that emerged around 1870, the distance between the lines of the grid was doubled, resulting in larger motifs (see catalogue no. 1 for the earlier style). A row of sparsely scattered starflowers contrasts with the blue-black ground of the *kepala* and fills the space between the rows of triangles, whose opposing apexes almost touch. The dainty motifs adorning the *papan* and *tumpal* are finely delineated in typical Lasem style. Butterflies and small, spiky birds flutter among the profusely flowering creepers; each triangle contains a carnation in full bloom and a small bird. *Cocohan* fill the ivory background sections. The borders are rather narrow; the end borders in the *kepala* show the traditional abstracted motifs, ending in two small tassels that meet in the middle. The stylish combination of blue-black with accents of blue and ivory is called *irengan* (blackened or lying fallow). Touches of reddish-brown crackle shimmer through here and there, due to breaks in the waxed background during the dye process.

MAKER

Peranakan entrepreneurs from Lasem started to mark cotton cloth with ink stamps of their names or initials around 1850. The ink stamp on this batik, made in a Peranakan workshop, is illegible, but it seems to resemble one within a small circle enclosing a tiny flower and the initials T. H. K. on a *sarung* with a similar design format in deep red and light yellow from Lasem. The *kepala* on that cloth, which was acquired in south Sumatra and is now in a private collection, is also in the middle. The present cloth was obtained in Sumatra. The carnation, referred to in Java by the Chinese name *celuki*, is typical of Peranakan batiks from Lasem.[1]

WEARER

The subdued colors and neatly arranged motifs made this cloth suitable for a middle-aged woman. In Java it might also have served for a condolence visit. This particular cloth was, in fact, obtained in Padang, in the Minangkabau area of Sumatra, where batiks traditionally form part of the ceremonial costume in contrast to the locally woven, gold-brocaded *songket* cloths. In such a situation wearing batik indicates lower social status. It is not known how the meanings of these motifs and colors differed among the Minangkabau and in Java.[2]

Catalogue no. 5
Hip wrapper,
sarung kepala pasung
Java, Lasem, c. 1870
Hand-drawn wax resist
on machine-woven
cotton; natural dyes
105.4 x 194.2 cm
(41 1/2 x 76 1/2 in.)
Los Angeles County
Museum of Art,
Inger McCabe Elliott
Collection,
M.91.184.75
See FIGURE 1

Catalogue no. 6
Hip wrapper,
sarung kepala pasung,
sarung prada
Java, Semarang, c. 1900
Hand-drawn wax resist
on machine-woven
cotton; natural dyes,
applied gold leaf,
and glazing
105.7 x 191.6 cm
(41 5/8 x 75 3/8 in.)
Los Angeles County
Museum of Art,
Inger McCabe Elliott
Collection,
M.91.184.340

An interesting mixture of elements marks the design of this *sarung*, still sewn to form a tubular cloth.[1] The *kepala pasung*, with its double row of triangles (top right), is positioned at one end in late nineteenth-century fashion. The undecorated lozenges between the triangles represent a style that was current at least fifty years earlier. The vigorous motifs of the *badan* are specific to Semarang during the last quarter of the nineteenth century. The motif type is called *Laseman* (in the style of Lasem), but the flowers and birds in the foreground are much larger than those in the classical Lasem style. Among the flowers and birds the poisonous *kembang sungsang* vine, the voluptuous Chinese butterfly (*kupon*), the fruit bat (*kalong*), and the bird of paradise (*cenderawasih*), with its long tail feathers, stand out. A subsidiary pattern of smaller floral creepers and a background dotted with *cocohan* add dimension to the design. The motifs in the symmetrical *kepala* and borders are of a more modest size. Carnations (*celuki*) abound; birds and corncobs (*janggel*) adorn both *papan*; the *tumpal* are alternately blue and cream. The *gandawari* border runs uninterruptedly along the *kepala* section and lacks the tassels in the middle. The colors show the *irengan* version of the western Pasisir, with its heavily oiled yellowish cream ground (*gumading*) and small accents of blue and red that set off the predominant blue-black of the motifs.

MAKER

This batik was made in a Peranakan workshop. It is a copy of an older Peranakan example, indicated by the undecorated field between the elongated triangles in the *kepala*, the oldest Pasisir style, and the Chinese motifs in the *papan* and *badan*, including a fluttering butterfly, which became a standard feature of Peranakan *batik Pekalongan* at the beginning of the twentieth century. One surface is glazed, a practice also common in the manufacture of Indian chintz for the European market and *sembagi* for the archipelago.

WEARER

Affluent Peranakan matrons expressed their status by wearing such batiks for weddings and other festive gatherings. This style with its large motifs does not suit young girls or slim women. The bat is a Chinese emblem for longevity and wealth, the butterfly stands for conjugal happiness, while the bird of paradise is linked to the mythical phoenix, which only appears in times of prosperity.[2] This particular cloth was never worn, as it still retains its luxurious glazed surface (*garusan*). It may have been part of a wedding gift and was probably kept as an heirloom for many years.

NOTES
1. Many *sarung* in private and museum collections have had the seam opened and therefore are displayed flat.
2. C. A. S. Williams, *Outlines of Chinese Symbolism and Art Motives*, 3d ed. (New York: Dover, 1976), 34, 51, 325.

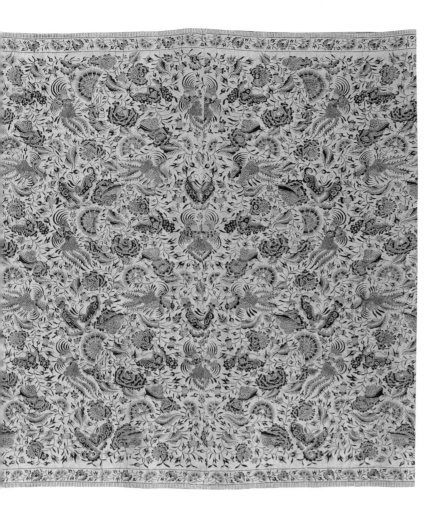

Catalogue no. 7
Hip wrapper,
sarung kepala pasung,
sarung prada
Java, Indramayu,
c. 1910
Hand-drawn wax resist
on machine-woven
cotton; natural and
synthetic dyes and
applied gold leaf
102.5 x 195.4 cm
(40 3/8 x 76 7/8 in.)
Los Angeles County
Museum of Art,
Inger McCabe Elliott
Collection,
M.91.184.296

Several elements of this early twentieth-century *sarung* are axiomatic for cloths belonging to a much earlier period. First, it has a *kepala* in the middle. While originally the classic *kepala* contained a plain, black central section, in this cloth starflowers were applied in gold leaf. The large, fluidly depicted florals, fruits, and leaves of the *badan* are neatly arranged in alternating rows. This structured combination of free style and abstracted motifs was another feature regularly found on earlier cloths as well. The red *cocohan*, which form a background layer in the *badan* and light border, were believed in Indramayu to have their origin in Lasem.[1] Third, the floral creepers in the *papan*, *tumpal*, and borders are of a smaller, more traditional size. The borders in the *kepala* section form a single unit and end at both sides in a kind of inverted tassel. A more recent development is the third, undulating border. Here, its form appears closer to the Indo-European bow border (catalogue no. 19) than to the original Pasisir-style serpentine. Unusual is its occurrence in both the upper and lower borders of the cloth and the differing colors, blue-black and cream. The *bang biru*, with the deep blue-black tones characteristic of Indramayu, is brightened by red and blue accents.

MAKER

Made in a Peranakan workshop, this batik is a mixture of an older style (the *kepala* with plain field between the elongated triangles in the middle of the cloth) and innovations (a wavy line at the top and bottom of the *badan* and borders with different color schemes). The result was a batik suitable for all ages; it could be worn "right side up" or "upside down," with red symbolizing youth and blue maturity. For the entrepreneur this was an advantageous sales point.

WEARER

Like the previous examples of sumptuously gilded cloth, this probably was a wedding gift. The unusual amount of gold decoration and the choice for the more appropriate light border to remain visible at the lower, gilded edge suggest its use by a Peranakan bride. The *kelengan* (blue-and-cream) border as a covering for the lower body, that is, the womb, may well have been intended to impart protective properties. A second possibility is that the cloth was meant to be worn at festive occasions by a grandmother. Not only are the dark tones and predominantly old-fashioned style of the cloth appropriate for an elderly woman, the separate rows of fruits and flowers can also be seen as a metaphor for a grandmother's position as the source for several successive generations.[2]

NOTES
1. Paramita Rahayu Abdurachman, "Dermayu Batiks: A Surviving Art in an Ancient Trading Town. *Spafa Digest* 8 (1987): 5.
2. "Tilling the Cloth and Weaving the Land: Textile Land and Regeneration in an East Javanese Area," in *Weaving Patterns of Life: Indonesian Textile Symposiu* (1991), eds., Marie-Louise Nabholz-Kartaschoff et al. (Basel: Museum of Ethnography, 1993), 161.

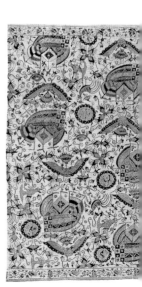

The motifs of this opened-up *sarung*, with its *kepala* at one end, mirror each other along an imaginary horizontal line in the middle of the *badan*, making it possible for the cloth to be worn with the design oriented in either direction. The designs are executed in the Lasem style, with its long, spiky details, but follow the fashion for larger designs of the late nineteenth century. The phoenix-in-the-egg (*sembagen buk*) is depicted enclosed in a roundel suggesting a valuable imported Chinese porcelain plate (*piring aji*). Turtles, goldfish, gamecocks, and fruit bats

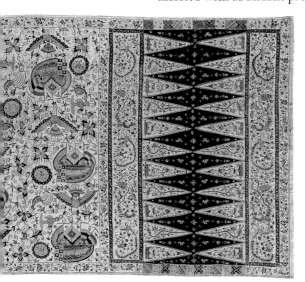

surround the ships that constitute the main theme of the batik. They can be recognized as European three-masters with a high stern and fully blown sails. Obviously, the woman who drew or copied the ships had scant knowledge of maritime detail and concentrated on abundant embellishment instead. The identical *papan* are adorned with large centipedes, scorpions, and flying birds. In addition to the usual starflowers, small fish and cocks are lined up in the *kepala*. Across the center a row of larger lozenges adds a vertical accent. Backgrounds and borders abound with finely delineated floral tendrils. Red and blue (*bang biru*) overlap to create black on the ivory ground. Gold leaf shimmers on the part of the cloth that will be visible when worn.

MAKER

Made in a Peranakan workshop, this type of batik in red overdyed with blue on a cream ground was made to be gilded. The drawing on the batik is characterized by a plethora of sharply defined, curling, elegant lines outside the motifs. This is characteristic of batiks from Lasem.

WEARER

This cloth was intended as a gift for an affluent Peranakan bride, although the scale of the motifs and color combination suggest that its use would only be appropriate later in life. The symbolism of the motifs expresses the wish that the owner of the cloth become a pillar of the community, prosperous and happily married with abundant progeny. Together the living creatures of sky, land, and sea grant the mystic power to achieve these ends. The *piring aji* has lost its original association with Islam and become, by association with imported Chinese porcelain, an emblem of prosperity instead. The heavily laden ships stand for the accumulation of riches and in the bridal context for the journey into marriage itself. The venomous creatures swarming the *papan*, an area sometimes compared with the womb, protect against danger. Particularly along the north coast the cock stands for male invincibility. In this case it probably serves as an emblem for the eminence of the groom's family. The reversibility of the cloth was lost after it was gilded on Sumatra.

Catalogue no. 8
Hip wrapper
sarung kepala pasung,
sarung prada
Java, Lasem, c. 1880
Hand-drawn wax resist
on machine-woven
cotton; natural dyes
and applied gold leaf
106.8 x 211.5 cm
(42 x 83 ¼ in.)
Los Angeles County
Museum of Art,
Inger McCabe Elliott
Collection,
M.91.184.329
See FIGURE 21
and pages 82-83

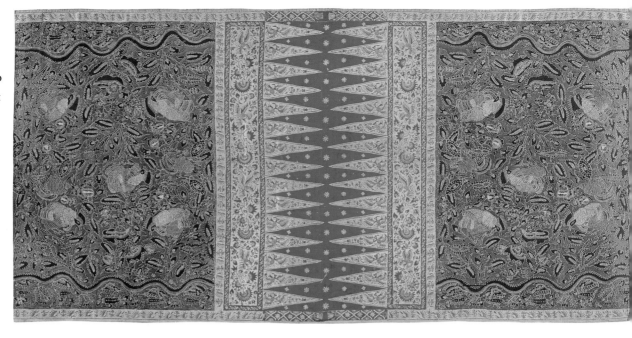

Catalogue no. 9
Hip wrapper,
sarung kepala pasung
Java, Semarang, c. 1910
Hand-drawn wax resist
on machine-woven
cotton; natural and
synthetic dyes
106 x 202.5 cm
(41 3/4 x 79 3/4 in.)
Los Angeles County
Museum of Art,
Inger McCabe Elliott
Collection,
M.91.184.475

The two *badan* sections, divided by the *kepala*, each show five stout gamecocks seated on comparatively delicate branches on a plain, blue ground. Although a horizontal division seems to have been intended, the placement of the central bird in each half undermines this concept. The borders and *kepala* were executed in Semarang in the traditional Lasem style and contain dainty red flowers and birds with a background of *cocohan*. The *kepala* border includes the classical tassels. A rather unusual version of the third border undulates along the upper as well as the lower edge of the cloth, climbing higher toward its ends. The design is a hybrid of motif types, a feature that also emerges in the color treatment. The traditional red-and-cream *bang-bangan* of Semarang contrasts with a now slightly faded combination of blue and brown in the *badan*, which continues, somewhat unusually, in the third border.

MAKER

This type of *sarung*, with the *kepala* in the middle, was made in large quantities in Peranakan workshops in Semarang and Lasem until the end of the last century. Most were exported to Sumatra, and until recently they could still be found in antique shops in Lampong and Palembang. The drawing in the *badan* is fairly bold, while the *kepala* and borders are refined. It is clear that this batik was either made by different workers within a single shop or by workers in more than one shop. Both parts, however, are in the nineteenth-century style of Semarang, so shops in two different batik centers can be ruled out.

WEARER

A hybrid cloth of this commercial type was generally meant for export to Sumatra, where the appreciation of good-quality batik was not as highly developed as in Java. The patterns and combination of colors may have reminded the Sumatrans of textiles imported from India in a time long past. The design does indeed resemble the imitations of this style that were made during the same period in the Netherlands. The Sumatrans probably associated the third border with the meandering rivers that were the actual and symbolic arteries of their community. A similar theme is encountered on *batik Jambi*.[1] The gamecocks (*jago*) stand for and provide a colloquial term for male prowess.

NOTE
1. Rens Heringa, *Een schitterende geschiedenis: Weefsels en batiks van Palembang en Djambi*, exh. cat. (The Hague: Museon, 1993), 26, 43.

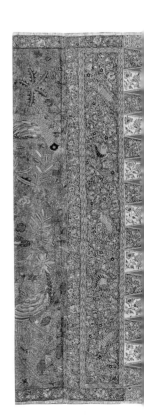

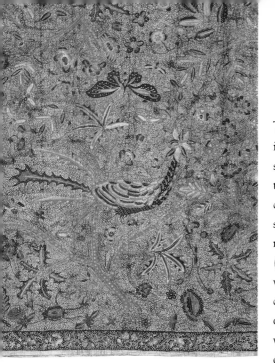

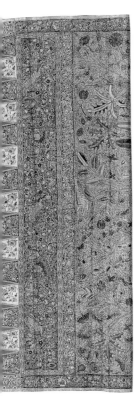

NOTE
1. C. A. S. Williams, *Outlines of Chinese Symbolism and Art Motives*, 3d ed. (New York: Dover, 1976), 323–25.

This elaborate batik, executed on heavy cotton cloth imported from England, is an early example of the *tiga negeri* style. The name *tiga negeri* (three regions) indicates that three different batik centers, in this case all on the north coast, contributed to its completion; the design and color styles fuse into a singularly prestigious batik. The cloth retains its tubular form, sewn together close to the *kepala* (below), where the seam would be invisible when the cloth was folded and worn. Six large birds with long tails perch clumsily on the branches of small, flowering trees, which owe a remote debt to Indian *palempore*. Butterflies, their wings outspread, flutter among the profuse vegetation, the effect of which is intensified by a background layer of reddish-brown, finely drawn tendrils (*ungkeran*). At first sight the main motifs appear to mirror each other along an imaginary horizontal line. An interesting vertical balance is attained by the arrangement of the male and female birds. Crested, seated males alternate with standing females, whose heads have turned into flowers. The *kepala*, with starflowers on a red ground formed by rows of opposing triangles, is in the traditional style, as is the *papan*, with its centipedes, fruit bats, and birds among small flowers. The symmetrical borders are edged with a plain upper and a finely striped lower selvage border (*seret*).

The complex use of color forms the main attraction of this batik. The deep orangy red is characteristic of batik made in Semarang; the golden sheen of the background *soga* differs from the more subdued tones produced in central Java. The borders show vibrant white accents outlining the red flowers and birds on a bright blue ground.

MAKER

The basic pattern of the *badan* and *kepala* in red on this Peranakan *sarung* was executed in Semarang; the filler motifs in blue were applied in Kudus; those in the background of the *badan* in light brown were added in Demak, although Surakarta in central Java was better known for such work (catalogue no. 13).

WEARER

Worn primarily by affluent Peranakan matrons, a *tiga negeri* batik might also be among the gifts for a wedding. It was viewed as an excellent investment, as it remained in fashion for a considerable time. The tree of life appears in many guises throughout the archipelago and may here, in combination with the profuse vegetation, symbolize prosperity and abundance. The long-tailed birds represent a variety of species: to the Javanese, the bird of paradise; to the Chinese and Peranakan, the pheasant, which represents beauty, good fortune, and the high status of the most honorable. It is further associated with the phoenix. Its Chinese name, *feng huang*, referring to both the male and female of the mythical species, bears the connotation of sexual pairing, which is particularly apt in this context.[1] The female bird's head transmuted into a flower is an instance of the Islamic notion discouraging the recognizable depiction of living beings. It later was adopted as part of the Pasisir design vocabulary. The link between women and flowers is, furthermore, a common concept throughout the archipelago.

Catalogue no. 10
Hip wrapper,
sarung kepala pasung,
sarung tiga negeri
Java, Semarang, Kudus, and Demak, c. 1880
Hand-drawn wax resist on machine-woven cotton; natural dyes
104.8 x 200.6 cm
(41 ¼ x 79 in.)
Los Angeles County Museum of Art,
Inger McCabe Elliott Collection,
M.91.184.24

Diversification: Batik from Peranakan and Indo-European Entrepreneurs

Close contact among racial groups increasingly perturbed the colonial government as the nineteenth century progressed. On the Pasisir the Javanese and
Chinese had been closely associated for centuries. European men continued to
form relationships with indigenous and Peranakan women. Gradually the descendants of these alliances came to feel a need to distinguish themselves ethnically.
Changes in batik styles apparently indicate that regionally determined designs
were in need of additional emblems for mixed-race identification.

The most obvious of these changes can be observed in the *kepala* of the *sarung*.
Although the traditional *kepala tumpal*, either in the middle of the cloth or at one
end, with or without starflowers, remained in use for the Javanese of the north
coast and for traditionalist Peranakan, two new styles developed in which the
kepala was transformed into the cloth's most striking element. Furthermore, the
manner of donning a *sarung* was adjusted in such a way that these new, more con-
spicuous decorations came into full view (see Appendix 2).

The *kepala* first showed increasing elaboration in a style Peranakan makers
and wearers called *gigi balang*, in which the central area of the *kepala* completely
overshadows the traditional triangles (FIGURE 62). A vertical row of large diamonds attracts the viewer's attention, in some cases using the triangles as counterpoint, in others incorporating them into a wealth of decorative detail. In the
other transformation of the *kepala*, primarily worn by Indo-European women, the
traditional triangles initially remained clearly discernible among the European
floral elements that were inserted in the central space. Soon, however, they were
replaced by floral designs suggestive of the large bouquets that were to come.

The origins of these changes remain obscure. Possibly they occurred simultaneously. It can be assumed, however, that mutual influences played a role, due
to the fact that maker and wearer did not necessarily belong to the same ethnic
group anymore. Peranakan and Indo-European workshops catered to the needs
of both groups, although each of the new *kepala* designs was initially intended for
one group of clients only.

In a second development the motifs on the *badan* also displayed an increasingly varied range of inspiration. Apart from the continuing use of traditional
motifs and mirrored designs, notions of European design were incorporated
into local patterns, resulting in a freer interpretation of tradition. Ever-larger
leaves and flowers, including Chinese flowers like the lotus, were depicted three-
dimensionally. Whereas previously each group had given its own interpretation
to a limited range of motifs, the need to designate one's mixed background more
clearly led to the combination of European elements with classic central Javanese
patterns, albeit in a color scheme adapted to Pasisir style.

A third development was the addition of a sinuous third border on the lower part of the cloth. Originally linked with the Sino-Javanese symbolic concept of a snake associated with both water and fertility, this border is most often encountered on batiks intended for Peranakan clients. A first intimation of the Indo-European "translation" of this decorative element, the imitation lace, or bow *(booh)*, border, eventually replaced the *papan*. Further variations were introduced in the selvages.

In most cloths color remained restricted to the limited classic palette. The Peranakan continued to adhere to the traditional color combinations, indicative on the Pasisir of various ages: the red-and-white *bang-bangan* cloth for young girls; the red-and-blue *bang biru* for women with children. Grandmothers were dressed in *irengan*, blue-black on white; a somewhat lighter blue version, the *kelengan*, was worn for mourning, as it was believed to guard against illness. In a new development green was added to the traditional north coast range of colors. On antique cloths the top-dyeing of yellow over blue has over time resulted in a faded tone (catalogue no. 16). More successful was the famous blue-green achieved by Carolina von Franquemont (catalogue nos. 17–18).

A final development involved silk batiks, the *lok can*, which in a finer version were already part of the traditional *batik Pasisir* repertoire. During this period commercial production and large-scale export to other islands began. On Sumatra and Bali they functioned as part of regional costume and as ceremonial hangings.

Throughout this period the production of *kain tiga negeri* continued, demonstrating that Peranakan contacts reached beyond the Pasisir to include central Java.

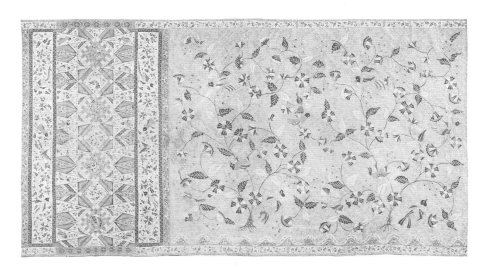

FIGURE 62
Hip wrapper,
sarung bang-bangan
Java, Semarang,
c. 1900–1910
Hand-drawn wax resist
on machine-woven
cotton cloth; possible
mixture of natural and
synthetic dyes
41 7/8 x 78 in.
(106.5 x 198 cm)
Los Angeles County
Museum of Art,
Inger McCabe Elliott
Collection,
M.91.184.87

This batik, though finished is called "unfinished" because of the many white areas left in the pattern to which blue could be added to create *bang biru* batiks. Big entrepreneurs in Lasem kept large stocks of diverse *bang-bangan* patterns as well as smaller supplies of the more expensive *bang biru*. When the latter were exhausted, the stock could be replenished by "completing" the former. This was less risky a venture than producing *bang biru* directly. The brownish red and yellowish cream of this *bang-bangan* are probably the result of an experiment with new synthetic dyes. These colors, however, make the cloth suitable for a young, marriageable Peranakan woman.

The Chinese pattern on this batik consists of two stylized *kembang teratai* (flowering lotus trees), mirrored along an imaginary horizontal line. Although the subject is Chinese, the design itself shows the influence of art nouveau. A single standing bird marks the center of the *badan*. The robust quality of the filler motifs indicates Cirebon influence. The background is decorated with *banji* in traditional Pasisir style. The triangles in the complex, Peranakan-style *kepala gigi balang*, are alternately long and short, while the central area is dominated by a row of diamonds on a ground of double diagonals. Each is adorned with an abstract pattern or a bird in classic Pasisir style. The *papan* and borders also show classic Pasisir motifs. Flowering vines, long-tailed birds, and rice stalks fill the available space. The style of the motifs in the borders is unusual, while the *seret* shows a new development, greater space between the vertical lines. Two shades of blue on white make up a perfectly executed *kelengan*.

Catalogue no. 11
Hip wrapper,
sarung kelengan
Java, Lasem, c. 1910
Hand-drawn wax resist
on machine-woven
cotton; natural dyes
107.2 x 197.3 cm
(42¼ x 77⅝ in.)
Los Angeles County
Museum of Art,
Inger McCabe Elliott
Collection,
M.91.184.44

MAKER

New designs like this one, executed in a Peranakan workshop, were based on pencil sketches on transparent paper, which were traced onto white cotton and copied with the *canting* in wax.[1] After the batik-maker had done this many times, she could draw the design by heart, as was the case with this cloth. The repeating pattern looks the same all over, but there are variations in it. This shows it was made in a Peranakan workshop where concept took pride of place. Indo-European entrepreneurs wanted their patterns to be rendered identically.

WEARER

Worn by Peranakan women, *kelengan* batiks such as this one served during the extended mourning period for close family members. In later life a woman rarely wore any other color. The sacred lotus, sprouting each year from the mud, and its pods, full of seeds promising renewed life, express a belief in reincarnation and the continuation of the family tree. The *banji* background multiplies this wish a thousandfold.[2]

NOTES
1. H. C. Veldhuisen, *Batik Belanda 1840–1940* (Jakarta: Gaya Favorit, 1993), 35–36.
2. C. A. S. Williams, *Outlines of Chinese Symbolism and Art Motives*, 3d ed. (New York: Dover, 1976), 257–58, 381.

Catalogue no. 12
Hip wrapper,
sarung bang biru
Java, Lasem, c. 1910
Hand-drawn wax resist
on machine-woven
cotton; natural and
synthetic dyes
106.7 x 170 cm
(42 x 66 7/8 in.)
Los Angeles County
Museum of Art,
Inger McCabe Elliott
Collection,
M.91.184.73

The subject of this tubular *sarung* is similar to that of the preceding batik. Only the colors differ. Two pairs of lotus trees, one smaller than the other, sprout from a tiny rock or island. Various sources for this often-used motif are known. On Indian chintz the tree of life usually stands on a small mountain or rock forma-tion, while Chinese porcelains show a tiny, rocky island. On Pasisir batik the tree is depicted with one type of flower and loosely hanging roots. The *papan*, bor-ders, and several of the diamonds in the Peranakan-style *kepala gigi balang* show detailed natural motifs in the Lasem style. The *bang biru* combination of red and blue is used to particularly good effect in the *kepala*. A wide, transparent band of red appears to be inserted between the diamonds and the abundantly embellished triangles. The contrast between the simplicity of a *badan* and complexity of a *kepala* reaches a climax in this cloth.

MAKER

The Peranakan maker of this batik as well as catalogue nos. 11 and 16 used the same style for depicting the lotus flower and leaves. Only the filler motifs differ. The same type of abstraction was applied to lotuses depicted on Chinese porcelains.[1]

WEARER

According to Pasisir tradition, the *bang biru* color scheme was intended for mar-ried women with children.[2] The lotus tree designates this cloth for Peranakan use; its details stress the hopes appropriate for a married woman: the flower is the emblem of summer and fertility; the pods, of abundant progeny. The tree, with white, blue, and red flowers growing from a single stem, indicates prosperity and marital happiness.[3] The cloth may have been a treasured heirloom, as its origi-nal, perfectly hand-sewn seam is still intact.

NOTES
1. J. Rawson, *Chinese Ornament: The Lotus and the Dragon* (New York: Holmes and Meier, 1984), 14.
2. Rens Heringa, "Dye Process and Life Sequence: The Coloring of Textiles in an East Javanese Village," in *To Speak with Cloth: Studies in Indonesian Textiles*, ed. Mattiebelle Gittinger (Los Angeles: Museum of Cultural History, University of California, Los Angeles, 1989), 123.
3. Jean Chevalier and Alain Gheerbrant, *Dictionnaire des Symboles* (Paris: Robert Laffont/Jupiter, 1988), 581; C. A. S. Williams, *Outlines of Chinese Symbolism and Art Motives*, 3d ed. (New York: Dover, 1976), 258.

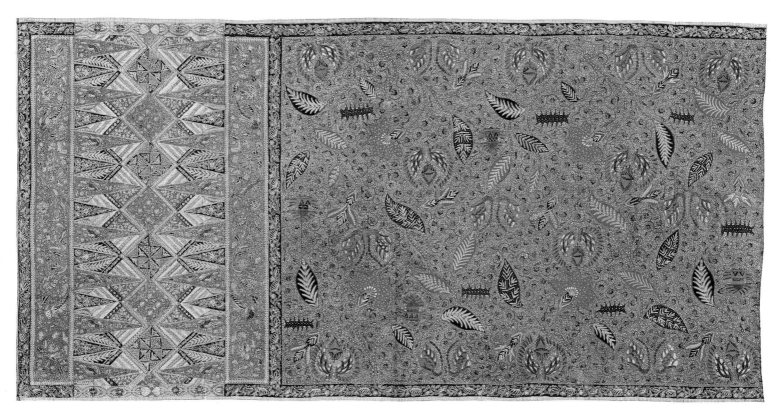

The upper layer of this *tiga negeri* textile consists of two sets of flowering trees in Lasem red and Kudus blue, one set somewhat smaller than the other. Their roots grow in clumps of rocky soil. (Two branches intrude from one edge, suggesting a continuation of the pattern.) The secondary central Javanese *semen* motif is itself made up of three layers: the large, double wings (*sawat*), an exuberantly meandering creeper, and a tangle of tiny tendrils (*ukel*). The *kepala gigi balang* in the Peranakan style is predominantly red on brown with blue and white accents and a background of *ukel*. The borders are decorated in typical Kudus style: scintillating white accents on bright blue. An obvious discrepancy exists between the bold and quickly drawn Pasisir styles and the minutely executed central Javanese work, especially noticeable in the filler motifs.

MAKER

This *tiga negeri* shows how difficult it is to work on one batik in three batik centers. The first of three Peranakan entrepreneurs established the basic pattern of flowering trees in red (hardly discernible because the traditional central Javanese secondary motifs dominate). The final entrepreneur, in Surakarta, had significant freedom to apply his background motifs in both brown and blue.

WEARER

The *semen* motif, originally restricted to members of the Surakarta court, was adapted for wear by outsiders. A cloth such as this, intended for an affluent, middle-aged Peranakan client, would have indicated she was part of a family network with branches across Java. This elaborate and most expensive of styles would have engendered pride of ownership in later hands.

Catalogue no. 13
Hip wrapper,
sarung tiga negeri
Java, Lasem, Kudus,
and Surakarta,
c. 1900–1910
Hand-drawn wax resist
on machine-woven
cotton; natural and
synthetic dyes
105.4 x 198 cm
(41 ½ x 78 in.)
Los Angeles County
Museum of Art,
Inger McCabe Elliott
Collection,
M.91.184.85

Catalogue no. 14
Hip wrapper,
sarung ganggeng
Java, Cirebon,
c. 1910–20
Hand-drawn wax resist
on machine-woven
cotton; natural and
synthetic dyes
104.8 x 202.5 cm
(41¼ x 79¾ in.)
Los Angeles County
Museum of Art,
Inger McCabe Elliott
Collection,
M.91.184.493
See FIGURE 47B

The *sarung* of this self-assured
Indo-European woman shows
a grapevine motif in the *badan*
and a wide lower border
adorned with birds perched
on branches. The upper edge
of the border is a new Indo-
European design, a sharp
zigzag, rather than the sinuous line Peranakan wearers
continued to prefer. Batavia,
c. 1900.
Koninklijk Instituut voor
Taal-, Land- en Volkenkunde,
Leiden.

Birds, mammals, and fish, surrounded by vegetal elements, fill the roundels of
this late example of the traditional Pasisir *ganggeng* motif. The mythical Chinese
qilin and dragon mingle with a scorpion and sea creatures that are fitting for a
fishing town like Cirebon. Shrimp, the local emblem, a lobster, and a variety
of fish are recognizable. The rather bold size and sparse filler motifs are also typical of Cirebon. The background is plain (*cocohan* were not normally used in
Cirebon). Birds and flowers alternate in the diamonds of the Peranakan-style
kepala gigi balang. The traditional *tumpal* triangles provide a counterpoint in the
heavily decorated space. The main colors are naturally dyed blue and a shade of
red that verges on orange due to the preliminary oiling, a treatment that had its
effect on the cream ground as well. This effect is exclusive to Cirebon. Accents of
synthetic pink, bright blue, and green were painted by hand, thus transforming
the *bang biru* into a multicolored cloth.

MAKER

The illegible remnants of a paper sticker probably bear the name of a Peranakan
entrepreneur. Colored weftlines are visible in one end border. These were applied
in Indian cotton mills to mark the start of a bolt, with the number of yards on the
bolt embroidered near one of the selvages at the left or right side of the weftlines.
Dutch textile mills adopted these markings in the headings of bolts made for
export to Java.[1] Often either the number or the weftlines or both were removed
in the batik workshop. In this case the weftlines remain, although they differ
from those applied to Dutch cloth, so probably the cotton was woven in India.

WEARER

This was likely a gift for a Peranakan bride, to be worn on formal occasions after
she had borne children. As the design is not oriented toward a particular border,
this cloth could be worn with either border down. To the Javanese *ganggeng* refers
to fertility-giving water and implicitly to women, whose role is to care for all living
things, expressed by the creatures of land, sea, and sky enclosed by the roundels.
The mythical animals and the venomous scorpion are apotropaic symbols.

NOTE
1. Piet den Otter and
Mienke Simon Thomas,
"Twentse tjaps," *Textielhistorische Bijdragen* 34 (1994):
107. In Dutch textile mills
an ink stamp and/or paper
sticker was also added in
the heading. This gave information about the firm that
imported the cloth into Java,
the quality, and the number
of yards.

NOTE
1. Beryl de Zoete and Walter Spies, *Dance and Drama in Bali* (Kuala Lumpur: Oxford University Press, 1973), pl. 105.

The classic bisected *badan* of this silk cloth is decorated with robust birds of paradise, which fly in pairs among large, densely packed floral motifs. The spiky outlines of the motifs, called *ren* (thorns), which are typical of the eastern Pasisir style, are clearly visible in this quickly drawn cloth, intended for export to Sumatra or Bali. The *cocohan* layer was omitted, and all motifs are much larger than in the daintily drawn styles of more luxurious cloths. The *kepala* shows a simplified version of the *gigi balang*, with three rows of diamonds, two of which form an underlying layer for the traditional rows of triangles. The borders are decorated with a basic version of the floral creeper; the edges are asymmetrical. The motifs of the *badan* and *papan* in brownish-black on a cream ground contrast with the *kepala* with its dark ground. Indigo was top-dyed with *kayu tingi* (*Ceriops candolleana*) to produce the brown-black *soga*.

MAKER

Batiks on silk were produced in Juana and Rembang by Peranakan entrepreneurs for Peranakan clients and for export to Sumatra or Bali.

WEARER

Although this type of batik was used on the Pasisir, most were exported to the Lampong area of southern Sumatra and to Bali, where they functioned as dancer's costumes.[1] Speedily executed batik work was less important to the Balinese than the silk base.

Catalogue no. 15
Hip wrapper,
sarung lok can
Java, Juana or Rembang,
c. 1930
Hand-drawn wax resist
on machine-woven silk;
natural dyes
96.5 x 160.5 cm
(38 x 63¼ in.)
Los Angeles County
Museum of Art,
Inger McCabe Elliott
Collection,
M.91.184.550

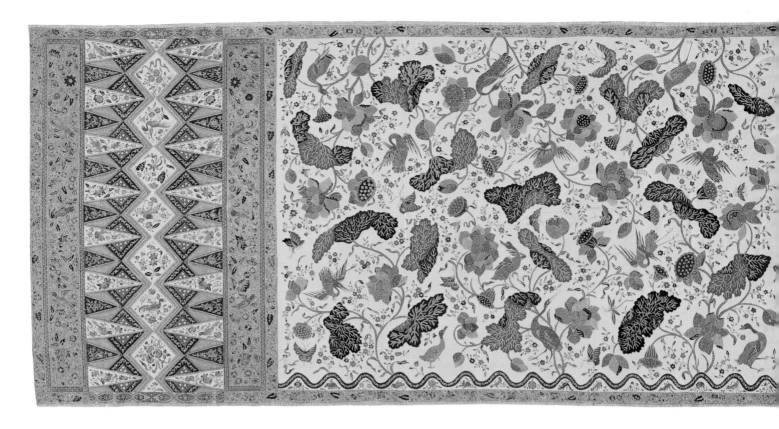

NOTES
1. H. C. Veldhuisen, *Batik Belanda 1840–1940* (Jakarta Gaya Favorit, 1993), no. 48.
2. C. A. S. Williams, *Outlines of Chinese Symbolism and Art Motives*, 3d ed. (New York: Dover, 1976), 51, 147, 323.

Catalogue no. 16
Hip wrapper,
sarung bang biru hijau
Java, Semarang, c. 1880
Hand-drawn wax resist
on machine-woven
cotton; natural dyes
104.8 x 200.5 cm
(41 ¼ x 78 ⅞ in.)
Los Angeles County
Museum of Art,
Inger McCabe Elliott
Collection,
M.91.184.309

Large, elegant lotus flowers, depicted in a European, three-dimensional manner, bloom on trees growing from the borders of this batik. Three trees, each different, mirror each other at the upper and lower ends of the *badan*. Smaller floral clusters sprout from the branches. Ducks waddle below, while egrets, butterflies, and other insects fly above. Each motif is enriched with delicate fillers. The *kepala gigi balang* shows a well-organized version of the Peranakan style, a pleasing composition of three rows of central diamonds, two of which underlie alternately long and short triangles on a dark ground. The lower border, in the form of a sinuous "snake," shows a unique feature: a small bird, mammal, or rosette filling the space under each curve. The animals impart a European sensibility. Red, blue, and somewhat faded green combine with the plain, ivory ground in this most elaborate color combination, *bang biru hijau*, of traditional Pasisir style.

MAKER

This batik was made in the workshop of a Peranakan who imitated an Indo-European design. The large variety of filler motifs is characteristic of Indo-European batiks from Semarang dating from the second half of the nineteenth century. The design is Chinese, but the style of the lotus flowers is Indo-European. The ducks are typical of Indo-European batiks from Semarang and later, around 1890, Pekalongan.[1] The jaunty impression created by the design has much in common with the following textile (catalogue no. 17) probably made by Carolina von Franquemont.

WEARER

This fine and intricate batik contains a multitude of lucky symbols for a Peranakan bride. Ducks, commonly depicted with the full-blown lotus of summer, stand for conjugal fidelity. The egret is here associated with the phoenix, summer, and harvest; the butterflies, sipping nectar from the flowers, are an emblem of felicity and the joys of married life. Together the living creatures express bounty and prosperity.[2]

Large egrets perched among the branches of the tree of life mirror each other across the *badan*. Some of the large leaves are depicted in a European, three-dimensional manner. Floral sprigs decorate the intervening spaces. The *kepala* shows a baroque treatment of the diamond outlines: "Europeanized," lengthened, and each enclosing a water creature, which is, however, depicted in Pasisir style. The *tumpal* rows are filled with small trees on alternately cream and green backgrounds. The red base of the *kepala* is elaborately decorated. The *badan* shows red, blue, yellow, the famous Von Franquemont green, and black on a cream ground and has a refined application of gold dust. A European interpretation has been given to the traditional Pasisir lower border.

MAKER

This batik is probably from the workshop of Carolina von Franquemont. The colors, perfection of work, richness of filler motifs, European interpretation of traditional Pasisir design with the tree of life and the European variation of the *tumpal* are characteristic of her batiks. The European influence is especially to be seen in the diverse sprigs and flowers and the semicurved leaves on the trees. Also the jaunty way of depicting the long-legged waders in diverse poses is neither traditionally Pasisir in style nor Peranakan.

WEARER

This was surely a wedding gift for an affluent Indo-European or Peranakan bride. The symbolism is Asian, in spite of the European design influences. The egrets, according to Javanese symbolism, protect against misfortune, as they take wing at the least sign of danger. These birds are further associated with the phoenix, which symbolizes summer, harvest, and prosperity. The trees of life form the axis of the universe, which connects the world of humans with that of the ancestors, particularly during critical life passages.

Catalogue no. 17
Hip wrapper,
sarung prada
Java, Semarang, c. 1850
Hand-drawn wax resist
on machine-woven
cotton; natural dyes
and applied gold leaf
106.7 x 204.3 cm
(42 x 80 3/8 in.)
Los Angeles County
Museum of Art,
Inger McCabe Elliott
Collection,
M.91.184.330

Catalogue no. 18
Hip wrapper, *sarung*
Java, Semarang,
c. 1860–67
Hand-drawn wax resist
on machine-woven
cotton; natural dyes
105.6 x 195.1 cm
(41 5/8 x 78 3/4 in.)
Los Angeles County
Museum of Art,
Inger McCabe Elliott
Collection,
M.91.184.381

The format of this Indo-European batik shows the classic division with the *kepala* bisecting the *badan*. Nevertheless, the impression is remarkably different, as the *papan* has been replaced by a wide, imitation lace border (*booh*)—rows of three-lobed leaves and floral sprigs—that also graces the horizontal edges of the cloth, one in red and the other a greenish *soga*, so the cloth can be worn with either edge on top. Although the colors resemble the traditional *bang biru*, this term was never used for Indo-European batiks. Moreover, the red and blue here were enlivened with *soga* in a shade that suggests green. The two halves of the *badan* are adorned with nosegays of roses and lovebirds, probably inspired by Dutch magazines. The *kepala* is decorated with a rather haphazard version of the earliest Indo-European floral *kepala* design. One selvage shows double lines; the other is plain.

MAKER

Like the preceding batik, this one is probably from the workshop of Carolina von Franquemont. The colors, perfection of work, richness of filler motifs, and European motifs are consistent with batik produced in her shop. The format, however, represents an innovation. The side panels of the *kepala* have disappeared, and the bow border, in red and *soga*, appears along each edge. This batik is only one example of Von Franquemont's repertoire of lovebirds. She also depicted the following stage of their love affair: two birds perched on the edge of a nest containing four eggs.

WEARER

Newly engaged or young married women of Indo-European and Peranakan background might have worn this cloth at home and for informal occasions. The lovebirds and abundant roses are appropriate for this stage of life. The surfeit of red, color of happiness and weddings, would appeal particularly to Peranakan taste. The more subdued greenish shade would have been preferred by Europeans.

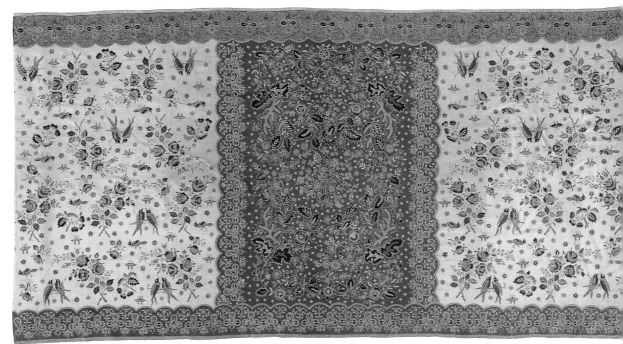

NOTES
1. Nian S. Djumena, *Batik dan Mitra; Batik and Its Kind* (bilingual) (Jakarta: Penerbit Djambatan, 1990), 16.
2. H. C. Veldhuisen, *Batik Belanda 1840–1940* (Jakarta: Gaya Favorit, 1993), no. 37.
3. Kartini, *Brieven aan Mevrouw Abendanon-Mandri*, ed. F. G. P. Jacquet (Dordrecht: Foris, 1987).

An interesting combination of Pasisir, Indo-European, and central Javanese elements marks this cloth. The *badan* is adorned with a variation upon a traditional motif from Banyumas,[1] known as *ayam puger* and consisting of a series of abstracted and naturalistic elements, including small chickens, double crosses, and stylized flowers, arranged in geometric precision on a background of very fine diagonal lines (*galaran*). The *kepala* is executed in the color style of Semarang and shows combined traditional Pasisir and Indo-European motifs. Rice stalks (often found on batik from Batavia), budding roses, and grapes on the vine fill the *papan* and the central area between the rows of triangles. Roses and grapes were well known in Batavia. White scallops delineate the triangles. A small, lacy border in Indo-European style, edged by a tiny *seret*, surrounds the cloth on three sides. The *gandawari* motifs bordering the *kepala* in earlier cloths have disappeared, a development that early on was encountered on cloths made in Batavia. The color is red with a few blue accents in the *badan*, an adaption of Pasisir *bang biru*, but the overall impression is that of a predominantly red and white (*bang-bangan*) cloth.

MAKER

Because Batavia did not have a local batik tradition, we can detect influences introduced by entrepreneurs from north coast centers who settled in Batavia. Possibly the Peranakan entrepreneur who made this cloth came from Semarang, where he had already made *sarung* with *kepala* in the Indo-European style for his European and Indo-European clientele. He then may have repeated the style for his clientele in Batavia. The pattern in the *badan* is known from *batik Banyumas* and was also executed by Indo-European entrepreneurs in Pekalongan. Around 1880 A. J. F. Jans depicted the same pattern on a *sarung* but in the Banyumas colors: blue and brown.[2] The imitation lace border on both selvages occurs in *sarung* from Batavia and differs from those used elsewhere.

Batiks with a fine *galaran* were among the most expensive. The time-consuming work was done by the best makers, often added to order on a finished batik without a background motif. In big workshops where both hand-drawn and stamped batiks were made, backgrounds were sometimes stamped. This could be done with intricate motifs but seldom with *galaran* because the breaking point of the lines was impossible to conceal.

WEARER

This cloth was probably meant for a marriageable girl of mixed European-Javanese descent, who, like a chicken in a coop (*ayam puger*), was confined inside the walls of her father's compound. This custom was widely followed among affluent families as late as the early twentieth century.[3]

Catalogue no. 19
Hip wrapper,
sarung bang-bangan
Java, Batavia (Jakarta),
c. 1870–80
Hand-drawn wax resist
on machine-woven
cotton; natural dyes
104.8 x 209.3 cm
(41 ¼ x 82 ⅜ in.)
Los Angeles County
Museum of Art,
Inger McCabe Elliott
Collection,
M.91.184.22

A young woman from Blora wearing the *ayam puger* motif, c. 1910, a year before her marriage.
Koninklijk Instituut voor Taal-, Land- en Volkenkunde, Leiden

Catalogue no. 20
Hip wrapper,
sarung bang-bangan
Java, Batavia (Jakarta),
c. 1880
Hand-drawn wax resist
on machine-woven
cotton; natural dyes
106.7 x 190.7 cm
(42 x 75 ⅛ in.)
Los Angeles County
Museum of Art,
Inger McCabe Elliott
Collection,
M.91.184.76

The horizontally mirrored halves of this tubular *sarung*'s *badan* teem with amphibians, birds, and other creatures, captured in lively poses. The *kepala*, once more with *papan* replaced by a border motif, is decorated with a coat-of-arms, similarly mirrored, with peculiar elements due perhaps to the unfamiliarity of the subject to the woman who drew the design. The escutcheon has become a vase of lotus flowers, embellished with a cross that resembles a medal. Like the Dutch coat-of-arms, it is supported by rampant lions that here look more like cats with swishing tails. The image is enclosed by an acanthus wreath. The asymmetrical borders are based on traditional Pasisir floral motifs, which have been combined into a lacy design in Indo-European style. The *bang-bangan* color scheme is reversed on the *kepala*.

MAKER

From the hybrid character of the design we may deduce that the batik was made by a Peranakan entrepreneur in Batavia, some of whom combined stylistic aspects from several batik centers. In this case the bow borders are in the Indo-European style of Pekalongan, while the row of upright leaves are known from batiks of Catharina van Oosterom, who worked first in Semarang and later in Banyumas. She also depicted many different animals in her *badan*,[1] which she copied from Dutch illustrations. In contrast, the animals on this batik were chosen for their Javanese symbolic meanings.

WEARER

The motifs of this interesting cloth are depicted in Europeanized style and combined with Peranakan and Pasisir elements. The cloth seems to depict a confrontational universe, not only among predators and their prey—the peacock and the worm, the snake and the bird—but also intraspecies—the gamecocks. The chickens alone move freely, being the only species that are reputedly immune to snake venom.[2] Apotropaic and medicinal powers are represented by the centipede and turtle. This powerful cloth may have been worn by a male of mixed descent who had overcome many of life's difficulties.[3] The fanciful coat-of-arms evokes the crests found in the four corners of Indian export textiles and on the carriage doors of Batavia's wealthy citizens. Many Europeans, the black sheep of aristocratic families as well as those of lowly birth, passed themselves off as aristocratic scions once they had made good.

NOTES
1. H. C. Veldhuisen, *Batik Belanda 1840–1940* (Jakarta: Gaya Favorit, 1993), no. 21.
2. Inger McCabe Elliott, *Batik: Fabled Cloth of Java* (New York: Clarkson N. Potter, 1984), 159.
3. Ibid., 220.

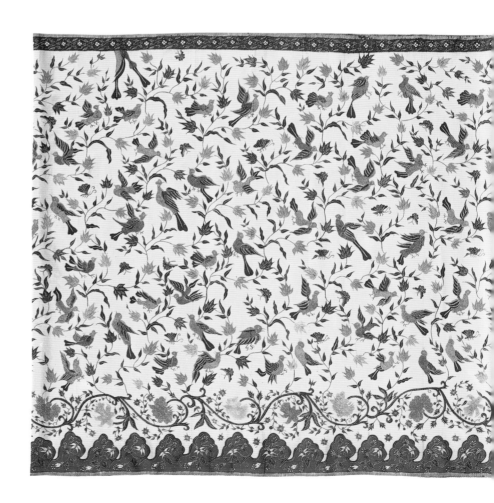

Catalogue no. 21
Hip wrapper, *sarung*
Java, Banyumas, c. 1890
Signed by
Nj. Gan Sam Gie
Hand-drawn wax resist
on machine-woven
cotton; natural and
synthetic dyes
105.4 x 217 cm
(41 1/2 x 85 3/8 in.)
Los Angeles County
Museum of Art,
Inger McCabe Elliott
Collection,
M.91.184.343

NOTES
1. H. C. Veldhuisen, *Batik Belanda 1840–1940* (Jakarta: Gaya Favorit, 1993), 122–24.
2. P. de Kat Angelino, *Batikrapport* (Batavia: Landsdrukkerij, 1930–31), 2: 5–12.

Floral vines in pastel colors wind diagonally across the plain, cream field of this tubular *sarung* in a style that largely follows the prescripts of traditional Pasisir design. Birds, each slightly different (doves and a cock are recognizable) and drawn in a European manner, flutter among the vines. In the *kepala* European flowers of the field—poppies, ears of corn, and trailing vetch—are loosely gathered on a blue ground sprinkled with tiny, six-petaled starflowers. Butterflies, drawn in the European style with fully opened wings, and a swallow nip at the honey. Along the lower border and one side of the *kepala* is a bold but finely depicted arabesque of orchids and roses in a style called *terang bulan* (full moon). The borders show the asymmetrical Indo-European treatment, though the bow borders are reminiscent of small mountains in Peranakan decorative style. The addition of purple accents, painted in diluted aniline ink on the otherwise red and blue cloth, results in a multicolored effect.

MAKER

The maker who signed the *kepala* of this batik "Njonja Gan Sam Gie Banjoemas" used her husband's name, Gan Sam Gie. (*Njonja* is Malay for *Mrs.*) This batik, though made in Banyumas (Banjoemas), follows an older Indo-European style used in Pekalongan about twenty years earlier; the colors are in the Peranakan taste. The *kepala* could have been copied from a design of Lien Metzelaar; the leaf in the upper border is also typical of her batik. Mrs. Gan must have been one of the earliest Peranakan entrepreneurs with a workshop in Banyumas. At that time, about 1890, workshops there were Indo-European, some even owned by male entrepreneurs, and Javanese.[1] *Batik Banyumas* with a pronounced European influence became popular after 1900 in Bandung and thus throughout Java and abroad.[2]

WEARER

Poppies and other European summer flowers, together with ears of corn, refer to harvest time. (To those unfamiliar with corn, this motif was perceived as a rice stalk, carrying its own symbolic meaning.) The luxurious orchids and fragrant red roses of the inner border both stand for the fullness of life and regeneration. The cloth is therefore suited to married women in the prime of life, either Indo-European or Peranakan.

Pekalongan: Stronghold of **Batik Belanda**

After 1860 Pekalongan developed into the most important production center of Indo-European batiks, which came to be known as *batik Belanda*. The innovative work of a few Indo-Europeans had far-reaching effects on the rest of production. Primarily in Pekalongan batik design became increasingly Europeanized in both inspiration and execution to suit the needs of Indo-European clientele. The possession of batiks from the workshops of A. J. F. Jans, Lien Metzelaar, Tina van Zuylen, and more particularly Lies van Zuylen became a must to express one's Dutch connections. First, by initiating the practice of signing their cloths, they emphasized the individuality of their designs and perfection of their work. The custom was soon adopted by Peranakan entrepreneurs as well. Imitation of successful designs was rampant, however, and the enforcement of copyright was completely unknown.

A second important change instigated by Indo-European designers can be seen in colors. Despite the continued predominance of blue and red, meticulous dyeing procedures resulted in a more varied scale with fine gradations of each color. The new light reds and blues were quite different from Pasisir *bang biru*; the same is true of Indo-European *kelengan* batik.

The third change consisted of several uniquely Pekalongan design styles. Although some Pekalongan designs followed traditional Pasisir precepts, such as the diagonal orientation of patterns in the *badan*, the best-known styles came to be dominated by two new concepts. The first was characterized by very simple lines and neatly arranged geometric motifs, not unlike wallpaper (FIGURE 63). It remained fashionable for a few decades, especially among recent Dutch immigrants. The second style contained an element generally referred to as *buketan* (decorated with bouquets), which has been widely considered the essence of *batik Pasisir* ever since: large bouquets of European stemmed flowers on the *badan* and a floral *kepala*. While initially the borders continued to be treated asymmetrically, ultimately identical borders appeared along the top and bottom edges of the cloth. Traditional background motifs were incorporated but lost their original meanings, which were probably beyond the Indo-European designers' understanding. *Cocohan*, for instance, came to be used in a novel decorative manner as color accents in white flowers. Dotted, white fillers (*isen*) were used increasingly to lighten and shade the colors in flowers. Further decorative innovations were the contour lines delineating flowers and diagonal lines used to decorate *kepala* backgrounds.

A simultaneous development was the adoption by Indo-European entrepreneurs of traditional central Javanese elements, which had already appeared on Peranakan cloths. The appeal of these elements to the Indo-Europeans was their simple lines and subdued colors. Motifs, such as *kawong* and *parang rusak*, which had been restricted to aristocratic use in the Principalities, were modified for the sake of propriety. The Indo-European entrepreneurs incorporated these new elements more harmoniously than the Peranakan, whose products went mainly to the lower-priced market.

The Indo-Europeans even adjusted the format of the cloths to the manner in which the batik was to be worn. The floral *kepala* was repositioned approximately one hand's width in from the end, a practical adaptation to the fashion for having most of the *kepala* visible instead of folding it in half (see Appendix 2). Accordingly, the seam could be neatly disguised. Tall European women, finding it difficult to wear standard-width batik at the prescribed ankle length, stitched a broad band of material onto the upper selvage. In most collections this addition has been removed, though the sewing holes are occasionally visible as evidence that

the wearer was probably European. The cloths were often worn with the inside out to protect the "good" side, which would only be shown on special occasions.

A final development was manifested among a growing segment of the Peranakan population, often educated and affluent. Needing to ally themselves with the ruling Dutch class, they eschewed traditional Peranakan styles in favor of Indo-European designs, though their meanings were frequently adapted to Peranakan cultural constructs. Although the new styles were made in Pekalongan, they were worn throughout the archipelago.

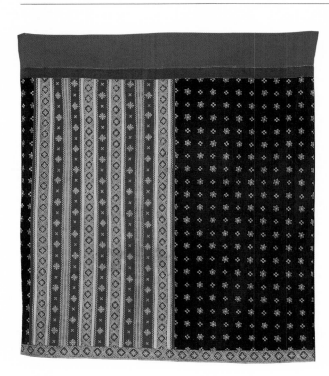

FIGURE 63
Hip wrapper, *sarung*
Java, Pekalongan,
c. 1900
Signed by
Maria Paulina Carp
Hand-drawn wax resist
on machine-woven
cotton; natural dyes
105 x 208 cm
(41 3/8 x 81 7/8 in.)
Private collection

Simple geometric *nitik* motifs, applied with different types of *canting*, are neatly arranged across the deep blue *badan* and saturated red *kepala* of this hand-sewn *sarung*. The style is reminiscent of the patterned bands woven in supplementary gold thread onto the well-known silk *songket* cloths of Sumatra and Bali. This batik was signed by Maria Paulina Carp, the only known Javanese with a European name to run a batik workshop in Pekalongan and imitate the European style. This cloth was made entirely in her workshop; she could not afford to send the piece out to an Indo-Arabian specialist in the *nitik* technique, as did her competitors Lies van Zuylen and Lien Metzelaar. Accordingly, the *nitik* is less precisely executed than theirs.

Catalogue no. 22
Hip wrapper, *sarung*
Java, Pekalongan,
c. 1900
Signed by A. J. F. Jans
Hand-drawn wax resist
on machine-woven
cotton; natural dyes
106.7 x 222.3 cm
(42 x 87 ½ in.)
Los Angeles County
Museum of Art,
Inger McCabe Elliott
Collection,
M.91.184.392

On the *badan* of this beautiful batik large irises in soft blue, green, and tawny
are combined with elegantly curling leaves in a design that reveals an art nouveau
source. Perfectly executed *galaran* cover the beige background, here used as a
purely decorative device. In the *kepala* two sets of clustered irises and pairs of
flirting swallows decorate the dark brown ground marked with diagonal *nitik*
lines. The border design follows the Indo-European asymmetrical division: the
upper consists of a variation on the simple floral band; the lower is embellished
with clusters of small orchids, but in perfect accordance with the rest of the
design. Note the extra space next to the *kepala*, permitting the entire *kepala* to
remain visible when worn.

MAKER

This batik, signed "J. Jans," was made in the workshop of A. J. F. Jans. The design
is probably after the English artist William Morris (1834–96), a founder of
the arts and crafts movement. It may have been copied from a magazine; Indo-
European entrepreneurs used these and other art nouveau sources, such as books
and postcards. The batik must have been made around 1900, when Jans ceased
signing herself as the widow of Th. J. Jans. The style here, with diagonal lines in
the background of the *kepala* (an adaptation of a design by Lien Metzelaar no earlier than c. 1880), is later than those made bearing the signature "Wed. J. Jans."[1]

The flower in the lower border is an orchid, not an iris, a possible misreading of the original source by the hired drawer. The same error often occurred as daffodils were transmogrified into orchids.

WEARER

NOTES

1. H. C. Veldhuisen, *Batik Belanda 1840–1940* (Jakarta: Gaya Favorit, 1993), nos. 38–39.

2. *De Echo: Weekblad voor dames in Indië* (1900–1901): 454.

3. Jean Chevalier and Alain Gheerbrant, *Dictionnaire des Symboles* (Paris: Robert Laffont/Jupiter, 1988), 524, 708.

This very expensive cloth of the finest quality would only have been chosen by a mature woman with a fashionable and quite personal Europeanized taste. Only a lady whose husband was of high status could afford to make such a striking choice. The European iris stands for opulence; its fragrance, for happiness and the fullness of life.[2] In the archipelago the flower may have been mistaken for an orchid, a flower that to Europeans represents graceful elegance.[3] As the Javanese link the orchid with regeneration, it was and is often used in wedding bouquets or as decoration of the nuptial chamber. The Peranakan relate it to summer and the mature phase of life.

Catalogue no. 23
Hip wrapper, *sarung*
Java, Pekalongan,
c. 1890
Signed and stamped by
Mevr. A. Simons
Hand-drawn wax resist
on machine-woven
cotton; natural dyes
106.7 x 218.3 cm
(42 x 86 in.)
Los Angeles County
Museum of Art,
Inger McCabe Elliott
Collection,
M.91.184.280

The striking *terang bulan* design on the *badan* of this hand-sewn *sarung* consists of seven large, abundantly decorated, red and cream triangles rising out of the lower border. The outlines are made of tiny dots that imitate the effect of the *tritik* (stitch-resist form of tie-and-dye) technique. Interspersed between the tri-angle/trees are cupids with bows drawn. *Cocohan* enliven their bodies and other cream sections of the design. Note the angelic, disembodied head of a final cupid to the right of the *kepala*. Nosegays of marigolds and daisies run in bands along the upper border on a green ground scattered with starflowers or sliced starfruit. The *kepala* contains an asymmetrical floral arrangement, cream and pink on deep red, somewhat resembling chrysanthemums, along with birds, butterflies, and other insects drawn in European style. The red ground is sprinkled with tiny, five-petaled flowers. An elaborate lace variation embellishes the left and lower borders and runs along the *kepala*; the upper border shows two interwoven gar-lands in empire style.

MAKER

Unfortunately there is no extant information on Mrs. Simons,[1] who signed the upper left corner of the *kepala* of this batik "Mevr. A. Simons Pekalongan"; the ink stamp in the left upper corner of the *badan* reads, "Batikkerij A. Simons Pekalongan." The stamp was applied to the white cotton, on which the batik maker was to work at home. It proved that Mrs. Simons was the owner of the waxed but undyed cloth and prevented its being sold by another or used as collat-eral. Many Lies van Zuylen batiks are similarly stamped,[2] a practice that she

NOTES
1. Only one other piece signed by Mrs. Simons is known: a *sarung* in the Linden-Museum (collection no. 78217), Stuttgart (see Brigitte Khan Majlis, *Indonesische Textilien: Wege zu Göttern und Ahnen* [Cologne: Wienand, 1984], 195). It shows a battle scene similar to that in catalogue no. 36.

2. H. C. Veldhuisen, interview with Lies Alting du Cloux and Frieda Lewis (both daughters of Lies van Zuylen), Rotterdam, 1981.

3. H. C. Veldhuisen, *Batik Belanda 1840–1940* (Jakarta: Gaya Favorit, 1993), no. 58.

4. Inger McCabe Elliott, *Batik: Fabled Cloth of Java* (New York: Clarkson N. Potter, 1984), 211.

alone among Indo-European entrepreneurs in Pekalongan shared with Mrs. Simons. The signature would have been added when the wax drawing was completed and Mrs. Simons had professed herself satisfied with its quality. Should there have been failures in the next step, dyeing, the batik would have been destroyed.

Precisely the same "faux *tritik*," standing triangles, decorate the *badan* of a Van Zuylen *sarung* of about 1890[3] and appear on other unsigned *sarung* and *kain panjang* from Pekalongan.

WEARER

The tree of life (in the form of triangles), cupids, and European spring and summer flowers make this cloth eminently suitable for an Indo-European bride or young married woman. The Javanese and many locally born women of mixed descent would see the cupids as *bidadari* (nymphs who descend from heaven on the eve of a wedding to protect the bride and provide her a celestial countenance).[4] This symbolism would have rendered the cloth suitable for a wide range of wearers. The color combination would have been particularly appealing to Indo-Arabian women.

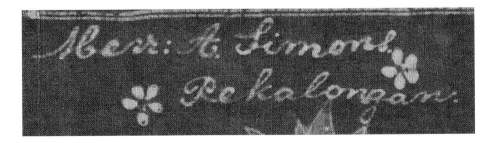

Catalogue no. 24
Hip wrapper,
sarung dlorong
Java, Pekalongan,
c. 1890
Signed by
Lien Metzelaar
Hand-drawn wax resist
on machine-woven
cotton; natural dyes
104 x 208.3 cm
(41 x 82 in.)
Los Angeles County
Museum of Art, Inger
McCabe Elliott
Collection,
M.91.184.491

The *badan* shows a variant of the central Javanese *geblak*, or *dlorong*, style, alternating diagonal bands decorated with garlands of chrysanthemums in blue, cream, and black on a *soga* ground, and a central Javanese *parang rusak* in traditional colors but slightly altered for wear by nonaristocrats. The *kepala*, a combination of art nouveau and Japanese design influences, shows a bamboo trellis with white lilies. Rudimentarily drawn birds and butterflies complete the design on a ground of dark blue with a sprinkling of small, four-petaled flowers. The lilies along the lower edge, complementing those of the *badan*, form an imitation-lace border. The upper border contains a very simple row of clustered flowers.

NOTE
1. M. J. de Raadt-Apell,
*De batikkerij Van Zuylen te
Pekalongan* (Zutphen: Terra,
1980), 44.

MAKER

The signature on this batik is "L Metz Pek" (for Lien Metzelaar Pekalongan), an abbreviation she adopted around 1890. This batik shows a new and recurrent Metzelaar motif in the upper border: four tiny flowers and seven leaves on a twig. The quality of drawing in the borders (which was delegated to younger, less experienced hands) fails to match that of the rest of the cloth, a result of specialization. Many of Metzelaar's batiks before 1890 show only the *badan* with a pattern and color combination—blue, brown, and cream—from the Principalities. The brown areas were dyed by Marjati, a Pekalongan specialist patronized by both Metzelaar and Lies van Zuylen.[1]

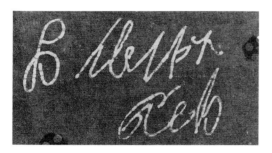

These batiks look like *batik dua negeri* in which *kepala* and *pinggir* were made in red with cream on the Pasisir and the *badan* in blue, brown, and cream in the Principalities. This method was used by Peranakan entrepreneurs, while Indo-European entrepreneurs from Pekalongan designed and executed the whole batik themselves. In this case Metzelaar used one color scheme for the *badan*, *kepala*, and borders. The chick in the right middle and lower right-hand corner of the *kepala* was one of her recurrent motifs, as was the lily, for which she and her friend Tina van Zuylen had a predilection.

WEARER

With its combination of European and central Javanese motifs and subdued color combination, this cloth is meant to be worn by an older Indo-European or possibly Peranakan woman. The chrysanthemum, flowering in autumn, is suitable for this time of life. The fragrant, white lilies, called *kerklelies* (church lilies) in Dutch, stand for purity and devotion. During the last quarter of the nineteenth century the simple lines of central Javanese design attracted a great deal of interest among Indo-Europeans.

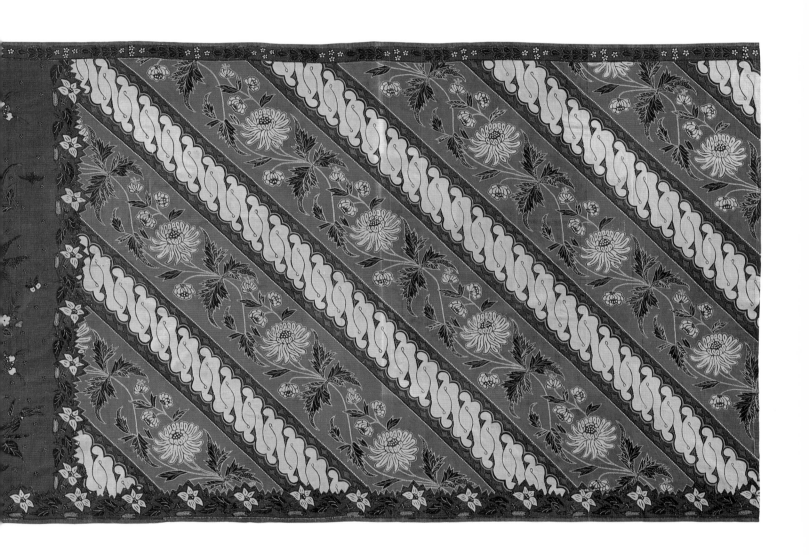

Catalogue no. 25
Hip wrapper,
sarung kelengan
Java, Pekalongan,
c. 1880–90
Signed by
Tina van Zuylen
Hand-drawn wax resist
on machine-woven
cotton; natural dyes
106.5 x 215 cm
(41⅞ x 84⅝ in.)
Los Angeles County
Museum of Art,
Inger McCabe Elliott
Collection,
M.91.184.474

This dainty batik is covered with nosegays in several tints of blue, arranged diagonally across the plain, white *badan*, giving a traditional Pasisir impression. Rows of small swallows form a horizontal counterpoint. A garland of carnations, morning glory, and bindweed runs diagonally across the *kepala*. In each corner a sprig of poppies, decorated with colored pinpricks, similar in technique to traditional *cocohan*, is surrounded by butterflies on the dark blue ground. The asymmetrical borders consist of closely striped selvage edges and clover leaves along the top and a finely delineated bow border of white flowers at the bottom.

MAKER

The signature of Tina van Zuylen, "T v Zuijlen Pk. [Pekalongan]," appears beneath the upper border in the *kepala*. The floral pattern on the *badan* closely resembles those on *sarung kelengan* produced by A. J. F. Jans as well as one known to be from A. Wollweber, both contemporaries in Pekalongan.[1] The *kepala* includes the rudimentarily drawn little bird (to the left and right of the broad, diagonal band), which Lien Metzelaar depicted in many of her batiks. Copying was a common practice among the entrepreneurs. What is more, Van Zuylen began her own workshop around 1880 with batik makers lent to her by Metzelaar, so it is not unlikely that the person who drew the chick in Metzelaar's workshop drew it for Van Zuylen as well. The embroidered number 16 in a corner of the cloth (not visible here) indicates that Van Zuylen used the best-quality cotton, machine-woven in the Netherlands.

WEARER

The gentle *kelengan* color scheme was worn by Indo-European brides on their wedding nights. Afterward such cloths were carefully stored and kept for funerary use. Though a *batik kelengan* could also serve as Peranakan mourning wear, the motifs here do not seem appropriate for that purpose. The fragrant, early summer flowers of the *badan* suit a young woman on the verge of mature life. The upper border of clover leaves stands for luck and married happiness. The swallow in the *badan* is the messenger of approaching summer. Although nineteenth-century wearers probably were not aware of this, in both Europe and China swallow's eggs were eaten during fertility rites in earlier times.[2]

NOTES
1. H. C. Veldhuisen, *Batik Belanda 1840–1940* (Jakarta: Gaya Favorit, 1993), nos. 38, 40.
2. Jean Chevalier and Alain Gheerbrant, *Dictionnaire des Symboles* (Paris: Robert Laffont/Jupiter, 1988), 506.

Catalogue no. 26
Hip wrapper, *sarung*
Java, Pekalongan,
c. 1900–1910
Signed and stamped by
Lies van Zuylen
Hand-drawn wax resist
on machine-woven
cotton; natural dyes
106.5 x 202 cm
(41⅞ x 79½ in.)
Los Angeles County
Museum of Art,
Inger McCabe Elliott
Collection,
M.91.184.423

This typical Lies van Zuylen batik, prototype of the style that later came to be called *batik Pekalongan* or even *batik Pasisir*, features rather stiff floral arrangements, which were probably intended as carnations, or perhaps peonies, and ferns in pastel blues, pinkish red, and a shade of green (now faded to blue-gray) on a ground originally cream, now bleached white. The *kepala* has a deep red ground and is decorated with another bouquet, white lilies with red pinpricks, a swallow, hummingbird, and butterflies in pink and white. This arrangement, with diagonal *nitik* lines in the background, became the norm in Indo-European *kepala* style. The borders show the usual asymmetry: the lower border is outlined by flowers instead of the bow line and edged by a double *seret*; the upper consists of a simple garland.

MAKER

This batik from Lies van Zuylen's workshop is signed "E v Zuylen" in white on a blue rectangle under the upper border to the left of the *kepala*. On earlier batiks her signature appears in the upper border itself. Those signatures also include "Pk" or "Pek," but it was not long before she considered this unnecessary; her customers knew the location of her workshop or could recognize *batik Pekalongan*. In one of the short ends is an oval ink stamp: "Batikkerij / Mevr. E. VAN ZUYLEN / Pekalongan."

The strong impression made by the bouquet in the *kepala* is due to the white flowers, a characteristic of Van Zuylen bouquets and imitated, even copied, by other entrepreneurs (see, for instance, catalogue no. 49). Around 1910 Van Zuylen and her followers started to repeat the bouquet from the *badan* on the *kepala*, although in different colors and mirrored. Such *sarung* were influenced by the tastes of European women, who were accustomed to wearing skirts with a single pattern. (For the entrepreneur, coincidentally, a repeated bouquet meant a smaller outlay for drawings.) The diagonal lines in the background of this *kepala* were introduced by Lien Metzelaar and often copied by her contemporaries.

WEARER

These colors, in a combination appealing to European taste, make this cloth suitable for young married Indo-European women. Flowers are universally related to women, though each ethnic group has its own symbolic concepts. To Europeans the carnation expresses delicacy, while the lily is an emblem of purity. According to Chinese and Peranakan views the peony is a symbol of mature feminine beauty; hummingbirds nipping at flowers represent males attracted by women; swallows announce the return of summer's heat. The universality of these symbols might have made this cloth appropriate as an emblem of status by a Peranakan woman who wanted to affiliate herself with the Dutch.

Catalogue no. 27
Hip wrapper, *sarung*
Java, Pekalongan,
c. 1900–1910
Signed by Tan Ien Nio
Hand-drawn wax resist
on machine-woven
cotton; natural dyes
106.8 x 192.2 cm
(42 x 75 5/8 in.)
Los Angeles County
Museum of Art,
Inger McCabe Elliott
Collection,
M.91.184.281

This perfectly hand-sewn *sarung*, with its floral sprigs—this time poppies in pink, blue, and well-preserved green with yellow veins on the leaves—gives an impression similar to the preceding cloth. Tiny birds and butterflies hover among the flowers on a cream ground, decorated with three-lobed leaves. The motifs are arrayed diagonally. The *kepala* shows a simple arrangement of lilies, which is also similar to the previous cloth, as are the background of *nitik* diagonals and asymmetrical borders.

MAKER

The Peranakan signer of this batik, Tan Ien Nio, used her husband's surname, Simonet, even before their marriage. Her batiks were made for Indo-Europeans and Europeans, who, when presented with a choice between two textiles in the same style and color scheme, preferred the one signed with a European name. In fact, Simonet was doing exactly as her Indo-European and Peranakan colleagues did, though the Indo-Europeans used their own initials before their husbands' surnames, while the Peranakan entrepreneurs used the abbreviation *Nj.* (Mrs.).

The borders are rather roughly drawn, which is not uncommon in batiks by Susannah Bouwer, Lien Metzelaar, and Lies van Zulyen and results from delegation to less-experienced batik makers. For the European clients the *badan* was more important than the *kepala*. Eventually the *kepala* on some of these cloths lost its distinctive pattern altogether.

WEARER

The symbolic meaning of this cloth is not unlike the last. The poppies stand for summer and harvest time; the lilies, for purity; and both are emblems of marital bliss and appropriate for a newly married European or Indo-European woman. The color scheme was especially popular among young women who had recently arrived from Holland. The cream-colored ground and the finely shaded reds and blues of the *badan* were widely appreciated by Europeans in the Netherlands East Indies as a characteristic of *batik Pekalongan*.

Neither the flowers in the elegant bouquets on the *badan* of this batik nor the others broadcast across the cream ground are readily identifiable. Butterflies, large and small, dragonflies, and swallows flutter about. The *kepala* shows a stiff arrangement of daisies, surrounded by the ubiquitous swallow and butterflies on a deep red ground with diagonal lines consisting of a tiny geometrical motif in *nitik* technique. The leaves of the chrysanthemum form the outline of the bow border; the flowers, neatly tucked beneath. The upper border shows a floral creeper, adapted from a traditional Pasisir motif. The familiar Indo-European pastel color scheme reaches a high point here in a palette of pinks, blues, and various shades of green created by overdyeing blue with ocher.

Catalogue no. 28
Hip wrapper, *sarung*
Java, Pekalongan,
c. 1900–1910
Signed by Susannah
Elisabeth Bouwer
Hand-drawn wax resist
on machine-woven
cotton; natural dyes
106 x 202.6 cm
(41³/₄ x 79³/₄ in.)
Los Angeles County
Museum of Art,
Inger McCabe Elliott
Collection,
M.91.184.282

MAKER

Susannah Elisabeth Bouwer signed her batiks "S E Bouwer Pekalongan." The stiff flower arrangement in the *kepala* is a good example of a type introduced by Lien Metzelaar around 1900, the precursor of the elegant bouquet in the *badan* of this *sarung*. This latter bouquet was undoubtedly inspired by European illustrations, because such seemingly natural arrangements of flowers were not in fashion in Pekalongan, where artificial arrangements prevailed.[1]

The execution of the design is fairly crude. The only other published Bouwer batik is similarly unrefined.[2] The number 16, embroidered in red with a tambour needle, is in the upper border next to the seam.

WEARER

This tubular, finely hand-sewn cloth was meant for a young married woman connected with the Indo-European community who may have interpreted the flowers as poppies, redolent of summer's harvest and therefore symbolic of the fulfillment of married life. Though the flowers are difficult to identify and may not even grow in the same season or region, their purpose is their association with things European. Therefore, the cloth might just as well have been given as a prestigious present to an affluent Peranakan bride for whom the reds and blues, the dragonflies, butterflies, and swallows would have expressed marital happiness.

NOTES
1. H. C. Veldhuisen, *Batik Belanda 1840–1940* (Jakarta: Gaya Favorit, 1993), 71, no. 67.
2. Ibid., no. 130.

Catalogue no. 29
Hip wrapper,
sarung dua negeri,
buket garuda sumping
Java, Pekalongan and
Paciran, c. 1910–20
Hand-drawn
and stamped wax resist
on machine-woven
cotton; natural and
synthetic dyes
104.8 x 192.9 cm
(41 ¼ x 76 in.)
Los Angeles County
Museum of Art,
Inger McCabe Elliott
Collection,
M.91.184.20

The abstracted, stamped motif on the *badan* of this *batik kombinasi* (in which some of the designs are hand-drawn) is called *garuda sumping* (ear pendants [with] garuda wings). It was inspired by a central Javanese design. A variation on the royal *sawat* motif, large double wings are combined with a motif that resembles a pineapple and is surrounded by feathers. Quadruple, fernlike flowers fill in the interstices, and rice grains (*wos utah*) are scattered in the background. Blue and cream accents are added to a *soga* brown with a yellow luster, yielding a rich, almost gilded effect. The hand-drawn *kepala* shows the familiar Indo-European bouquet (*buket*) made up of small, round flowers and ferns tied with a bow and a background of starflowers. The flowers in the light and elegant bouquet resemble a traditional Pasisir motif, *brondong mentul* (crackling popcorn). Lovebirds pursue one another, and butterflies flutter about. The borders are decorated in the asymmetrical Indo-European Pasisir style. The upper border consists of a band of simple, stringed flowers; the lower shows the same floral bow border that outlines the *kepala*. A bright synthetic red sets the *kepala* and the borders off against the *badan*.

MAKER

From the beginning of this century and continuing until about 1930 large quantities of unfinished batiks, with *badan* as yet undrawn, were produced in Pekalongan and sold to entrepreneurs along the Pasisir and in the Principalities to be finished as *batik dua negeri*. The work on this batik was divided between two Peranakan workshops. The *kepala* and borders in red and cream were hand drawn in Pekalongan and the *badan* hand-stamped in the eastern part of the north coast, possibly in Paciran.

WEARER

During the early twentieth century a cloth such as this, with its vaguely central Javanese flavor, European florals, and Pasisir red, would have been acceptable to a varied group of urban women who did not feel inclined or were unable to choose an explicit statement of ethnic or racial affiliation. Its medium-quality material and uneven workmanship (the stamps of the *badan* do not parallel the borders) brought this cloth within reach of the lower middle class, while its golden *soga* gave it a pretense of elegance.

NOTE

1. Greet de Raadt-Apell, oral communication, Lochem, the Netherlands, 1985.

This tubular cloth shows an elegant floral arrangement, including European carnations, repeated in several shades of blue on a plain, white *badan*, scattered with insects and tiny flowers. Large European carnation species were cultivated during the late nineteenth century in the mountains and sold door to door in nearby Pekalongan. (Very old people still remember the itinerant sellers who came through European neighborhoods in Javanese cities shouting *anjelier*, the Dutch name for the flower.)[1] In the *kepala* Prince Charming leads Cinderella to the dance. The couple is dwarfed by surrounding floral arrangements, whose intermingling stems end at the upper border, where a swallow and two butterflies hover. The bright blue ground is decorated with dotted diagonal lines. A fine lace border on a rather dark blue ground decorates the lower border and edges of the *kepala*; the upper border shows a neatly drawn floral chain.

MAKER

Lies van Zuylen's signature appears upside down in the middle of the *kepala* under the upper border. She signed in pencil on the cotton after she had approved the completed wax drawing of the entire cloth. Her best-qualified batik maker than traced the signature in wax, on one side of the cloth only, thus determining which side was the front. After dyeing, the signature was only vaguely visible on the back. Van Zuylen copied illustrations from books. The fairy-tale characters and floral arrangement seen here could have been adapted from European book jackets. Van Zuylen added the diagonal lines, seen on so many Indo-European *kepala* from Pekalongan, and the bird in flight and butterflies, commonly presented in context of floral arrangements on the same batiks. The birds, butterflies, and bouquets were then imitated by local Peranakan entrepreneurs, on whose batiks the butterflies, at least, became increasingly elaborate and "exotic."

WEARER

This finely hand-sewn *kelengan* cloth was likely used by an Indo-European bride on her wedding night. The fragrant carnations in full bloom refer to the bride, Prince Charming and Cinderella to the bridal couple, and the mingling stems to their marriage. The sprinkling of small flowers evokes the fragrance of *melati* blossoms that are scattered on the floor of the nuptial bedroom. Obviously, though the blue-and-white color combination was considered suitable to the occasion, the design was not appropriate for a Peranakan mourning cloth.

Catalogue no. 30
Hip wrapper,
sarung kelengan
Java, Pekalongan,
c. 1900–1910
Signed by
Lies van Zuylen
Hand-drawn wax resist
on machine-woven
cotton; natural dyes
108 x 194.3 cm
(42 ½ x 76 ½ in.)
Los Angeles County
Museum of Art,
Inger McCabe Elliott
Collection,
M.91.184.269

Catalogue no. 31
Hip wrapper,
sarung kelengan dlorong
buketan, sarung porselen
Java, Pekalongan,
c. 1900
Signed by
Lies van Zuylen
Hand-drawn wax resist
on machine-woven
cotton; natural dyes
109.2 x 222.2 cm
(43 x 87 ½ in.)
Los Angeles County
Museum of Art,
Inger McCabe Elliott
Collection,
M.91.184.473

Vertical bands (*dlorong*) of varying width in the *badan* are decorated with undulating garlands of carnations and cornflowers in shades of blue; fine diagonal lines (*galaran*) decorate the narrowest band. Three floral bands and butterflies fill the dark blue ground of the *kepala*, the central band forming an overlay on an eye-catching double meander. The treatment of the flowers shows art nouveau influence, while the meander was inspired by Chinese iconography. Delicate white *kemuning* flowers grace the wide lace border.

NOTE
1. Inger McCabe Elliott, *Batik: Fabled Cloth of Java* (New York: Clarkson N. Potter, 1984), no. 43.

MAKER

Lies van Zuylen used the same design in a multicolored version.[1] Both were produced for inventory. (Successful Peranakan entrepreneurs, such as The Tie Siet in Pekalongan, followed the same practice.) The pattern in this *badan* was also combined with a diversity of patterns in other *kepala*. The precision of these replications resulted from their having been traced in wax with the *canting* from life-size drawings on paper pinned to the back of the white cotton.

WEARER

This *kelengan* batik with its summery flowers could have been worn by an Indo-European bride on her wedding night, but unlike the previous cloth, it might also have served as Peranakan mourning dress. This was made possible by the double meander, reminiscent of the *fu*, one of twelve auspicious Chinese ornaments. Furthermore, the motif gives strong intimations of the protective *banji* motif. The *kemuning* flowers in the lower border are used both to ornament the hair of a married woman and in garlands covering a bier. The fine shades of blue, which evoke for the Peranakan community blue-and-white Ming porcelains, gave the cloth its additional name, *kain porselen*. The Dutch associated these colors with Delft blue plates.

Finely delineated bouquets of large chrysanthemums in several shades of pink, red, blue, and green grace the perfectly executed *badan* of this cloth. Butterflies with widespread wings and birds, both depicted in European style, embellish the bouquets. Two elegant floral designs decorate the diagonal bands of the *kepala*. Each band is outlined by a zigzag *nitik* edge. The lower border shows chrysanthemums in pink, blue, and white; the upper is filled with a dense, abstracted garland.

MAKER

Lies van Zuylen's name stamp appears under the *pinggir*, at the left side of the *kepala*, to the right of the seam. This is the first Van Zuylen batik shown here on which every aspect was completed with utmost perfection, which was to become her trademark. Pencil guidelines still dimly visible in the *kepala* indicate that the drawing began in the upper right corner and ended in the lower left with a band somewhat smaller than its counterpart. The simple nitik outlines were the specialty of Indo-Arabian entrepreneurs in Pekalongan, from whom local Indo-European entrepreneurs commissioned such work.

WEARER

The style and color scheme of this exquisite cloth made it suitable for young married Indo-European women. The chrysanthemums, Chinese emblem of autumn and, hence, middle age, also made it appropriate for affluent Peranakan matrons, who generally used lighter colors than was customary for Europeans and Indo-Europeans of the same age group. Van Zuylen numbered all three among her customers during the period this batik was made.

Catalogue no. 32
Hip wrapper, *sarung*
Java, Pekalongan,
c. 1900–1910
Stamp of
Lies van Zuylen
Hand-drawn wax resist
on machine-woven
cotton; natural dyes
105.4 x 210.8 cm
(41 1/2 x 83 in.)
Los Angeles County
Museum of Art,
Inger McCabe Elliott
Collection,
M.91.184.555

NOTE
1. H. C. Veldhuisen,
interview with Lies Alting
du Cloux and Frieda Lewis,
Rotterdam, 1981.

The space provided by the length of the cloth proves barely wide enough to accommodate four simple but elegant bouquets of poppies in red, bright blue, tawny brown, and green on a cream ground. Nontraditional, feathery tan lines, which run diagonally, provide a background layer. The *kepala* is quite similar to catalogue no. 32, although its diagonal *dlorong* bands are narrower and its garlands less spontaneous. Delicate filler motifs add detail to each small flower, none of which belongs to recognizable species, though their European flavor is obvious. A neat but rather stiff bow border consisting of poppies and carnations decorates the lower edge; the upper border is a very fine version of the garland of small flowers.

MAKER

This batik is signed by Lies van Zuylen and bears her name stamp. It is of the finest quality but of a type more costly than the preceding example because of the refined, Van Zuylen-designed background motif in the *badan*, the drawing of which was not only time-consuming but risky when applied to such an expansive area.

Therefore Van Zuylen had only a few such batiks in stock to show to dealers and private customers.[1]

The art nouveau bow border had appeared earlier in Van Zuylen's repertoire. Such combinations of new and old were not unusual. The color scheme, however, differs from earlier Van Zuylens. It is no longer specifically European, but more to the taste of Peranakan matrons. Since the *sarung* and *kabaya* combination fell out of fashion in the European communities of the larger Javanese cities in the 1920s, the preponderance of Van Zuylen's most affluent customers were, in fact, Peranakan.

WEARER

This flawless and very expensive piece, through its multiple colors and choice of summer flowers, depicts the high season of life and is therefore suited for a middle-aged Indo-European or Peranakan woman of ample means. Though the flowers are European, they are depicted rather vaguely, so they may be identified as peonies or carnations, flowers closer to the hearts of the second group.

Catalogue no. 33
Hip wrapper, *sarung*
Java, Pekalongan,
c. 1900–1910
Signed and stamped by
Lies van Zuylen
Hand-drawn wax resist
on machine-woven
cotton; natural dyes
104.1 x 215.8 cm
(41 x 85 in.)
Los Angeles County
Museum of Art,
Inger McCabe Elliott
Collection,
M.91.184.134

An Indo-European woman wearing a *kain kompani*, a *sarung* decorated with images referring to the military campaigns that consolidated the colonial power of the Dutch. Padang, west Sumatra, 1930. Koninklijk Instituut voor Taal-, Land- en Volkenkunde, Leiden

Emblems of Colonial Power

As the nineteenth century came to a close, easier transportation over land and across the sea set into motion a chain of overwhelming changes in the archipelago, one of the most influential being the expansion of Dutch colonial power throughout the outer islands. These developments inspired a body of completely new batik designs with naturalistic images in a kind of comic-book style, which remained in vogue throughout the following half century. The subjects of steamboats, trains, and, later, airplanes are prime examples of this modern batik style. Another subject, the conquest of the island of Lombok, evokes colonial expansion. Other European contributions to the colonial lifestyle, card games and the opera, which had already been introduced on batik, persisted. A longtime favorite, European fairy tales, came to be regarded as substitutes for local myths and moralistic legends addressed to women of various ages.

More than merely being modern, these new designs represented Dutch hegemony. Interestingly, these are also the designs several early twentieth-century scholars disparage as lacking in taste and refinement, thereby obviously overlooking their meaning for Indo-Europeans.[1]

A second important change was the development of synthetic dyes, first used in Java around 1890. Though the new colors looked rather harsh, their ease of use and broad range of shades made them the obvious choice, especially for cheaper, lower-quality commercial batik and for popular designs that were produced in large quantities. A further time-saving device to which the synthetic dyes lent themselves was *colet* (the painting of small areas by hand). The fine details in human faces, which were difficult to execute in wax, were in some cases directly drawn in india ink.

NOTE

1. J. E. Jasper and Mas Pirngadie, *De batikkunst*, vol. 3 of *De inlandsche kunstnijverheid in Nederlandsch Indië* (The Hague: Mouton, 1916), 2: 9; G. P. Rouffaer, "Beeldende Kunst in Nederlandsch Indië," *Bijdragen van het Koninklijk Instituut voor Taal- Land- en Volkenkunde van Nederlandsch-Indië* 89 (1932): 653.

Catalogue no. 34
Hip wrapper,
kain panjang
Java, Pekalongan,
c. 1900
Signed and stamped by
Lies van Zuylen
Hand-drawn wax resist
on machine-woven
cotton; natural dyes
109 x 234 cm
(42 7/8 x 92 1/8 in.)
Los Angeles County
Museum of Art,
Costume Council and
Museum Associates
purchase,
M.77.121

The meeting of Little Red Riding Hood and the Big Bad Wolf is the subject of this fairy-tale batik. The background is decorated with a traditional Javanese motif called *gedekan* (like a wall of plaited bamboo), or *bilik*. It is yet another example of the purely decorative use of such a motif. Each hand-hemmed, narrow edge shows, instead of a *kepala*, a series of decorative borders, one of which is a row of small triangles, called *gigi walang*, a term obviously related to the traditional Peranakan *kepala gigi balang*. The bow border consists of narcissus, while tiny triangles decorate the upper border. The method of applying the filler motifs in the green areas provides a realistic shaded effect.

MAKER

Lies van Zuylen's signature appears in a blue rectangle in the upper left-hand corner; beneath it, her name stamp. The opposite border contains within a narrow band brown and red weftlines, denoting the head of the bolt, and embroidered in chain stitch the number of yards. One of her daughters, Frieda Lewis, claimed that the cotton used by Van Zuylen was absolutely flawless. Before cutting the bolt into desired lengths, a worker checked for imperfections in weaving and cut them out. Thus, one *sarung* or *kain panjang* could be shorter than the others. Customarily the heading with weftlines would never be used in Van Zuylen's workshop.[1] This batik is an exception, but Van Zuylen addressed the problem ingeniously: the weftlines are virtually invisible because they form one of the narrow, colored bands with tiny motifs in the end border.

Batiks with scenes from European fairy tales had become very popular in Pekalongan by the end of the nineteenth century. Freelance artisans made enlarged

NOTES

1. H. C. Veldhuisen,
interview with Frieda Lewis,
The Hague, 1992.

2. H. C. Veldhuisen, *Batik
Belanda 1840–1940* (Jakarta:
Gaya Favorit, 1993), 40–41,
based on interviews and the
comparison of batiks depicting fairy tales in collections
and publications.

3. M. J. de Raadt-Apell,
*De batikkerij Van Zuylen te
Pekalongan, Midden-Java
1890–1946* (Zutphen: Terra,
1980), 34.

4. H. C. Veldhuisen,
interview with Eliza Christina
Metzelaar, The Hague, 1992.

copies of book illustrations and reproduced them many times in pencil on paper. The drawings were sold to batik entrepreneurs, Van Zuylen among them, and used as the basis of wax tracings.[2] Not surprisingly, we encounter identical patterns on batiks from different workshops.

The picture of Little Red Riding Hood on this batik, however, differs from ones that she executed on other examples[3] and also from those executed by her colleagues. Here the wolf resembles a lion; the basket looks Indonesian; and the slender, flowering tree is unlike those more commonly seen, with thick branches and with few leaves. Probably Van Zuylen's artisan created his own design from her instructions. Van Zuylen made many copies of Little Red Riding Hood. Her niece, Eliza Christina Metzelaar, who worked for her around 1920, remembers they were especially popular with Indo-Arabian dealers from Batavia.[4]

WEARER

The fairy tale about the little girl who is sent into the forest, where her excess of trust results in her being gobbled up by a wolf, then rescued by a hunter, represents a kind of female initiation myth. Similar stories about the adventures of young heroines that end happily through the intervention of heroes abound in Java. The Western tale was thus comprehensible to a wide audience, explaining why this type of batik was so popular. The cloth could be given as a present to a young woman, thereby expressing hopes for her to succeed in contracting a happy marriage. The use of the apotropaic *gigi walang* (cricket's teeth) in the borders was probably not merely a decorative device in the original design, while the use of a broad range of dyes, resembling multicolored ceremonial textiles may also indicate the almost ritualistic importance of this cloth.

Catalogue no. 35
Hip wrapper, *sarung*
Java, Batang, c. 1910
Hand-drawn wax resist
on machine-woven
cotton; natural and
synthetic dyes
105.4 x 203.7 cm
(41 ½ x 80 ¼ in.)
Los Angeles County
Museum of Art,
Inger McCabe Elliott
Collection,
M.91.184.259

NOTE
1. *Gedenkbock 10 jaar:*
De Huisvrouw in Indië (1941)
465; H. C. Veldhuisen, *Batik*
Belanda 1840–1940 (Jakarta:
Gaya Favorit, 1993), no. 16.

Scenes from opera were often depicted on batik as early as 1860, when local, amateur companies first performed on Java.[1] The designs were generally copied from illustrations in Dutch books or magazines. The scene on this cloth suggests a Wagnerian source. A person in a braided tunic, with flowing hair, steers a chariot pulled by swans through a lake resplendent with flowering lotus. Large butterflies flutter among the flowers. In the center of the lake a young boy is guided by a winged guardian across the lotus leaves toward an undefined goal. A pair of officers with sabers at their belts, dressed in great coats and German helmets, stand on the shore. The connections among these elements is unclear. The *kepala* is decorated with an elegant bouquet of lilylike flowers, while the borders offer an asymmetrical variant. Bright natural red and synthetic indigo on a green ground are enlivened with synthetic pink and bright blue. Along the lower border and interspersed with a garland, the Malay text *"slamet pakei"* (wear [the cloth] in good health) can be deciphered.

MAKER

The Peranakan batik entrepreneurs in Batang, near Pekalongan, followed the style of Pekalongan, but their color schemes tended to be deeper.

A remarkable feature of this batik is the Malay text, which is known on woven textiles from Sumatra but was not the fashion in Java; possibly this batik was ordered for a Sumatran woman on a special occasion.

The design of the *badan* has much in common with the opera scenes popular on Indo-European *sarung* from Semarang around 1860 and with the fairy-tale batiks from Pekalongan. Because there are so many inconsistencies among the depictions, we can easily conclude that in this case the batik maker did not use a drawing on tracing paper. This might indicate that she knew the pattern by heart because she had already drawn it so many times.

WEARER

This rather fanciful cloth was probably presented to convey fond wishes to the recipient. The chosen scene must have had a personal meaning, which regretfully has not been discovered.

NOTES
1. M. C. Ricklefs, *A History of Modern Indonesia since c. 1300*, 2d rev. ed. (London: MacMillan, 1993), 135.
2. H. C. Veldhuisen, *Batik Belanda 1840–1940* (Jakarta: Gaya Favorit, 1993), 43–44.

This cloth depicts the Dutch conquest of the island of Lombok in 1894 after almost twenty years of contention.[1] Vivid scenes of the colonial army's campaign are depicted on the cream-colored *badan* (below). A trumpeter precedes the soldiers, who march in single file along a grassy road with their rifles shouldered. Officers on horseback ride with their swords drawn. Two men carry a palanquin loaded with supplies. A cannoneer singlehandedly pushes his weapon. Tents have been erected along the way. Interestingly, the officers and soldiers, with their red and black faces, are accurately shown to have been recruited from both the Dutch and native populations. The *kepala* is decorated with a stamped combination of floral motifs that give a rather haphazard impression. The term *kain kompeni* relates the cloth to "the Company," the term originally used in the archipelago for the VOC. Even during the colonial period the Dutch forces continued to be denoted as such.

Catalogue no. 36
Hip wrapper,
*sarung perang Lombok,
kain kompeni*
Java, Pekalongan,
c. 1920–30
Hand-drawn and stamped wax resist on machine-woven cotton; synthetic dyes
103.5 x 182 cm
(40 3/4 x 71 5/8 in.)
Los Angeles County Museum of Art,
Inger McCabe Elliott Collection,
M.91.184.380

MAKER

This cloth came from an Indo-Arabian batik-stamp workshop, of which there were many in Pekalongan. Their synthetic-color schemes differed notably from those of their Peranakan colleagues, and they made batik with Indo-European designs, which had become as popular as *batik canting*. A batik depicting soldiers of the Java War (1825–30) was made in Semarang before 1894 and the battle for Lombok.[2] After that similar scenes occurred on *sarung* from the workshops of Lien Metzelaar, A. Simons, A. Wollweber, and Tina van Zuylen.

WEARER

An important event for the Europeans, the battle for Lombok, which exemplified the successful "pacification" of the outer islands, was widely illustrated on *sarung*. When the design appeared later on stamped batik, it became popular with the native and Indo-European consorts of soldiers in the garrisons. This type of cloth remained fashionable for many decades among Indo-Europeans throughout the Dutch East Indies who wished to express their pride in Dutch accomplishments (see FIGURE 42).

Catalogue no. 37
Hip wrapper, *sarung*
Java, Pekalongan,
c. 1930
Stamped wax resist on
machine-woven cotton;
synthetic dyes
107.9 x 182.5 cm
(42 1/2 x 71 7/8 in.)
Los Angeles County
Museum of Art,
Inger McCabe Elliott
Collection,
M.91.184.486

Two passenger trains chug along the borders of this batik toward the *kepala*. (The letters on the train—BLKSM DJSMR—have so far eluded interpretation.) Full-masted steamers carve the waters in between. Lobsters and nosegays fill the remaining spaces. The blue dye was dipped, while the synthetic red dye was painted by hand as was the yellow, painted over the blue to achieve a green, which has now faded. In the *kepala* blue top-dyed with red results in a purplish shade called *wungon*.

MAKER

Mechanized modes of transportation were symbols not only of modernization but of colonial power as well, yet batiks with trains and steamboats were not produced by Indo-European entrepreneurs, although it was their tradition to depict important events. This *sarung* may have been made in the same Indo-Arabian workshop that produced catalogue no. 36. The floral *kepala* are certainly similar, and the stamps for the *badan* are again large-sized. The upper border of this batik is still in the Indo-European fashion (Peranakan entrepreneurs had by 1920 begun repeating the bow border along both horizontal edges). While batiks such as this were not made for Europeans, the motifs are themselves Western, which probably accounts for the old-fashioned upper border used for customers who associated themselves with the ruling class.

This batik was acquired in Sumatra, and there are records showing that this type was made for export there.[1]

WEARER

Batik of this sort was worn all over the archipelago by those who, even in a modest way, felt themselves part of the colonial state. A local symbolism is contained in the choice of elements here. Together they express the idea of *tanah air*, the fatherland consisting of water (the ships and sea creatures) and land (the trains and floral motifs).

NOTE
1. Inger McCabe Elliott, *Batik: Fabled Cloth of Java* (New York: Clarkson N. Potter, 1984), 223.

NOTES

1. H. C. Veldhuisen, *Batik Belanda 1840–1940* (Jakarta: Gaya Favorit, 1993), 89.

2. K. R. T. Hardjonegoro, oral communication, Surakarta, January 1995.

Hybrid steamships with masts and sails, possibly denoting patrol vessels, and two fanciful, early airplanes navigate the *badan* of this batik. On the coast helmeted men tread their way through marshes. They are probably soldiers on patrol, with their sabers drawn. Various shades of blue and black are combined on the plain, cream ground. In the *kepala* an elegant bouquet, held by a bow and consisting of lilies and ferns, is surrounded by birds and butterflies on a dark ground scattered with small, white flowers. The borders are asymmetrical; the bow consists of small, generic flowers.

MAKER

The lengthy inscription on the ink stamp—"*Dilarang Masoek Gade atau di djoeal* [Forbidden to pawn or to sell] *Yap Loen Tik. Pek*"—indicates that the maker was a Peranakan entrepreneur; they often used such "ban stamps." The ban in this case was intended for the hired maker. On many stamps the words *Auteurswet 1912* (copyright law 1912) appear along with a proscription, "*dilarang meniroe*" (forbidden to copy), which was intended for colleagues. Both bans were at times combined on a single stamp.[1]

WEARER

The design may well have been made with modernization in mind, but the men on patrol and the patrol boats can also be seen as a variation of the *perang Lombok*. In spite of the thoroughly Western subjects, the design implicitly incorporates the three traditional Javanese realms—sky (airplanes), land (trees and human beings), and sea (boats)—that together constitute the universe.[2] This feature transforms the scene into a present-day cosmological concept. Cloths of this type were used by a varied group of Indo-Europeans, Peranakan Chinese, and possibly others all over the archipelago.

Catalogue no. 38
Hip wrapper, *sarung*
Java, Pekalongan,
c. 1930
Stamp of Yap Loen Tik
Hand-drawn wax resist
on machine-woven
cotton; synthetic indigo
106.7 x 198.5 cm
(42 x 78 1/8 in.)
Los Angeles County
Museum of Art,
Inger McCabe Elliott
Collection,
M.91.184.266

Catalogue no. 39
Hip wrapper, *sarung*
Java, Pekalongan,
c. 1930–40
Stamp of Haji Ehsan
Stamped wax resist on
machine-woven cotton;
synthetic dyes
105 x 177.4 cm
(41 3/8 x 69 7/8 in.)
Los Angeles County
Museum of Art,
Inger McCabe Elliott
Collection,
M.91.184.498

A variation on the theme of modernization and colonial power. The motifs are in blue and brownish-purple on a plain, cream ground. The *kepala* is decorated with flowering boughs, among which fluttering birds nip at the flowers, as do a couple of hungry ducks below. The asymmetrical borders contain a neat bow of daisies and an undulating floral creeper.

MAKER

The stamped signature of the Indo-Arabian entrepreneur H[aji] Ehsan appears in the upper right corner of the *kepala*; his name and address, on the sides of the steamboats. *Haji* is the title assumed by a Muslim man who has successfully completed the pilgrimage to Mecca. In Java the desire to make the pilgrimage was especially strong among the devout Indo-Arabian and Javanese adherents of Islam on the north coast.

The long-legged wading bird was often depicted by Lien Metzelaar. Because the image is so prominent, we can conclude that it had a special meaning, possibly the mother country feeding her colonial children. In those days the political discussion in Holland and her East Indies colony was about which process of independence would be best for both parties.

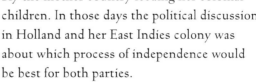

WEARER

Compared with the two previous examples, the third batik of this type seems to combine most explicitly notions of progress and tradition: the steamers and airplanes on the one hand, the fish, flying birds, and herons or storks on the other. The latter are drawn in traditional Pasisir style. Again the tripartite division of the universe is implied, thereby incorporating emblems of modernity and colonial power into an age-old view of the universe. Only large women with ample hips could wear a cloth with motifs this size.

OTE

1. H. C. Veldhuisen, *Batik
elanda 1840–1940* (Jakarta:
aya Favorit, 1993), no. 101.

Playing cards in ones, twos, and threes are deployed in informal rows on a dark blue ground, decorated with floral sprigs and small flowers. The *kepala* was executed with large-size stamps and corrected by hand. Its decoration consists of a bouquet of grapes and grape leaves in pink and white, surrounded by the ubiquitous birds and butterflies. The red ground is sprinkled with the suggestion of flowers, each made up of seven dots, which also were applied by hand. The upper and lower border are similar and consist of a bow, outlined in leaves, with flowers that may have been intended as marigolds.

Catalogue no. 40
Hip wrapper, *sarung*
Java, Pekalongan,
c. 1930–40
Stamp of
H[aji] Achmad
Stamped wax resist on
machine-woven
cotton; synthetic dyes
105.4 x 188.8 cm
(41 1/2 x 74 3/8 in.)
Los Angeles County
Museum of Art,
Inger McCabe Elliott
Collection,
M.91.184.558

MAKER

The depiction of playing cards on batik was quite popular. The same pattern, but with some variation in particular cards, appears on a hand-waxed *sarung* from the Pekalongan workshop of the Indo-European entrepreneur S. B. Feunem, made around 1900.[1] It appears again on a *kain panjang* in a Japanese collection. The signature stamped in the *kepala* of this example informs us that the entrepreneur was H[aji] Achmad. It is the only batik in this small series in which the bow border is repeated along the upper edge, a Peranakan innovation of about 1920.

At the right side of the *kepala* (left of the seam) is a narrow band of brown and red weftline threads, the usual way of marking a bolt of cloth in the Dutch mills.

WEARER

The playing of bridge or whist at the club (Societeit) was considered a modern and slightly frivolous pastime for emancipated women of the upper strata of the European and Indo-European communities. If a particular game was illustrated here, it is no longer possible to say what it was. The grapes may indicate another activity indulged in by women in the club, the drinking of wine. This rather inexpensive cloth may have been worn by those who were not actually included in these social activities but wanted to present themselves as associated with the ruling class.

A Chinese woman wearing an
Indo-European-style *sarung*
produced by a Peranakan
workshop, perhaps in
Pekalongan. Riouw archipelago, c. 1920.

Modifications by Peranakan Entrepreneurs for Peranakan Wearers

After 1910, with the official imposition of increasing racial distinctions, the gap between Dutch and non-Dutch residents widened, a development that was exacerbated by the negative attitude of newly immigrated Dutch women toward Indies lifestyles and dress. Furthermore, in 1920 the Chinese, including the Peranakan, were declared legally equal with the Dutch, a considerable change in their status.[1] Dress codes were adjusted to make the existing social hierarchy within both the Dutch-affiliated and Peranakan communities apparent. For the upper class of the colonial establishment the *sarung* costume was considered appropriate for nothing more than housewear. Although many among this group were of obvious mixed descent, they did their utmost to imply by their Dutch behavior and dress that they were indeed Dutch. Only the middle class, primarily those who openly acknowledged their mestizo background, continued to show themselves publicly in *sarung* and *kabaya*.

The Pekalongan style remained fashionable as private and public dress among both Dutch and Indo-European women of this class. Of newer designs a single type of bouquet, at most in different colors, now decorated both the *badan* and *kepala*. The symbolic meanings attributed to the particular flowers or to their fragrances appear to have remained important to the Indo-Europeans. Plain grounds gave some of these batiks an elegant simplicity. Furthermore, the *kain panjang* came to be similarly designed, with a series of identical bouquets on a plain ground. The return to popularity of the rectangular cloth can be seen as the forerunner of the *pagi sore* style of the 1930s. Identical upper and lower borders continued, with a slightly wider type appearing in those from Peranakan workshops. By the 1930s new types of synthetic dyes provided a palette that supplanted the traditional reds and blues.

Class distinctions among the Chinese were expressed more subtly. Though the upper echelons of the Peranakan population now often donned European dress for public occasions, in private and for family festivities they also maintained the latest Pasisir styles, albeit recognizable by the pastel shades that had become their particular fashion. The luxurious qualities of the batik work and an abundance of colors, rather than the symbolism of a cloth, became the most accurate indicators of status. This occasioned the development, first in the borders and *kepala*, later in the *badan*, of increasingly elaborate background motifs, a trend that reached its zenith in the *tanahan Semarangan* style. The new Peranakan batiks in their seemingly Europeanized designs retained some traditional signifiers of apotropaic protection, fertility, and prosperity, and the layered quality can still be recognized in textiles of this period.

More and more Peranakan workshops were established, most in Pekalongan and others in different towns of the Pasisir. Some of these towns developed their own recognizable styles. While joining in the imitation and reinterpretation of the Indo-European design repertoire, they developed their own color schemes with a gamut of mixed tints. Many of these entrepreneurs signed their work and sometimes forged the signature of the Indo-European maker Lies van Zuylen. Financial considerations occasioned the production of cloths that were suitable for more than one group of wearers.

NOTE

1. Colonial rules did not distinguish between immigrant and Peranakan Chinese.

Catalogue no. 41
Hip wrapper, *sarung*
Java, Tegal, c. 1920–30
Hand-drawn wax resist
on machine-woven
cotton; natural dyes
105 x 218.5 cm
(41 3/8 x 86 in.)
Los Angeles County
Museum of Art,
Inger McCabe Elliott
Collection,
M.91.184.97

Three large, elegant bouquets of white foxgloves and hydrangea fill the *badan* of this striking cloth. The leaves show varied filler motifs; their unusual—now slightly faded—deep bottle-green consists of a top-dye of *soga* brown on blue. Red pinpricks show in the white flowers, while the bright red ground has been decorated with sprigs of blue carnations, tiny insects, and swallows in flight. The same design with blue foxgloves and red hydrangea graces the white ground of the *kepala*. Both borders are adorned with a delicate garland of red carnations and green leaves.

MAKER

The Peranakan entrepreneurs of Tegal followed the batik style of Pekalongan but with local variations in color and motif. Here the variation occurs in the cream background of the *kepala* and bow borders; in Pekalongan the custom was a cream *badan* instead.

WEARER

Although the design is European in inspiration, bright colors, and associations evoked by several details, this cloth would suit a married woman in the prime of life of either Indo-European or Peranakan heritage. The poisonous foxglove, or digitalis, is the source of a well-known medicine for cardiac complaints and, in a modern manner, provides the traditional protective element in this cloth. To the Peranakan woman the form of the hydrangea would have been reminiscent of the fragrant *kemuning*, which on Java may only be worn by a married woman, while the swallow is an emblem of summer.

NOTE
1. *De Echo: Weekblad voor
mes in Indië* (1900–1901):
54.

The *badan* is adorned with bold bouquets of lilies in several pastel shades of blue on a white ground, with a host of small blue bees forming a diagonal background pattern. Swallows and butterflies in both Peranakan and Indo-European styles hover near the fragrant flowers. In the *kepala dlorong* a diagonal, lobed band is embellished with lilac sprigs in two shades of blue on a fine *galaran* base. Two smaller bouquets of lilies in the left and right corners, based on soft blue sprinkled with lighter curlicues give an early intimation of the style that a few decades later was known as *tanahan Semarangan*. Both bow borders show a design of stylized lilies on dotted blue. The selvages are edged in triangles.

MAKER

The batik is signed in the upper right corner of the *kepala* "Lie Sian Kwi." The row of tiny triangles, replacing the stripes above the upper and below the lower borders, is an innovation here and on the next *sarung*. This was used on *kain panjang* from the north coast around 1930 but was not common on *sarung*. Small motifs, in this case a bee, were not used as backgrounds on *badan* in Pekalongan. Lilies, well-known as an Indo-European motif on batiks from Pekalongan, were also depicted on *sarung* from Tegal.

WEARER

This cloth with its exquisite work in the *kepala* and borders, could have been worn by either upper-class Indo-European or Peranakan women, as the flowers depicted had significance for all three. The blue-and-white cloth with its fragrant flowers—lilies, emblem of purity; and lilacs, emblem of love, youth, and gracefulness[1]—could have served an Indo-European woman on her wedding night and subsequently as housewear and eventually for her burial. The lily was associated with a locally grown, poisonous flower, the datura; it offered protection to Peranakan women during periods of mourning for close relatives. The richly dotted backgrounds of the *kepala* and borders expressed in a new form the old concept of abundance and prosperity showered on the living by the ancestors.

Catalogue no. 42
Hip wrapper,
sarung kelengan
Java, Tegal, c. 1930
Signed by Lie Sian Kwi
Hand-drawn wax resist
on machine-woven
cotton; synthetic dyes
107 x 203 cm
(42 1/8 x 79 7/8 in.)
Los Angeles County
Museum of Art,
Inger McCabe Elliott
Collection,
M.91.184.99

Catalogue no. 43
Hip wrapper, *sarung*
Java, Tegal, c. 1930–35
Hand-drawn wax resist
on machine-woven
cotton; synthetic dyes
106.6 x 200.6 cm
(42 x 79 in.)
Los Angeles County
Museum of Art,
Inger McCabe Elliott
Collection,
M.91.184.60

An art nouveau influence, probably taken directly from a European magazine illustration, is evident in the swooning, turquoise lilies on this tubular cloth of top quality. Elegant stems bend in contrast with the perfectly drawn, intricate background in yellow, grass green, and olive green, which consists of vertical bands of equal width. Each band is decorated with a traditional motif of central Javanese inspiration, among them *banji, galaran, gedekan,* and *kawong.* These devices are used in a purely decorative manner. The *kepala dlorong,* in which the lilies are both turquoise and white, shows a series of diagonal bands, with filler motifs that differ from those of the *badan.* Its generally darker colors also work to set the *kepala* off. The upper and lower bow borders display an early form of *tanahan Semarangan,* in which the background is solidly covered with *pasir* (grains of sand).

MAKER

The color scheme of this Peranakan batik is typical of Tegal. The layout, displaying vertical or diagonal bands, was the creation of Lies van Zuylen, but she never combined vertical and diagonal bands on a single batik or used them as background, nor did she ever use so many diverse motifs in the bands at one time.

The art nouveau arrangement of the lilies was possibly after an Indo-European design from Pekalongan, but more likely copied directly by the Peranakan entrepreneur from a European illustration. Dutch magazines and the European lifestyle were de rigueur for Peranakan students of Dutch schools. Probably the entrepreneur had been one of them.

An innovation here is the difference between the color scheme of the upper bow border and that on the left side of the *kepala* and the lower border and that on the right side of the *kepala.* As this *sarung* must be oriented in just one direction, only the latter contrast would be visible when the cloth was worn.

The seam, originally machine-sewn, is now hand-sewn. Sewing a cloth into a tube by machine was often done in the workshop or by the batik dealer. After being purchased, expensive batiks were unstitched and then restitched by hand. The owner did this herself or had it be done by a servant or indigent relative, who showed her gratitude by doing this sort of work. Sometimes inexpensive, hand-waxed batiks and stamped batiks are found with incredibly fine hand-sewing. For a less affluent owner the purchase of such a batik was an investment, and it was treated with care.

WEARER

The combination of European design and Chinese colors permitted several readings of this cloth by the Indo-European and Peranakan women who might have worn it. The colors were appropriate for either a young Indo-European or middle-aged Peranakan woman. To the former the implied fragrance of lilies connoted purity and modesty; for the latter, who believed them to be the heavily scented but poisonous datura lily, a different species, they averted illness and bad luck.[1] The European design expressed a Peranakan woman's legal equality with the Dutch. The aristocratic flavor of the Javanese background motifs may have added a touch of extra status for both.

NOTE
1. H. C. Veldhuisen, interview with Kwee Hin Goan, Rotterdam, 1990.

This *kain panjang* is decorated in the same style as the preceding cloth. Two sets of three mirrored bouquets consisting of orchids in pink, purple, and white and pink strawberries are surrounded by a scattering of small flowers, swallows, and butterflies. The intricate background is adorned with diagonal bands, each covered solidly with traditional central Javanese filler motifs in shades of green, modified by the varied intensity of the fillers. Instead of a *kepala*, the end section on one side contains a series of borders, among them a row of small triangles (*gigi walang*). The other side shows a plain, white edge. Pink borders enclose the *badan* on all four sides and are made up of a miniature version of the orchids in the bouquets.

MAKER

Made in a Peranakan workshop, the color scheme of this batik is typical of Tegal, where wild strawberries were also a popular motif.

WEARER

Despite its Europeanized design, this cloth's striking pastels accord with Peranakan taste.

NOTE
1. C. A. S. Williams, *Outlines of Chinese Symbolism and Art Motives*, 3d ed. (New York: Dover, 1976), 301.

The fragrant Chinese orchid *(lan hua)* has a wide range of associations; it is an emblem of love, beauty, and numerous progeny. It also represents elegance and refinement.[1] Thus the cloth was suitable for an upper-class Peranakan woman of middle age with numerous grandchildren. This notion is enhanced by the strawberries, which might at first seem incongruous.

The cloth could be worn with the decorated end section on the outside or tucked underneath. In either case, the cricket's teeth would ward off untoward influences.

Catalogue no. 44
Hip wrapper,
kain panjang
Java, Tegal, c. 1930–35
Hand-drawn wax resist
on machine-woven
cotton; synthetic dyes
106.7 x 266.6 cm
(42 x 105 in.)
Los Angeles County
Museum of Art,
Inger McCabe Elliott
Collection,
M.91.184.26

Pairs of red and pink peacocks perch in trees in the form of bouquets of white chrysanthemums or possibly daisies. Pinpricks accentuate the flowers. The stunning green ground of the *badan* is solidly covered with small, white, geometrical, *nitik* motifs aligned in crossing diagonals. The *kepala* repeats the main theme of the *badan* but with a background that differs in color—red—and second-layer motifs in a single diagonal direction. The borders are dissimilar, in the earlier Indo-European style, with stylized daisies along the lower edge and traditional European garlands at top.

Catalogue no. 45
Hip wrapper, *sarung*
Java, Sidoarjo,
c. 1910–20
Signed by
Njo. Tan Sing Ing
Hand-drawn wax resist
on machine-woven
cotton; natural and
synthetic dyes
105.4 x 204.3 cm
(41 1/2 x 80 3/8 in.)
Los Angeles County
Museum of Art,
Inger McCabe Elliott
Collection,
M.91.184.180

NOTES
1. H. C. Veldhuisen, *Batik Belanda 1840–1940* (Jakarta: Gaya Favorit, 1993), no. 69.
2. C. A. S. Williams, *Outlines of Chinese Symbolism and Art Motives*, 3d ed. (New York: Dover, 1976), 317.

MAKER

The Peranakan woman who signed this batik in the upper portion of the *kepala*, between the diagonal lines "Njo. Tan Sing Ing Sda" used her husband's name: Tan was his family name; Sing, his generation name; Ing, his first name. (Sda. is the abbreviation for Sidoarjo, where the cloth was made.)

A relatively small peacock was often repeated on the *badan* of traditional Pasisir batiks. Indo-European entrepreneurs in Pekalongan also employed this motif. Tan in this case imitated a design of Lies van Zuylen.[1] The chrysanthemums, however, were executed in the Peranakan style.

The batik is of the highest quality, a good example of the way that diverse cream filler motifs can, against a red ground, create the impression of a light tint of red; the more cream, the lighter the tint appears.

Other batiks from Tan's workshop, produced in 1915–25, were also excellently executed, though with a smaller range of filler motifs. Around 1920 she began repeating the bow border along the textile's upper edge in the then-fashionable Peranakan manner.

WEARER

The combination of strong red and deep green was particularly appealing to the Indo-Arabians; to the Peranakan the festive red was the specific color for a wedding. The peacock pair alludes universally to a wedding or marriage. According to Chinese symbolism, the peacock stands for beauty and dignity.[2] Europeans consider a pair the epitome of faithfulness, as they are wont to remain together throughout their lives. Although the flowers resemble chrysanthemums, daisies, which represent youth and early summer, may in this case be more appropriate.

Catalogue no. 46
Hip wrapper, *sarung*
Java, Pekalongan,
c. 1910
Signed by
Oei Khing Liem
Hand-drawn wax resist
on machine-woven
cotton; synthetic dyes
106 x 192 cm
(41 3/4 x 75 5/8 in.)
Los Angeles County
Museum of Art,
Inger McCabe Elliott
Collection,
M.91.184.144

Clumps of iris rise from the lower border, giving the impression they grow in water. The flowers are orange-red and green on a cream ground, which is decorated with a variety of small central Javanese *parang* motifs, also in orange-red. Small insects, butterflies, and a comparatively large dragonfly adorn the upper half of the cloth. Birds fly in pairs, one of each pair carrying a twig. The *kepala* (right) shows a simple bouquet of chrysanthemums, flowering grasses, and ivy in orange-red, cream, and green and a single butterfly in European style, with spread wings, on a dark green ground sprinkled with small, five-petaled flowers. The borders are asymmetrical.

NOTE
1. Openwork is more durable than lace and was thus more suitable to the *kabaya*, which was changed several times a day and laundered often.

MAKER

The batik is signed upside down in the middle of the *kepala* under the *pinggir* "Oei Khing Liem" and has an illegible ink stamp on the back in the upper portion between the *kepala* and seam. This and another batik from Oei's workshop in the collection are more or less in the European style and have the European upper border. The bow border is an imitation of *broderie d'Anglaise* (openwork), which had become popular as borders on the white *kabaya* worn by European and Indo-European women.[1]

The *parang* motifs in the *badan* give the impression of having been stamped, because they were so perfectly executed. On closer examination, one sees, however, that the red stripes in the background vary in thickness. This would have been unacceptable to critical customers.

WEARER

With its European design and rather muted Peranakan palette, this tubular cloth would have been suitable for a mature and probably affluent Peranakan woman. Although the iris is absent from Chinese symbology, the European style, especially in combination with the aristocratic *parang*, expresses high status. The motifs in the *badan* and *kepala*—butterfly, dragonfly, and nest-building birds—designate the cloth for a married woman. The chrysanthemum, emblem of autumn, indicates middle age.

Catalogue no. 47
Hip wrapper,
sarung dlorong buketan
Java, Pekalongan,
c. 1915
Stamp of
Oei Khing Liem
Hand-drawn wax resist
on machine-woven
cotton; synthetic dyes
106.7 x 191 cm
(42 x 75 ¼ in.)
Los Angeles County
Museum of Art,
Inger McCabe Elliott
Collection,
M.91.184.187

Strongly contrasting synthetic hues color this tubular batik. The *badan* is divided conceptually into two horizontal sections. The lower shows small egrets taking flight and larger ones searching for fish in a lake, in which blue and crimson lotus or water lilies and greenish reeds grow abundantly. In the upper section decorative clusters of six-petaled flowers are combined with cascades of blue and crimson wisteria and interspersed with small, diving egrets. The cream ground is embellished with a brownish-red herringbone pattern, vaguely reminiscent of a traditional central Javanese motif, which runs diagonally. Floral arabesques bloom in *dlorong* bands with undulating borders in the *kepala*; the bands are alternately deep crimson, brownish red, and cream, the latter showing *galaran*. The bow border shows the wavy Peranakan lines and consists of chrysanthemums and leaves on a crimson base with a dotted, cream motif.

MAKER

The *kepala* with diagonal bands was introduced by Lies van Zuylen. Peranakan entrepreneurs created variations. This batik is from the workshop of Oei Khing Liem; it is not signed, but his name stamp appears inside, between the *kepala* and the seam. Oei himself made the drawings for the *badan*, though parts of it

NOTES
1. H. C. Veldhuisen, *Batik Belanda 1840–1940* (Jakarta: Gaya Favorit, 1993), no. 69.
2. Ibid., no. 86.

were copied from Indo-European batiks. The wisteria, for instance, almost replicates some Van Zuylen depicted.[1]

The design with egrets and aquatic flowers is after one used by Lien Metzelaar around 1900.[2] Her sources were nineteenth-century European paintings, which were in turn inspired by Japanese screens. Oei changed the proportions of her birds and lilies and imposed a sense of depth on the picture.

WEARER

This cloth, with its Peranakan interpretation of European design, may have been intended for a grandmother about forty years old. Traditional motifs were modernized, but the symbolism remained constant. Egrets, which alight at the first sign of danger, signify protective impulses. The large bird and smaller ones represent a mother and her offspring; the large lotus and small, clustered seed pods, abundant fertility and regenerative power; the chrysanthemum, middle age. The bower of wisteria, reminiscent of laburnum, whose Dutch name translates "golden rain," indicates a shower of prosperity. The somewhat gaudy colors accorded with Peranakan taste of the day.

This elaborate tubular *sarung* shows airy bouquets of tulips and daffodils, surrounded by multicolored birds and butterflies in both the *badan* and *kepala*.
The *badan* adds a background of sweeping ferns interspersed with dots in *tanahan*
style. The cream tulips are veined in orange and decorated with pinpricks; the
fantastically shaped blue and orange ones are embellished with finely shaded
fillers. The ground of the *kepala* is plain pink with a scattering of fine cream
flowers with red centers. Garlands of daffodils on a pink ground embellish the
borders. A gamut of fine mixed shades, effected by intricate dyeing procedures—
colet, dipping, and top-dyeing—resulted in the pink, orange, blue, green, yellow,
and lilac of this extraordinary work of art. The once-shiny glazed surface has
partially faded.

Catalogue no. 48
Hip wrapper, *sarung*
Java, Pekalongan, 1937
Signed by
Oei Khing Liem
Hand-drawn wax resist
on machine-woven
cotton; synthetic dyes
106 x 192 cm
(41 3/4 x 75 5/8 in.)
Los Angeles County
Museum of Art,
Inger McCabe Elliott
Collection,
M.91.184.344

MAKER

Oei Khing Liem signed and dated this piece in the upper left corner of the *kepala*.
Dating was rare, though there are other examples in the collection. In this case
the year was noted with the *canting*. On examples by some other makers the full
date is stamped in ink (see catalogue no. 51).

The tulip and the daffodil are popular Dutch flowers. Oei had studied drawing through a Dutch correspondence course; these flowers may have been used
as exercises. What he did not know is that the daffodil exudes a liquid that destroys
the tulip; hence, they are never used together in the same bouquet. Such verisimil-
itude was unimportant to designers and their clientele; Lies van Zuylen and her
followers combined flowers from different countries and seasons in their bouquets.

The batik is in the style of The Tie Siet, who included big, white flowers
with ribs and contour lines in his bouquets and introduced the very crowded
background, repeated in this case with ferns.

WEARER

This stupendous cloth would have been in the dowry of a Peranakan bride or a
gift from the groom's family. With its European spring flowers, it could have been
worn on a honeymoon. The tangle of ferns and the myriad grains of sand contain wishes for fertility and prosperity. Although the colors primarily appealed
to Peranakan taste, the flowers would also have been appreciated by young Indo-
European women.

Catalogue no. 49
Hip wrapper, *sarung*
Java, Pekalongan,
c. 1940
Signed by
Oei Khing Liem
Hand-drawn wax resist
on machine-woven
cotton; synthetic dyes
108 x 200 cm
(42 1/2 x 78 3/4 in.)
Los Angeles County
Museum of Art,
Inger McCabe Elliott
Collection,
M.91.184.214

The *badan* and *kepala* of this tubular *sarung* are adorned with large bouquets of irises, lilacs, and sprigs of small flowers in pinks and purples, white, red, and olive green with leaves in olive green on an elegant, plain, blue-gray ground. Color shading and white filler motifs have been used to effect a sense of depth. The bouquet in the *kepala* is identical in form but set on an unusual tawny ground with small, white starflowers with red hearts. Purple and red birds swoop down to drink nectar. The borders consist of elegantly stylized irises and sprigs of white flowers on the same tawny ground.

MAKER

The design of this batik, signed by Oei Khing Liem in the upper right corner of the *kepala*, lacks originality. The bouquet accented with small, white flowers is typical of Lies van Zuylen's work; she used exactly the same design around 1937–40 in at least two different color schemes on *kain panjang*.[1] Even Oei's bow borders copy Van Zuylen's, as do the colors. Oei added only the starflowers in the *kepala*, a popular background motif for *kepala* in those days, and the background colors for the *kepala* and *badan*. A penciled notation in Dutch in the upper left corner of the *badan* indicates the color to be used: *creme-grijs* (creamy gray). The result, however, is bluish.

Oei was not the only entrepreneur to copy this bouquet. Oey Soe Tjoen and Liem Giok Kwie, both from Kedungwuni, copied it with slight variations (see catalogue no. 67).

WEARER

An affluent, mature, married Peranakan woman would have been attracted by the European design and Peranakan palette of this batik. The lilacs, irises (resembling orchids), and brightly colored birds in search of honey all refer to happy marriage. This sizable design could not be worn properly by a slim, young girl.

NOTE
1. H. C. Veldhuisen, *Batik Belanda 1840–1940* (Jakarta: Gaya Favorit, 1993), no. 147; M. J. de Raadt-Apell, *De batikkerij Van Zuylen te Pekalongan, Midden-Java 1890–1946* (Zutphen: Terra 1980), no. 30.

This *sarung* shows stylized *cempaka mulya*, the fragrant flowers of the tulip tree, which mirror each other across the cloth. A pink, stamped variation of the *parang menang* (cape of victory or winning daggers) motif provides the background for the *badan*. The *kepala* is adorned with a delicate bouquet consisting of poppies, lilies, and sprigs of unrecognizable flowers in apple green, yellow, turquoise, and orange-brown on a pink ground with a sprinkling of floral rosettes that resemble the central Javanese *truntum* motif. Symmetrical borders of garlands are edged by tiny, striped selvages.

MAKER

The name of the maker, Kwee Liem Hok, Pekalongan, and an illegible text appear in an ink ban stamp in an end border. The design, with stylized flowering trees in mirror image in the *badan*, is a variation on an earlier design from Lasem with lotus trees (see catalogue nos. 11–12), which could be worn with either horizontal edge up. The Indo-European–style bouquet in the *kepala*, however, cannot be turned upside down.

WEARER

The fragrance of the *cempaka* flower, like love, was said to have an intoxicating effect. Combined in this design with the *parang menang*, this batik may have been offered as a gift from the groom's family to a Peranakan bride. *Encim* (Chinese for aunt) would have been the term of address used by her husband's nephews and nieces once she came to live in their compound. This particular combination of pastel tones was suited to the young bride recently added to the household, hence *sarung Encim* (sarung for the aunt). In Peranakan families adhering to Javanese customs, the *cempaka mulya* motif, which is associated with the lotus, could be worn by the mothers of both bride and groom.[1] The colors in this cloth, however, seem a shade too light for that purpose. The design shows a modern variation on a traditional theme which still incorporates all the defining elements. The paired "lotus" trees represent wishes for a close relationship between the families and a happy marriage. The background motifs add an aristocratic Javanese association. The *parang menang* also contributes the wish that the wedding ceremony and marriage be successful.

Catalogue no. 50
Hip wrapper,
sarung Encim
Java, Pekalongan,
c. 1930
Stamp of
Kwee Liem Hok
Hand-drawn
and stamped wax resist
on machine-woven
cotton; synthetic dyes
106.7 x 193.6 cm
(42 x 76 ¼ in.)
Los Angeles County
Museum of Art,
Inger McCabe Elliott
Collection,
M.91.184.173

NOTE
1. Inger McCabe Elliott, *Batik: Fabled Cloth of Java* (New York: Clarkson N. Potter, 1984), 214.

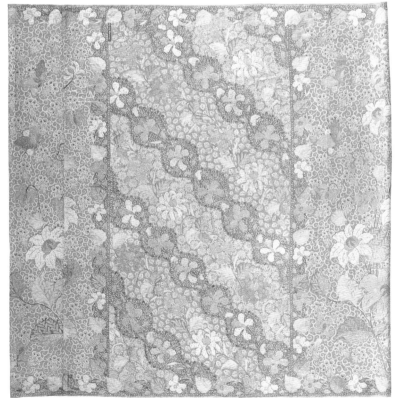

Catalogue no. 51
Hip wrapper,
sarung Encim,
dlorong buketan
Java, Pekalongan,
12 April 1934
Signed by
Nj. Oeij Kok Sing
Hand-drawn and
stamped wax resist on
machine-woven cotton;
synthetic dyes
104.7 x 200.8 cm
(41 ¼ x 79 in.)
Los Angeles County
Museum of Art,
Inger McCabe Elliott
Collection,
M.91.184.223
See FIGURE 57

This is a technically complex piece with three delicate bouquets of orchids and lilies in the *badan.* The *kepala* is adorned with a series of lobed, diagonal *dlorong,* each embellished with a floral arabesque consisting of orchids and chrysanthemums, among others, on an intricate background in *tanahan Semarangan* style with a variety of tiny filler motifs: *paden, pasir,* and *semanggen.* The borders of orchids and leaves are also on a ground of *tanahan Semarangan.* The flowers are veined and outlined in red with small red pinpricks in the petals. The finely balanced combination of pastel colors consists of the mint-green ground with flowers in salmon, orange, baby blue, grass green, yellow, and cream.

MAKER

Nj. Oeij Kok Sing signed this batik in a green rectangle in the left upper corner of the *kepala.* Her ink stamp and the date, 12 April 1934, appear in an end border. Such complete dating was rare; this is the only example in the collection.

The white flowers in the bouquet and the crowded background are in the style of The Tie Siet. The background pattern in the *badan* is intricate and gives the impression that it could not have been done with the *canting.* It seems to have been stamped, but close examination reveals that it was, indeed, applied with the

canting. The use of stamps for a background was often done on top-quality batiks from Peranakan workshops, especially those in Sidoarjo. These batiks were no less expensive than ones executed with the *canting* alone.[1]

WEARER

The symbolism of the flowers, the soft colors, and the small filler motifs in the background all combine to make this batik eminently suitable as a Peranakan dowry cloth or bridal gift. The orchids stand for love and beauty and are also symbolic of numerous progeny. The lilies are apotropaic. The *paden, pasir,* and *semanggen* add wishes for riches and numerous offspring.

NOTE
1. H. C. Veldhuisen, field notes, Jakarta, 1979.

Four elegant bouquets, three in the *badan* and one in the *kepala*, consist of generic flowers in the European style. All four share the same palette: two shades of blue, ocher, pink, and white on a perfect plain, green or salmon-pink ground. Shading provided by various filler motifs give the flowers their depth (detail). The background of the *kepala* is sprinkled with small, intricate flowers. Outside the finely delineated floral bow borders are selvages exquisitely striped in ocher.

Catalogue no. 52
Hip wrapper,
sarung Encim,
buketan kembang suket
Java, Pekalongan,
c. 1935
Signed by The Tie Siet
Hand-drawn wax resist
on machine-woven
cotton; synthetic dyes
107.2 x 198 cm
(42¼ x 78 in.)
Los Angeles County
Museum of Art,
Inger McCabe Elliott
Collection,
M.91.184.377

MAKER

This batik was signed in the *kepala* by The Tie Siet, one of the leading Peranakan batik entrepreneurs in Pekalongan. Executing all four bouquets in a single color scheme simplified the dyeing process, while the intricacies

of the shading simultaneously complicated the work. Oey Soe Tjoen was the innovator behind this particular linear use of dots to create shading. Lies van Zuylen had employed dots earlier but rather rigidly. Oey's lines are omnidirectional—different for each petal—and the effect is even more lifelike and three-dimensional. Varying tints enhanced the effect. The Tie Siet and other producers of fine batiks imitated Oey's style.

WEARER

This very precise and intricate cloth, with its fine pastel shades and artistic treatment of the Europeanized flowers, is an eminent example of the elegant, high-status batik style worn during the mid-1930s by affluent Peranakan matrons at family gatherings. The flowers, though resembling poppies, may have been considered peonies, the Chinese emblem of summer. Although the treatment of the flowers and plain backgrounds might have appealed to Indo-European taste, the price of this cloth would probably have been prohibitive for the lower middle-class Indo-Europeans who still wore batik in 1935.

Catalogue no. 53
Hip wrapper,
kain panjang
Java, Pekalongan,
c. 1910–20
Signed by
Lies van Zuylen
Hand-drawn wax resist
on machine-woven
cotton; natural dyes
107.2 x 264 cm
(42¼ x 103⅞ in.)
Los Angeles County
Museum of Art,
Inger McCabe Elliott
Collection,
M.91.184.131

One bouquet of poppies or peonies repeated six times with varied colors adorn the *badan* of this *kain panjang*. Dragonflies, swallows, and European-style butterflies with wings widespread hover among the flowers. The colors, though primarily attractive to Indo-Europeans, were adapted slightly to Peranakan taste with shades of blue, red, green, and cream on a plain, tawny ground, reminiscent of central Javanese *soga* brown. The bow border of similar flowers in blue and cream decorates the left and bottom edges of the cloth. The left edge also features a rudimentary *kepala* of small triangles. The opposite edge has an even smaller row of triangles, while both long sides show fine, ocher lines in the selvages. The natural dye work is of an extraordinary quality with the special deep tones of Lies van Zuylen.

MAKER

The signature is in cream on a red rectangle in the upper left corner: "E v Zuylen." The floral arrangement is still simple, not yet the rich bouquet of many species, which she depicted later on. She achieved a three-dimensional effect by using several filler motifs in each flower.

Van Zuylen's daughters recall that around 1935 a Peranakan customer showed their mother a Oey Soe Tjoen batik and asked her if she could imitate his style of tints and tiny dots in her own bouquets and color scheme. She discussed this with her principal batik maker, and they decided to try it. Afterward she continued to make use of Oey's technique.[1] The result, while meticulous, never achieved the delicate shadings and jauntiness of Oey's makers, who were past masters in this art.

On other *kain panjang* Van Zuylen repeated the bow border at either end and after around 1930 repeated it along all four edges in the manner of her Peranakan colleagues.

WEARER

During the early twentieth century elegant, affluent, and mature European, Indo-European, and Peranakan women, all belonging to the elites, started wearing the dressier, more formal *kain panjang* as an alternative to the *sarung*. While the Dutch and upper-class Indo-Europeans would only use such batiks as housewear, the Peranakan women would also appear in them at family gatherings. For the lower echelons of Indo-Europeans this highly priced cloth would have been out of reach. The fashionable plain background was particularly appealing. The flowers, whether seen as poppies or peonies, indicate summer. Swallows, dragonflies, and butterflies evoke marital happiness and prosperity. The recognizable style of this "*panselen*" (a local pronunciation of Van Zuylen) batik gave its owner high status.

NOTE
1. H. C. Veldhuisen, interview with Lies Alting du Cloux and Frieda Lewis, Rotterdam, 1981.

NOTE

1. H. C. Veldhuisen, *Batik Belanda 1840–1940* (Jakarta: Gaya Favorit, 1993), nos. 54, 138.

Roses and daffodils in pastel shades of salmon pink, lilac, purple, yellow, green, and cream, accentuated in bouquets with sprigs of smaller flowers, decorate the *badan* of this *sarung*. Cream-colored flowers are outlined in green. One brightly colored swallow and one Dutch-style butterfly hover near the top of each bouquet on the plain, tan ground. The floral *dlorong* design of the *kepala* was a revival of an earlier fashion. Smaller bouquets on a lilac ground flank the diagonal band. The symmetrical bow borders are edged by a delicate, extremely finely striped *seret*. The cloth was originally glazed.

MAKER

A hand-drawn number 129 appears in the upper left corner beside the signature, "E v Zuylen"; her ink stamp, in the cream area below. Her daughter-in-law and assistant, Elfriede Bäumer, introduced the practice of numbering each pattern and color scheme after 1937, facilitating reorders. Formerly the batiks were numbered chronologically; each had its own number on a paper label.

In 1935 Van Zuylen started to use synthetic dyes, as did her contemporaries, the Peranakan entrepreneurs. She also followed the Peranakan manner of repeating the bow border along the upper selvage. By then her only clients were the affluent Peranakan of Java, Sumatra, and Singapore.

The layout of the *kepala* with its diagonal band was executed in diverse variations from 1890 onward[1] and was also used by Indo-European and Peranakan entrepreneurs.

WEARER

This is an example of a cloth produced by Van Zuylen for a Peranakan wearer and not for her earlier affluent Dutch and Indo-European clientele, who by the late 1930s would have preferred a Japanese kimono or long housedress for domestic use. The flowers, recognizably European, are a mixture of spring and summer bloomers, suggesting that their symbolic meanings had become rather muddled or were of little import by this late date. The pastel palette was the result of adjustment for the tastes of Peranakan women of mature years, to whom the daffodils would have appeared as orchids, emblem of beauty and refinement, and the roses as peonies. As always, a recognizable Van Zuylen batik carried a certain fashionable cachet.

Catalogue no. 54
Hip wrapper, *sarung*
Java, Pekalongan,
1937–42
Signed by
Lies van Zuylen
Hand-drawn wax resist
on machine-woven
cotton; synthetic dyes
107.2 x 212.2 cm
(42 1/4 x 83 1/2 in.)
Los Angeles County
Museum of Art,
Inger McCabe Elliott
Collection,
M.91.184.483

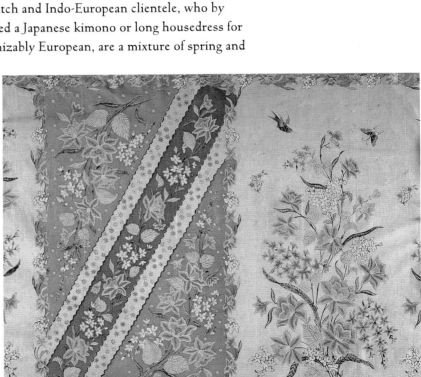

Catalogue no. 55
Hip wrapper, *sarung*
Java, Pekalongan or
Kedungwuni, c. 1940
Forged signature of
Lies van Zuylen
Hand-drawn wax resist
on machine-woven
cotton; synthetic dyes
107 x 202 cm
(42 1/8 x 79 1/2 in.)
Los Angeles County
Museum of Art,
Inger McCabe Elliott
Collection,
M.91.184.533

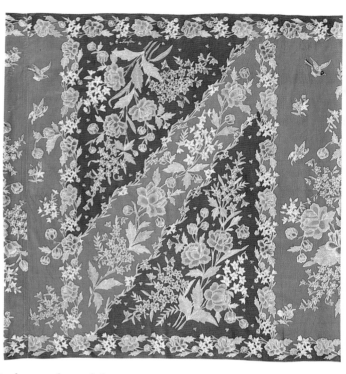

When compared with the preceding cloth, this imitation Lies van Zuylen batik, despite the considerable effort expended, makes a clumsy and mechanical impression. As the colors contrast rather harshly and the shading in the motifs is less refined, the effect produced by the design is flat. The *badan* shows similar bouquets of roses and floral sprigs, while the *kepala* also contains a diagonal band and smaller floral arrangements in opposing corners.

MAKER

Although this batik is signed "E v Zuylen," the work is not to her standard. The white flowers are not enhanced with *cocohan*, a Van Zuylen staple, and the signature is in another hand. This must be a Peranakan forgery from either Pekalongan or Kedungwuni. One sometimes doubts the authenticity of the Van Zuylen signa-

ture on later examples because the writing is so strange. Of course, a Van Zuylen ink stamp compensates for this; but absent the stamp, style is the only clue. There are forgeries with perfectly copied signatures,[1] and others where the name is misspelled "Panselen," according to the Indo-European pronunciation. One entrepreneur took the trouble to imitate her ink stamp but misspelled the name "Zeylen." Other Peranakan entrepreneurs, mainly in Pekalongan but also in Kudus and Demak, imitated her batiks and under their own signatures added "M. D. Van Zuylen" (for *model dari* [made in the style of]).[2]

NOTES
1. H. C. Veldhuisen, *Batik Belanda 1840–1940* (Jakarta: Gaya Favorit, 1993), no. 150.
2. Ibid., 144–45.

WEARER

This hand-sewn cloth looks enough like a Van Zuylen batik to be appreciated by an older Peranakan woman who probably could not discern the difference. Moreover, as the price of fakes was at most only a fraction lower than that of originals, the cost could not have been a "give-away." The blue-gray and purple are suitable for middle age. Someone with an untrained eye might also be taken in by the signature. Today many "signed" fakes come onto the market, most of them of lower quality than this example.

A large bouquet, repeated three times in the *badan* and once in the *kepala*, decorate this postwar batik. An outsized butterfly with wings spread flutters near the top of each bouquet in the *badan*; two, in the *kepala*. Three smaller ones embellish the otherwise plain space to the left of the *kepala*. The flowers might be poppies, roses, or peonies. Although the arrangement is rather stiff, the flowers themselves were embellished with the perfect three-dimensional shading for which Oey Soe Tjoen's designs are well known. The colors show a strong contrast between the blues and ochers of the flowers and the golden orange and bottle green of the backgrounds, which were fashionable during the 1950s. The narrow borders provide a neat outline to the cloth, which is further defined by the refined stripes on the selvages.

Catalogue no. 56
Hip wrapper, *sarung*
Java, Kedungwuni,
c. 1950
Signed by
Oey Soe Tjoen
Hand-drawn wax resist
on machine-woven
cotton; synthetic dyes
106.7 x 209.3 cm
(42 x 82 3/8 in.)
Los Angeles County
Museum of Art,
Inger McCabe Elliott
Collection,
M.91.184.244

MAKER

The batik is signed "Oey Soe Tjoen Kedoengwoeni 104." (After 1950 Oey adopted the town's modern spelling, Kedungwuni. 104 is not the number of this design, but the number of his house.)

This design, with two very large butterflies above the bouquet in the *kepala* and one in the *badan*, is characteristic of his practice after the Japanese occupation and for a long time afterward. The same butterfly hovering above a bouquet of carnations on a *sarung* from Oey with the modern spelling of Kedungwuni can be dated around 1955.[1] The crowded filler motifs in the leaves were also created during the Japanese occupation.

WEARER

This cloth, with its typical Peranakan style, was most likely worn by a mature, affluent Peranakan woman for evening receptions and family gatherings. Some Indonesian women of the Jakarta upper class with modern tastes, that is, women who were not wedded to traditional central Javanese design, might have chosen it for semi-official occasions, such as a ladies' morning at an ambassador's residence.

Return of the Kain Panjang

The pluralistic colonial society came to its culmination in the decades just preceding World War II. The immigrant colonial establishment completely dissociated itself from the native lifestyle and costume. Among the locally born population of mixed descent, the stratifying trends that defined batik styles during the first quarter of the twentieth century manifested themselves through increasingly complex designs, in which Europeanized floral motifs continued nevertheless to form the main component.

A series of interconnected developments can be noted primarily in the *kain panjang*, which came to be worn in the central Javanese manner on the Pasisir, tapering down toward the lower legs, as a more elegant substitute for the tubular *sarung*. The first design changes had their origins in the prewar years. In the *pagi sore* style the *badan* of the rectangular cloth is bisected along an invisible diagonal line, each half decorated with a different motif and/or color scheme (see Appendix 1). This contrast gave the style its name, *pagi sore* (morning/ late afternoon). The old standby, the *tiga negeri*, was also adapted to this style. Generally the dark half of the cloth was worn on the outside during the daytime, while the lighter half served as evening dress. Immediately prior to and during the Japanese occupation, patterns became larger and increasingly striking, with deeper, more contrasting mixed tones. The device of shaded fillers and the application of darker shades of a color used in the flowers were perfected as were the increasingly intricate *tanahan Semarangan* backgrounds. Between the 1940s and 1960s the wide, undulating *terang bulan* borders came to their finest flowering on the *pagi sore* batiks.[1] The most effusive examples of these elaborate batik styles

NOTES
1. Earlier the term *terang bulan* was used for a design with large triangular motifs rising vertically on a plain background (see catalogue no. 23).

2. The Indonesian spelling *Djawa* remained in use until 1972.

3. A rare example of a *Djawa Hokokai* is illustrated in Pepin van Roojen, *Batik Design*, rev. ed. (Amsterdam: Pepin Press, 1994), 144–45.

4. Inger McCabe Elliott, *Batik: Fabled Cloth of Java* (New York: Clarkson N. Potter, 1984), 186.

are the *Djawa Hokokai* textiles, which originated during the occupation.[2] Combining the characteristics of *pagi sore*, *terang bulan*, and *tanahan Semarangan*, these batiks show a profusion of background layers that merge with the overlay of floral elements in a burst of color.[3]

As a result of Indonesian independence new styles came to express feelings of national unity. Several Indo-Arabian workshops perfected the *Hokokai* style, renamed *Djawa baroe*, using the strongly contrasting color palette that hitherto had been utilized exclusively by Indo-Arabians. Both the modern Indonesian elite and those of upper-class Indo-Arabian descent wore these colors, which were thereby fused into a single symbolic reading. Central Javanese motifs were also combined with traditional Pasisir colors in a style known as *batik nasional*.[4] This term was soon adopted indiscriminately for other variations on more or less traditional central Javanese motifs in any Pasisir colors. Less elaborate designs continued to be executed in the traditional Peranakan pastel shades. The intricate *terang bulan* borders were ultimately combined with plain backgrounds in the vibrant styles of The Tie Siet and other Peranakan designers.

In the midst of all these developments, the classic *buketan panselen* of Lies van Zuylen and her imitators remained in vogue.

FIGURE 64
Hip wrapper,
kain panjang
Java, Pekalongan,
c. 1970
Hand-drawn wax resist
on machine-woven
cotton; synthetic dyes
104 x 227.4 cm
(41 x 89½ in.)
Los Angeles County
Museum of Art,
Inger McCabe Elliott
Collection,
M.91.184.81

NOTE
1. H. C. Veldhuisen, interviews with Raden I. Prawira Koesoemah, The Hague, 1979, and Raden N. Kalsoem Gastina, Jakarta, 1979, both influential fashionable Sundanese noblewomen.

This batik is a late example of the *batik nasional*, initiated in the 1950s by President Sukarno. Its promotion was based on the development of a truly national style acceptable to all women who considered themselves Indonesian first and foremost rather than Javanese, Sundanese, or Peranakan. For many different reasons this never succeeded.[1] The cloth shows a free but rather stiff variation on the *semen* design from the Principalities, in which the double Garuda wings can still be recognized. A Hindu symbol and once representative of the central Javanese rulers, who had the exclusive right to wear it, it now graces the official seal of the Republic of Indonesia.

Made in an Indo-Arabian workshop, the cloth exemplifies the *colet* technique: applying synthetic dyes directly to the cotton cloth with a brush. *Colet*'s early use, around 1900, was as a labor-saving device for the application of colors featured only sparingly in a batik. After 1945 *colet* was used for more, sometimes even most of the colors on a batik in order to create a multicolored cloth for an attractive price; in such cases resorting to *colet* was essential to the survival of a batik entrepreneur.

Catalogue no. 57
Hip wrapper,
kain panjang pagi sore
Java, Pekalongan,
c. 1930
Hand-drawn wax resist
on machine-woven
cotton; synthetic dyes
105 x 263 cm
(41³/₈ x 103¹/₂ in.)
Los Angeles County
Museum of Art,
Inger McCabe Elliott
Collection,
M.91.184.549

Neatly arranged, art-nouveau–inspired bouquets in two styles cover both halves of this cloth: white carnations or peonies with red veins and blue pistils combined with blue forget-me-nots and green and red leaves on a plain, salmon-pink ground (*tanahan polos*) in the darker half; irises and double tulips in red, pink, and blue on a pale yellow background of waving ferns in *Semarangan* style on the lighter half. Brightly colored swallows and butterflies flutter among the flowers. The end sections are decorated with *nitik* borders, both ending in a row of *gigi walang*, a vestige of the traditional *kepala tumpal*. The flowers in the dissimilar bow borders harmonize with those in one of the bouquets. Tiny striped edges run along the upper selvage; the lower repeats the *gigi walang* decoration of the left end section.

MAKER

This batik, while unsigned, is typical of the *kain panjang pagi sore* from the workshop of The Tie Siet and his wife, with large, white flowers gathered in a bouquet on a plain ground in one half and a different bouquet with a crowded background in the other. In this case that background is adorned with ferns, a motif often used by The and his followers (for an example by Oei Khing Liem see catalogue no. 48). We may assume that this batik is one of many *kain panjang* unsigned, not because the quality was insufficient but because even well-known entrepreneurs often did not sign *kain panjang*.

The art-nouveau–style bow border of irises resembles one used earlier by Lies van Zuylen with a poppy in place of the iris (see catalogue no. 33), which leads to the conclusion that The also adapted designs from successful colleagues.

WEARER

This finely worked cloth was delicately hand-hemmed. The shimmering pastel colors in *Encim* style and the neatly arranged florals would appeal to a young woman of affluent Peranakan background, to whom it would have been presented as a bridal gift. In her eyes the flowers intimated wishes for marital happiness and beauty; the profusion of ferns signified prosperity and numerous progeny, preferably sons.

In this intricate *tiga negeri*, with a background in a rather dark shade of Solonese *soga* brown, it is the complex central Javanese background motifs that form the *pagi sore* juxtaposition. The motifs are called *geblak tempel buketan* (slanting bands with an overlay of bouquets motifs). The striking motifs consist of rows of squares climbing diagonally across one half, while diagonal rows of a *sekar jagat* (flowers of the universe) variation shimmer on the other. Each alternates— and contrasts—with bands of floral creepers on a background of *ukel* tendrils. An overlay of six floral arrangements in red and blue with extremely fine, white filler motifs almost fuses with the busy background. These too show a division along the central diagonal, the central bouquet among the two mirrored sets stopping at the dividing line. One end section is embellished with a row of tiny triangles, which form a rudimentary *kepala*. The borders are asymmetrical, and each style runs along one long and one short edge. The predominantly blue border is in an Indo-European style; the other, predominantly red and more sinuous, is in a Peranakan style. Tiny red stripes edge the selvages.

Catalogue no. 58
Hip wrapper,
kain pagi sore,
kain tiga negeri
Java, Lasem, Kudus
or Demak,
and Solo (Surakarta),
c. 1930–35
Hand-drawn wax resist
on machine-woven
cotton; natural and
synthetic dyes
106.7 x 261.5 cm
(42 x 103 in.)
Los Angeles County
Museum of Art,
Inger McCabe Elliott
Collection,
M.91.184.310

MAKER

The ink stamp in an end border is illegible but for the particle "Nji." From this, however, we may conclude that the entrepreneur who started this cloth was a Peranakan woman and that she worked in Lasem, because the bouquets and bow borders in red are in the Lasem style, and this was nearly always the case in the

making of *batik tiga negeri*. Furthermore, we know that the entrepreneurs in Lasem were Peranakan. On the north coast red was the first color applied on a multicolored batik, and the entrepreneur who started a batik to be completed in several workshops was its owner; she ordered each of the following steps from colleagues and paid them for their work. The light blue color with the filler motifs is in the style of Kudus or Demak; the background pattern in dark blue, light brown, and black was added in Solo. The patterns themselves are not traditional, but new designs. Because one half is lighter in tone, this batik can be identified as *pagi sore*.

In the cream band of one end border are the letters P.R.T.D. in wax. These must have been added after the batik was finished and the pattern in wax used for the last stage of dyeing had been boiled away. The only explanation is that these letters refer to the person who ordered the background to be done in Solo.

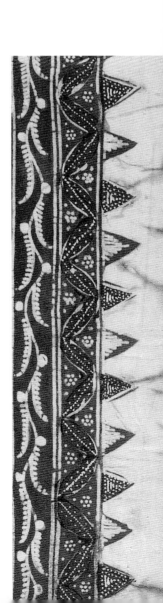

WEARER

The styles of the north coast and central Java were fused completely in this rich cloth. Its complex variety of decorative elements and filler motifs, executed with the finest *canting*, must have made it a very costly possession for an affluent Peranakan lady of middle age. Originally it may have been part of her dowry or the bridal gift of her in-laws. Even today cloths such as this are kept as valuable heirlooms by many upper-class Peranakan women.

Catalogue no. 59
Hip wrapper, *sarung
tanaban Semarangan*
Java, Kudus, c. 1950
Signed by O. S. Hwa
Hand-drawn wax resist
on machine-woven
cotton; synthetic dyes
105.4 x 201.8 cm
(41 1/2 x 79 1/2 in.)
Los Angeles County
Museum of Art,
Inger McCabe Elliott
Collection,
M.91.184.57

This intricate tubular *sarung* is decorated with four similar bouquets, three in the *badan* and one in the *kepala*. Composite, shaded flowers of an unidentifiable but Europeanized type may have suggested peonies to a Peranakan wearer. The leaves are adorned with finely detailed filler motifs. The profusion of saturated pastel shades includes salmon, lilac, blue, green, ocher, and accents of teal. Both the *kepala* and *badan* are adorned with an elaborate maze of tiny motifs in *tanaban Semarangan* style: *lung ganggeng* (seaweed) and *pasir* cover the golden brown *badan*. *Ceblong* (tadpoles) with red accents can be seen in the purple *kepala*. Smaller flowers in the same color combinations on intricately decorated purple grounds make up both borders, which are edged by very fine, contrasting *gigi walang*.

MAKER

This batik was signed in a red rectangle in the upper left corner of the *kepala* by O. S. Hwa, a Peranakan entrepreneur in Koedoes (Kudus). The floral arrangements no longer resemble Lies van Zuylen's bouquets. Indeed, the flowers themselves defy a botanist's taxonomy, a trend that became increasingly pronounced. The filler motifs in the leaves are known from *Djawa Hokokai*.

Remarkable is the very crowded *tanaban Semarangan* background in both

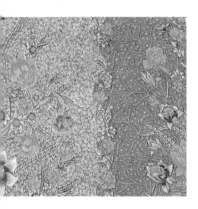

badan and *kepala*. In the former it comprises a third layer, behind the background motif composed of seaweed. This intricate work is a variation of the Kudus batiks made before the occupation and called *buketan Semarangan*. The new, even more crowded style typifies batiks made by Peranakan entrepreneurs for Peranakan customers after independence.

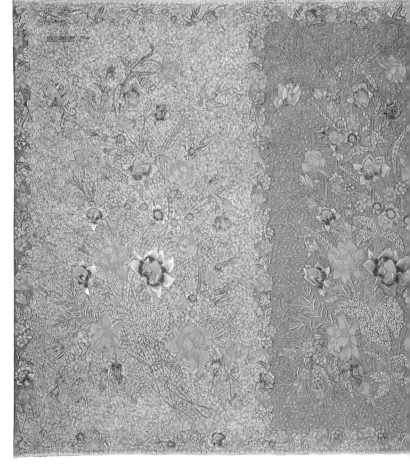

WEARER

This type of cloth found a substantial clientele among the affluent trading families in the bustling port of Semarang. The rich variety of color and the abundance of tiny background motifs clearly spread the message that its wearer, an older woman of Peranakan descent, was part of a prosperous clan with many descendants and links to the sea.

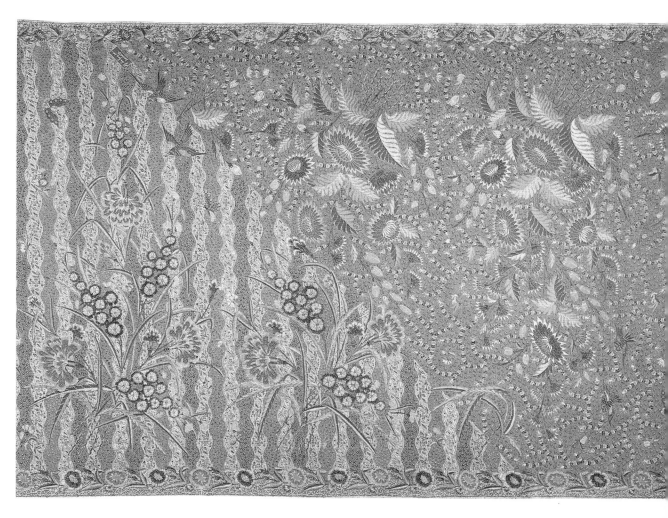

Half the cloth shows bouquets of carnations and asters in subdued shades of deep red and purple with yellow-green stems and leaves on a background of fine, undulating vertical bands decorated with floral creepers in muted shades on a *Semarangan* base in yellow and brown. The other half is adorned with bouquets of chrysanthemums in blues and reds with intricate leaves in various shades of yellow, green, and brown. The background is decorated with a variation of the traditional *lung* (tendril) motif, also in the shade of brown that was widely used in Kudus. There are two rather modest floral bow borders; each occupies one long and one short edge of the cloth. The short ends show additional floral bands; the selvages, finely divided stripes.

MAKER

This batik, like the last, is in a Peranakan-made style popular with Peranakan consumers after independence. The signature, which is difficult to find in the crowded background, is that of Nj. Lie Eng Soen of Kudus.

WEARER

This cloth in *Djawa baroe* style, showing the muted shades typical of the 1950s, would have been worn by an older Peranakan woman of ample means. By this period the symbolism of flowers had been largely forgotten. Only the backgrounds retained such meaning; in this case, prosperity and abundance. Status was evidenced by the elaborateness of this textile, especially during the economically difficult period of early Indonesian independence.

Catalogue no. 60
Hip wrapper,
kain panjang pagi sore
Java, Kudus, c. 1950–60
Signed by
Nj. Lie Eng Soen
Hand-drawn wax resist
on machine-woven
cotton; synthetic dyes
106.7 x 250.1 cm
(42 x 98 1/2 in.)
Los Angeles County
Museum of Art,
Inger McCabe Elliott
Collection,
M.91.184.71

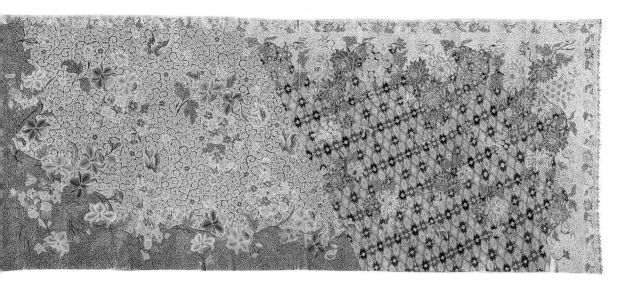

Catalogue no. 61
Hip wrapper,
kain panjang pagi sore
Java, Kedungwuni,
c. 1950
Signed by
Oeij Siok Kiem
Hand-drawn wax resist
on machine-woven
cotton; synthetic dyes
106.5 x 253 cm
(41 7/8 x 99 5/8 in.)
Los Angeles County
Museum of Art,
Inger McCabe Elliott
Collection,
M.91.184.230

NOTE
1. The new spelling, Kedungwuni, dates officially from 1972, but around 1950 such changes were already in common use.

Sprigs of orchids in pink, blue, orange, and golden yellow spread over an elaborate brown background with a maze of tendrils on one half of this cloth, returning in the wide *terang bulan* border. Large roses or possibly chrysanthemums and sprigs of forget-me-nots on the other half embellish the wide border and background, which consists of a grid of elongated lozenges (*limaran*) linked by abstracted starflowers in a haze of pink, blue, purple, and dark olive green. A voluptuous, brightly colored butterfly in Chinese style flutters among the flowers, though it is hardly visible on the latter half. A sense of depth is added to all flowers by the use of darker central areas and shaded filler motifs. The beautiful golden yellow in particular lights up against the muted background shade. Both selvages show a finely striped, yellow *seret*, while the short end borders are finished with a small floral edge on a plain, white band.

MAKER
The batik is signed in the upper left corner "Oeij Siok Kiem Kedoengwoeni."[1] Oeij was a successful batik entrepreneur before the Japanese occupation. He worked for the Japanese, and this cloth is a good example of the *pagi sore* type, with a complete *terang bulan* border in both halves, which was characteristic of the *Djawa Hokokai* batiks. In this case, however, the border is composed of flowers, and instead of a bouquet, we see the same flowers in posies in the field above the border. This was an innovation introduced after the occupation.

WEARER
Another example of the *Djawa baroe* style, this glazed cloth must have been an eye-catcher when it was worn for festive occasions by its Peranakan owner, a middle-aged woman of ample girth and means. The intricately decorated flowers, the riot of colors, and the elaborate backgrounds all express opulence.

Catalogue no. 62
Hip wrapper,
kain panjang pagi sore
Java, Pekalongan,
c. 1960
Signed by
Mohamed Djohari Ali
Hand-drawn wax resist
on machine-woven
cotton; synthetic dyes
105.8 x 244 cm
(41 5/8 x 96 in.)
Los Angeles County
Museum of Art,
Inger McCabe Elliott
Collection,
M.91.184.240

The light half of this cloth shows pairs of rice birds (*glatik*) perched on clusters of flowers in purple, greens, and blue on a background of ocher-colored *parang klithik seling kawong*, that is, alternating bands of *parang* and *kawong* motifs, in Pasisir colors. The motif is somewhat less detailed than its central Javanese version. The dark half is decorated with large pairs of butterflies hovering above clusters of flowers in darker green, purple, and reds on a multicolored background, in which ocher and green predominate. The chrysanthemumlike flowers almost disappear into the background, in which seaweed and seastars can be recognized. The intricate, wide floral borders only seemingly follow the *terang bulan* style, as they are applied solely to the long edges of the cloth and not to the ends. Smaller, asymmetrical floral borders on dark green and purple grounds enclose the *badan*, further edged by rows of tiny triangles in ocher, each filled with a single purple dot. The dark side shows a series of slanting floral bands, while the light side is embellished with a multicolored floral design, which is in its own way relatively structured. The end sections thus form a half *kepala* that is different at each end.

MAKER

The batik is signed in the *seret* "Mohamed Djohari Ali." Were his name not enough, the color scheme itself would prove the cloth's Indo-Arabian origin. Next to the entrepreneur's name is that of the design, *pantjawarna boenga rampai* (diverse multicolored flowers). The name is somewhat generic, however, as were those given to designs on stamped

batiks. Entrepreneurs were known to name designs for their children or even popular songs.[1] The format is one of the Arab variations on *pagi sore* with *terang bulan* borders in both halves. The filler motif in the left-hand end panel consisting of tiny dots arranged in concentric circles was frequently used by Indo-Arabian batik makers.

NOTE
1. H. C. Veldhuisen, field notes 1979, and interview with Kwee Hin Goan, Rotterdam, 1980.

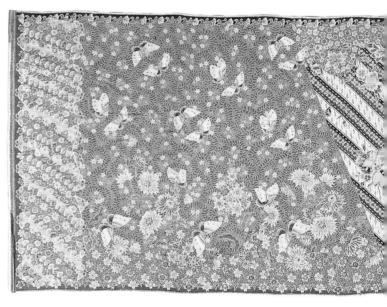

WEARER

The rather muted colors of this richly decorated cloth were traditionally worn by affluent Indo-Arabian women of middle age. Although the various design elements probably contained specific meanings for this group, little is remembered among its current members. During the postwar decades this type of cloth with an indigenous Indonesian bird and *pantjawarna boenga rampai* was also worn by upper-class women in Jakarta in preference to their own ethnic or regional dress for occasions when they felt such a cloth was better suited to the expression of their feelings of national unity. Previously such feelings hardly existed; most people in the archipelago felt most closely affiliated with their ethnic group. The Indonesian name of the design evokes the many different ethnic groups that all were united in the new Indonesian Republic.

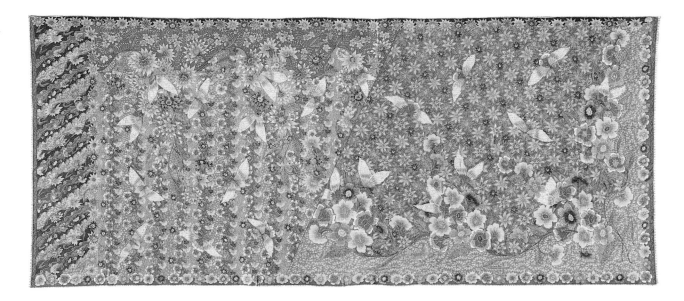

The darker half of this *pagi sore* cloth shows huge, brightly colored butterflies fluttering across a grid of abstracted starflowers in purple and pink. They also hover above the clusters of multicolored peonies or poppies rising from the wide *terang bulan* border, whose background is bursting with a maze of winding tendrils in white on ocher. In the lighter half the butterflies and clusters of chrysanthemums or sunflowers almost disappear into the intricately patterned background with three alternating bands of *Semarangan* motifs. On this half the short end shows a half *kepala* of diagonal floral bands in dark olive green, purple, and ocher. Two types of bow borders and a tiny *seret* in ocher decorate the edges.

MAKER

This batik is from an Indo-Arabian workshop. The predominantly purple color scheme was consistent with Indo-Arabian taste. The format is an Indo-Arabian variation on the *kain panjang pagi sore* with a complete *terang bulan* in one half and an incomplete border with half a *kepala* in the other. The flowers on the *terang bulan* are in the Peranakan fashion with the colors shading into one another and tiny, white dots, but now executed in the Indo-Arabian style of Pekalongan, which renders them indecipherable. In an end border is the name of the design, *mana suka* (liked by everybody), which nicely expresses what the national style was about: a design for all Indonesians.

WEARER

The strong color combination in this cloth of extraordinary technical quality was for a long time specific to the taste of affluent Indo-Arabian women. Such batiks were, however, in the late 1950s and early 1960s also worn by Indonesian women close to the establishment. Better than their own regional colors and motifs, such a cloth was felt to express sentiments of national unity, which were also reflected in the name of the design. The machine-hemmed cloth is still glazed, indicating that it was worn only a few times.

Catalogue no. 63
Hip wrapper,
kain panjang pagi sore
Java, Pekalongan,
c. 1950–60
Hand-drawn wax resist
on machine-woven
cotton; synthetic dyes
107.5 x 243 cm
(42 3/8 x 95 5/8 in.)
Los Angeles County
Museum of Art,
Inger McCabe Elliott
Collection,
M.91.184.237

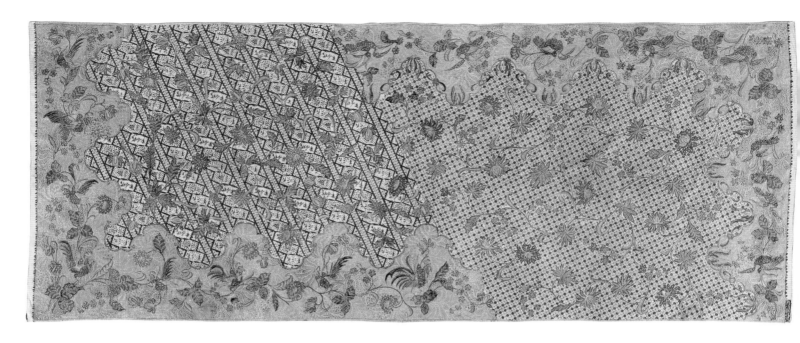

Catalogue no. 64
Hip wrapper,
kain panjang pagi sore
Java, Solo (Surakarta),
c. 1960
Hand-drawn wax resist
on machine-woven
cotton; synthetic dyes
104.8 x 257.7 cm
(41¼ x 101½ in.)
Los Angeles County
Museum of Art,
Inger McCabe Elliott
Collection,
M.91.184.254

This batik is an example of the designs in Pasisir style that were made in central Java in Peranakan workshops. The batik work, especially the filler motifs, are finer and more varied, in accordance with central Javanese style.

The two halves of this *pagi sore* cloth are distinguished, not by color, but by background motif. On each half floral creepers start from a single source at the end and spread horizontally toward the middle. The flowers, in soft shades of red, blue, and a particularly beautiful green, may represent either roses, chrysanthemums, or carnations, but all suggest the lotus. One half the background is covered with a grid of small *kawong* motifs in an unadulterated central Javanese style. The other half shows diagonal bands filled with a strongly stylized *banji* variant. Both motifs superimpose a plain, cream ground. Inside the wide, clearly delineated *terang bulan* borders egrets and gamecocks are depicted, both surrounded by vines. The backgrounds are adorned with small motifs in *Semarangan* style. Plain, white end borders show a single row of *gigi walang*. The selvages are finished with an unusually minuscule, striped *seret*.

MAKER

Baji Product (the words appear in one end border) was a trade name used by Baji, a Peranakan entrepreneur. His workshop in Solo began producing *kain panjang pagi sore* in a vivid color scheme—blue, yellow-green, and purple—around 1930. This cloth was not hemmed originally, which means that it was acquired in Sumatra. The hand-sewn hems were probably the work of a relative of the dealer in Jakarta.[1]

WEARER

This type of cloth with its clear design and muted colors accorded with the preferences of older Indo-Arabian women in Java, but it was also exported to Sumatra, where Baji Product was especially appreciated by the elite because of its green accents, as appropriate to Muslim dress.[2] For a short period in the early 1960s batiks such as this, which combined shades of green and central Javanese detailed batik work, were also in fashion among the non-Javanese urban Indonesian elite.

NOTES
1. H. C. Veldhuisen, interview with Adrian Idris, Jakarta, 1979.
2. H. C. Veldhuisen, field notes 1979. In Sumatra such cloths were referred to as *batik Baji*, though many are unsigned and were produced in other workshops.

NOTES

1. J. Thomas Lindblad, "De handel in katoentjes op Nederlands-Indië, 1824–1939," *Textielhistorische Bijdragen* 34 (1994): 104.

2. H. C. Veldhuisen, field notes, Pekalongan, 1979.

The brightly colored *terang bulan* borders of this *pagi sore* cloth contrast sharply with the plain grounds (*tanahan polos*) of the *badan*. Small arrangements of double chrysanthemums in blue, pink, and white, brightly colored butterflies, and peacocks spreading their tails embellish the orange half of the cloth. The border is decorated with the same flowers on a bright blue ground. The other half shows sprigs of chrysanthemums and ferns surrounded by lovebirds on a beige ground with an orange border. The small bow borders, one in Indo-European, the other in Peranakan style, each show a sinuous garland of flowers using the same color scheme and running along one short and one long edge. The end sections are adorned with vestigial *kepala tumpal*, consisting of bands with small, stepped mountains alternating with triangles.

MAKER

This batik, signed in the orange upper corner "The Tie Siet Pekalongan," is a variation on the Peranakan version of *Djawa Hokokai*, virtually free of background motif. The quality of the work is good, but this type was far less time-consuming to make than those with complicated background motifs. The Tie Siet produced this simple variation for his exploratory foray into the old export markets of Singapore, Malaysia, and Thailand, which he succeeded in reopening for his batiks. At home in Java he also created a market for this style. This example bears a cotton stamp, the legible portion of which reads, "Geo Wehry & Co.," a Dutch trading firm with branches in Java. The firm purchased cloth on consignment from a mill in the Netherlands and sold it in Java. This continued until 1952, when the production of white cotton cloth came to a halt because of the mounting financial losses it entailed for Dutch manufacturers.[1] At that time

the Indonesian economy was in a deplorable state, and batik entrepreneurs could not afford to keep much yardage in stock. These facts, along with first-person observations in the field, help to date this batik to around 1950.[2]

The format is noteworthy in that it was The who introduced a crowded background to *batik Pekalongan* around 1930 but did not use it after independence, while Indo-Arabian entrepreneurs continued to do so in the *Djawa Hokokai* style, and Peranakan entrepreneurs perfected the very intricate *tanahan Semarangan* background style.

WEARER

This finely hand-hemmed cloth with its striking colors would have been worn by a well-to-do Peranakan woman of middle age. A younger, slimmer woman would not have been able to wear such sizable motifs, and the color combination would have been deemed too bright to be worn by autochthonous Indonesians.

Catalogue no. 65
Hip wrapper,
kain panjang pagi sore
Java, Pekalongan,
c. 1950
Signed by The Tie Siet
Hand-drawn wax resist
on machine-woven
cotton; synthetic dyes
106.7 x 257 cm
(42 x 101 1/8 in.)
Los Angeles County
Museum of Art,
Inger McCabe Elliott
Collection,
M.91.184.455

Catalogue no. 66
Hip wrapper,
kain panjang pagi sore
Java, Kedungwuni,
c. 1960–70
Signed by
The Kwie Tjoen
Hand-drawn wax resist
on machine-woven
cotton; synthetic dyes
107.5 x 250.4 cm
(42 3/8 x 98 5/8 in.)
Los Angeles County
Museum of Art,
Inger McCabe Elliott
Collection,
M.91.184.199

The design of this cloth resembles the previous one, although it is not as finely wrought. The orange and blue-green of the *badan* and borders contrast with each other. Small bouquets of purple and salmon chrysanthemums and hibiscus combined with sprigs of white *kemuning* seem to grow out of the orange *terang bulan* border, where tiny chicks scratch for worms. Three birds perch on a branch along the green border. Purple and salmon roses in a simpler style are scattered across the orange half of the *badan* and outline the blue-green border. The white flowers show orange pinpricks; the purple and salmon flowers have been shaded through darker *colet* accents and dotted, white relief effects. The bow borders are adorned with the same flowers arranged in a garland. Rows of triangles again form a vestigial *kepala tumpal* in both end sections.

MAKER

There were numerous Peranakan batik entrepreneurs in Kedungwuni, many related to each other and to batik entrepreneurs in nearby Pekalongan. The batik style of Kedungwuni is the same as that of the better-known center. The signature on this batik in the upper left corner is "The Kwie Tjoen / Kedungwuni." It is in the style of the preceding one by The Tie Siet. When an entrepreneur scored a success with a new design, it was not long before it was imitated by others. That is true of The's roses with their stark contour lines. The himself probably copied them from Dutch get-well cards popular between the wars.

WEARER

Boldly colored *terang bulan* cloths were worn predominantly by affluent Peranakan women of middle age. The flowers evoke a festive and prosperous atmosphere, the small chicks and other birds may indicate that the wearer had grandchildren.

Catalogue no. 67
Hip wrapper,
kain panjang
Java, Kedungwuni, 1982
Signed by
Oey Soe Tjoen
Hand-drawn wax resist
on machine-woven
cotton; synthetic dyes
103 x 259 cm
(40 ½ x 102 in.)
Los Angeles County
Museum of Art,
Inger McCabe Elliott
Collection,
M.91.184.300

OTE
1. P. Hutton, *Guide to Java*
Hong Kong: Apa Produc-
on, 1974), 155. "Even if
ou're not buying, visit the
orkshop just to see what
eally fine batik is all about."

The *badan* of this perfectly executed recent cloth shows the classic bouquets of
the 1930s. Six large arrangements of iris in salmon and blue, combined with sprigs
of salmon and blue starflowers and green leaves are neatly divided on the plain,
dark blue ground (*tanahan polos*). Large and small butterflies, inspired by Chinese
designs, hover nearby. The available space has been used to the utmost advantage.

MAKER

The hand-waxed information in the upper left corner reads, "Oey Soe Tjoen /
Kedungwuni 104 / 82 Java." 104, as noted earlier, is the number of his house
and workshop on the Jalan Raya; 82, the year of production, a datum seldom
included; "Java" was added for the tourists and collectors, who had read in a
guidebook that Oey was still producing his finest batiks.[1]

The lower portion of the bouquet replicates precisely the one designed by
Lies van Zuylen and depicted by her on many *kain panjang pagi sore* between
1935 and 1937 and copied by Oei Khing Liem, Pekalongan, and Liem Giok Kwie,
Kedungwuni, around 1940. The relatively restricted palette, albeit with shading,
and the fairly simple filler motifs in the leaves were simplifications chosen by Oey
in order to be able to offer the batik for a price not too shockingly high in comparison with other, less-perfect, hand-waxed batiks on the market.

WEARER

This type of cloth was often bought by foreign residents in Jakarta to be framed
and hung on a wall like a painting. This example is unhemmed and has never
been worn. It was purchased at Oey's workshop for the collection.

Minangkabau Muslim
headman wearing a head cloth
decorated with stylized Arabic
script imported from the
Pasisir.
Koninklijk Instituut voor
de Tropen, Amsterdam

Additions to Traditional Pasisir Dress

Although the principal item of Pasisir dress was the hip wrapper, additional, smaller-sized batik cloths formed part of traditional costume for both men and women during the nineteenth century. Muslim men used to cover their heads with the *iket kepala* (head cloth), which coincided in size with a single square of the imported cotton specially machine-woven for hip wrappers. Each age group, region, and occasion called for its own style of folding or wrapping these cloths, as with *sarung*. The format, design, and colors also differed by region. Pasisir *iket kepala* were worn on Java but also exported to Sumatra in large quantities particularly from Lasem. There a layer of gilding (*prada*) was applied to cloths worn on ceremonial occasions.

In addition to their *kain panjang* or *sarung* Muslim women wore a *selendang* (shoulder cloth), *kemben* (breast cloth), or *kudhung* (head covering). These cloths are all of the same length as the hip wrapper but of different widths. Motifs and colors bore the same symbolic import. Due to more conservative tastes there, traditional cloths continued to form part of regional costume among various Sumatran groups far into the twentieth century. Furthermore, in Sumatra and Bali their functions varied somewhat from those in Java.

For urban women the *selendang* was generally made of silk and in Java loosely draped over the shoulder as an elegant accessory. The same cloth could be worn as a *kemben*. In Sumatra and Bali commercially produced, imported silk batiks generally served a ceremonial function. Obviously the silk *selendang* was not suitable as a carrying cloth. A *gendongan* (baby carrier) was more likely to be made of cotton, with its width adjusted for easier use. This was also the width for the *kudhung* that modestly covered the head and shoulders of Muslim women when they left their private quarters. An orthodox women would cover the lower part of her face with an edge of the cloth, clenching it between her teeth to leave her hands free for other activities.

With the disappearance of the traditional Pasisir style, smaller antique cloths were only worn as part of regional costume in Sumatra or Bali. Other unusual sizes date to the 1940s and 1950s. During and shortly after the Pacific War cotton was scarce, and even scraps were used for batik. The function of these cloths is no longer evident, but their elaborate designs derive from the *Djawa Hokokai* and *Djawa baroe* styles.

Catalogue no. 68
Breast cloth,
kemben bang biru hijau
Java, Lasem, c. 1910
Hand-drawn wax resist
on machine-woven
cotton; synthetic dyes
52.1 x 237.4 cm
(20½ x 93½ in.)
Los Angeles County
Museum of Art,
Inger McCabe Elliott
Collection,
M.91.184.127

Two lotus trees, with red and blue flowers and green leaves (now faded to grayish blue as the yellow top-dye has deteriorated), grow from a minute, rocky base on a cream ground covered in small, red, circular motifs called *grinsing*. The trees meet midway along the main field, surrounding the elongated diamond (*sidhangan*) in the center of the cloth. A solid row of pointed, slanting motifs (*cemukiran*) encloses this plain, cream area. A threefold border encircles the main field: a row of mountainlike triangles decorated with a vegetal element; a series of alternating blue and red bars; and a *seret* with rather wide stripes.

MAKER

The tree of life on this Peranakan batik blossoms with lotus flowers typical of the Lasem style. This cloth is hemmed on both ends and one long side, as the fabric is half the width of a bolt of machine-woven cotton. After cutting flaws that occurred in even the best cotton, the smaller pieces were used for *kemben* or *selendang*.

WEARER

This type of cloth was exported to western Sumatra, where it may have served as *selendang* or *tengkuluak* (elaborately wrapped headdress) for Minangkabau women. There the lotus trees were perceived as trees of life. This is feasible given the rather late date, although the cloth may also have been used as a *kemben* by a Peranakan bride from a traditionalist family with strong Javanese affiliations. Though this use was common in central Java, it was not generally practiced on the Pasisir, especially during the early twentieth century. The plain lozenge in the center, with its clearly female symbolic associations, could only be worn by a bride or a married woman. The pointed arrows that surround this space, provide protection. The pair of lotus trees represents the couple ready to grow together and the progeny that may issue from their union. The threefold border forms an enclosure, which includes the ubiquitous row of triangles, in this case pictured as a wooded mountain chain.

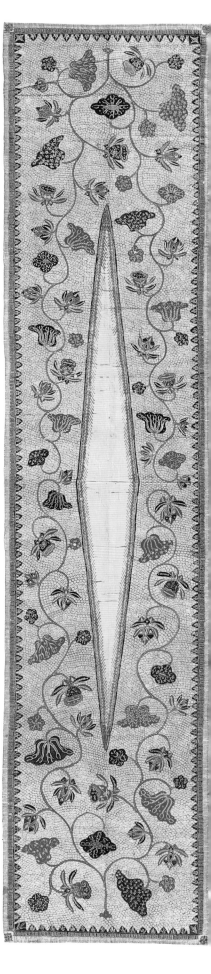

NOTES

1. Cloth with a width of about 75–90 centimeters (30–35 in.) was machine-woven in India especially for this purpose. The Dutch did not produce this particular width.

2. Francine Brinkgreve and David Stuart-Fox, *Offerings: The Ritual Art of Bali* (Sanur, Bali: Image Network Indonesia, 1992), 146.

Abstracted floral patterns create a solid grid across the dark blue main field of this cloth. (The combination of geometrical, white motifs on a dark background is called *irengan*.) Traditional Pasisir motifs in miniature, such as this *banji serong* (banji motif set on its side), were becoming rare during the last quarter of the nineteenth century. The main field is enclosed on all sides by a threefold border, including a floral arabesque. A plain, white *seret* edges the selvages. Both short ends are decorated with a traditional *selendang* border: a wide band of vertical stripes called a *kemadha*. The pattern in gold leaf applied to one side of the cloth does not coincide precisely with the resist, because the glue was applied with a stamp that did not replicate the original pattern.

Catalogue no. 69
Wall hanging,
selendang prada
Java, Lasem, c. 1880
Stamped wax resist on machine-woven cotton; natural dyes and applied gold leaf
76.9 x 321.1 cm
(30 1/4 x 126 3/8 in.)
Los Angeles County Museum of Art,
Inger McCabe Elliott Collection,
M.91.184.323

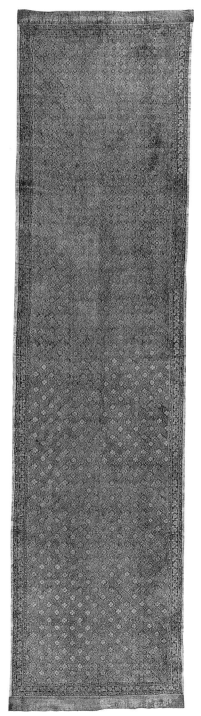

MAKER

This is a good example of the batiks crudely stamped in blue and white in Lasem by Peranakan entrepreneurs for export in large quantity to Sumatra and Bali, where they were gilded. Widths and lengths vary, but when the width was about half that of the bolt of cotton, the cloth was intended for use as *kemben* or *selendang*.

WEARER

If this cloth had only been gilded at one end, it might have served as a *kemben*. Somewhat wider, it could have been used by Muslim women in Sumatra as a *kudhung* or *tengkuluak*.[1] Since this checkered combination of "black-and-white" is symbolic for the Balinese of the equilibrium of the cosmos,[2] this gilded cloth may have been used as covering or hanging in a sacred Hindu venue to ward off evil influences. When the cloth, like this one, was relatively long, it could be wrapped around the pillars beneath the roof of a Balinese temple or pavilion during Hindu rituals. This cloth was indeed purchased on the island of Lombok, neighboring Bali.

The traditional *Laseman* motif, consisting of floral and faunal elements, was known in different guises all along the Pasisir. In this delicately hand-waxed example it reveals its Chinese inspiration. Birds, including birds of paradise, quail, and cocks, mingle with butterflies and deer, whose antlers give the appearance of trees. Floral sprigs embellish the intermediate spaces. The *kelengan* color scheme features dark indigo motifs on a cream ground, the latter covered with *cocohan* in the same dark blue. An unusual, stylized garland makes up the encircling border. As usual, the end sections show the *kemadha*. All motifs have been delineated with a beautifully detailed *prada*.

NOTES

1. A small tablecloth (H. C. Veldhuisen collection no. 1060) in the same style, but blue on cream, was presented in 1955 to Dr. Frits Cramer by a grateful patient in Jakarta. She was a Peranakan woman from Indramayu, and the batik was one of the many she had made for her trousseau around 1895.

2. C. A. S. Williams, *Outlines of Chinese Symbolism and Art Motives*, 3d ed. (New York: Dover, 1976), 51, 116, 199, 323, 336.

Catalogue no. 70
Shoulder cloth,
selendang prada
Java, Indramayu,
c. 1900–1910
Hand-drawn wax resist
on machine-woven
cotton; natural dyes and
applied gold leaf
50.2 x 210.1 cm
(19 3/4 x 82 3/4 in.)
Los Angeles County
Museum of Art,
Inger McCabe Elliott
Collection,
M.91.184.295

MAKER

This is a perfect example of a *selendang* on which the glue for the gold leaf was applied to the original pattern with a thin brush. Around 1890 Indo-European batik entrepreneurs in Pekalongan started to place orders for this technique on wall hangings, and a high grade of craftsmanship was achieved. Lien Metzelaar and Lies van Zuylen also made use of the technique on bridal *sarung*.

The drawing style seen here is typical of Lasem, but Indramayu is a better conjecture for several reasons. The *cocohan* were made, not with a needle, but with a *cemplongen*, a piece of wood studded with needles, developed as a labor-saving device in Indramayu to imitate the *cocohan* of Lasem batik. The very dark indigo dye is also characteristic of Indramayu batik.

It is possible that this batik with a design uncommon for commercial production was made, not in a workshop, but by a young woman eager to demonstrate her ability as batik maker to her future husband. This once-common Pasisir custom was still practiced in old-fashioned communities at the beginning of the twentieth century.[1]

WEARER

Replete with a combination of male and female symbols, this sumptuous cloth may have been used as a hanging in the bridal chamber. The bird of paradise is associated with the male phoenix, most honored of birds and emblem of regeneration. The cock is raised on the Pasisir as a fighter. Chinese symbolic lore furthermore considers the gamecock the chief embodiment of the *yang*, warmth, and life of the universe. The crown on its head refers to its literary spirit; the spurs on its feet, to its warlike disposition. Its counterpart, the female fighting quail, is considered the emblem of courage. The floral sprigs are associated with feminine beauty. The deer, in this case with antlers in the shape of a tree, stands for the ancestors and the family tree that springs from them. The butterflies refer to conjugal felicity.[2]

NOTE
1. Nian S. Djumena, *Batik dan Mitra; Batik and Its Kind* (bilingual) (Jakarta: Penerbit Djambatan, 1990), 22–23.

The main field of this *selendang* is decorated with a Pasisir variation on the central Javanese *semen ukel* motif, neatly arranged sets of wing and sun motifs surrounded by a profusion of plant tendrils. The arrangement was changed slightly to accommodate its use by nonaristocratic wearers. The main field is enclosed with a *banji* border; the end sections show the *kemadha* band and are finished with self-fringes, which were hand-twined and knotted at each end, a feature typical of Pasisir *selendang*.

MAKER

Rembang and Juana were the centers for the production of silk *selendang* and *sarung* by Peranakan entrepreneurs. *Selendang* with a rich yellow color, of which this is a good example, were highly appreciated by the Hindu Balinese, as, indeed, were those with a green ground. The same pattern sold with an undyed ground was favored by elderly Peranakan women. At the beginning of the twentieth century silk *selendang* from Juana and Rembang were offered in Bandung and proved a success with fashionable Sundanese women. Because of their fragility only a few specimens survive. After World War I production declined along with the economy, and fashions changed; a younger generation of women looked upon the silk *selendang* as old-fashioned.

WEARER

The *semen ukel* motif relates this batik to fertility. In Java it was suitable for use by itinerant dancers. Generally demeaned as of low repute, they originally performed the role of sky nymphs, harbingers of rain and thus of fertility. The wings and plant tendrils in the design seem appropriate for these flying creatures. The cloth was wrapped around the waist as a sash, with its ends hanging down in front and sometimes flung into the air in a semblance of flight.

Such silks were also exported in large quantities to other islands in the archipelago. In Bali they were known as *kain Rembang* after their port of embarkation. They served as sashes or formed part of ceremonial and dancing costumes. In Sumatra they were known as *kain tanah liat* (clay cloth) after their principal color. Heirloom pieces function even now as part of Minangkabau ceremonial wear: men drape the cloth loosely around their necks; women use it as *kudhung*.[1]

Catalogue no. 71
Shoulder cloth,
selendang lok can
Java, Rembang,
c. 1900–1910
Hand-drawn wax resist
on machine-woven silk;
natural dyes
52.1 x 270.4 cm
(20 1/2 x 106 1/2 in.)
Los Angeles County
Museum of Art,
Inger McCabe Elliott
Collection,
M.91.184.385

Catalogue no. 72
Shoulder cloth,
selendang lok can
Java, Juana or Rembang,
c. 1900
Hand-drawn wax resist
on machine-woven silk;
natural dyes
28.2 x 225.8 cm
(11⅛ x 88⅞ in.)
Los Angeles County
Museum of Art,
Inger McCabe Elliott
Collection,
M.91.184.553
See FIGURE 40

A variant of the *Laseman* pattern adorns this silk, which is typical of the eastern Pasisir, with each motif outlined by long, sharp spikes. The benevolent *qilin*, birds of paradise with their long tail feathers, and circular sun motifs line up in the middle of the main field, surrounded by floral creepers and passion fruit (*buah delima* or *salakan*). A wide, threefold border consists of two rows of *banji* enclosing a series of stepped, triangular motifs, each embellished with a starflower. Indigo was top-dyed with reddish-brown *kayu tingi* for the brownish black in the motifs on a cream ground. The short ends show the ubiquitous *kemadha* and are perfectly hand-hemmed. Each hand-twined fringe ends in a small knot.

MAKER

Like the previous example, this silk batik was made in a Peranakan workshop. Many silk *selendang* with this *Laseman* pattern but on a plain, green or yellow ground were exported to Bali.[1] This design with its decorated border is an older version.

WEARER

In Java this type of cloth was worn as a shoulder cloth but was also used as a covering for gifts or food on ceremonial occasions. The birds of the sky and flowers of the earth, together with the life-giving sun and resulting fruits, represent the universe and all its living creatures. The *qilin* stands for prosperity, while the *banji* borders provide protection.

In Bali and Sumatra its uses would have been similar to those of the previous cloth.

NOTE
1. H. C. Veldhuisen, field notes, Bali, 1971.

West Sumatra, c. 1910. The attendants of a Minangkabau bride and groom wearing *lok can* shoulder cloths from the Pasisir. From *Indië in Beeld* (Haarlem: De Tulp, 1911).

NOTES
1. Another example was signed by Gan Tjioe Liam, a well-known entrepreneur in Pekalongan. The batik has the same format as the present example but different *wayang* figures in the end panels and elegant bouquets in the *badan*. Important for dating this type of design is the ink stamp, which reads "Gan Tjioe Liam/Bawakan [a quarter in Pekalongan]" and the date the batik was begun: "9 Aug 1925" (private collection).

2. H. C. Veldhuisen, field notes, Palembang and Lampong, 1992.

In the main field two trees of life on a deep green ground, with flowers in blue and white and leaves in reddish brown, sprout from composite mountains and spread toward each other and the center of the cloth. The trees show elements of the *buketan* style. Birds depicted in the European manner flutter among the branches, while ducks scratch the soil below. The dark main field contrasts with the wide, bright cream borders of floral arabesques in blue, green, and yellow. These borders, enclosed within *banji* bands, surround the *badan* and the end sections. The latter depict the four servants—Semar, Bagong, Petruk, and Gareng—familiar from Javanese shadow plays *(wayang)*. Standing on a black-and-white tiled floor, they flank a large vase of flowers on a three-legged table. For some reason the *kemadha* at either end has been cut off.

MAKER
Numerous Peranakan entrepreneurs in Pekalongan produced batik illustrating scenes with *wayang* figures in the end panels.[1] Many of these cloths were exported to south Sumatra as *kudhung* for devout Muslim women.[2] There the Javanese symbolism would have gone undeciphered.

WEARER
Each infant in an affluent Peranakan family in Java was cared for by a servant and carried around in a multicolored *gendongan* such as this. Even after walking, toddlers were placed in carrying cloths to be fed or to nap. The *wayang* servants set an example for the child's caretaker. The tiled floor is reminiscent of the apotropaic, checked *poleng* motif, while the tree of life, as the axis of the universe, stands for harmony and balance. The duck is an emblem of felicity.

Catalogue no. 73
Carrying cloth,
kain gendongan
Java, Pekalongan,
c. 1920–30
Hand-drawn wax resist on machine-woven cotton; synthetic dyes
83.8 x 227.3 cm
(33 x 89½ in.)
Los Angeles County Museum of Art,
Inger McCabe Elliott Collection,
M.91.184.510

Catalogue no. 74
Head cloth,
iket kepala prada,
setangan, destar
Java, Lasem, c. 1880
Stamped wax resist on
machine-woven cotton;
natural and synthetic
dyes and
applied gold leaf
91.5 x 92 cm
(36 x 36 ¼ in.)
Los Angeles County
Museum of Art,
Costume Council Fund,
M.74.18.1

NOTES
1. H. C. Veldhuisen, field notes, Palembang, 1992.
2. Nian S. Djumena, *Batik dan Mitra; Batik and Its Kind* (bilingual) (Jakarta: Penerbit Djambatan, 1990), 74.

The *prada* decoration, added in Sumatra, changed the format of this cloth, with its large, diamond-shaped, abstracted floral motifs in deep red and small accents of white arranged in a regular pattern on a blue-black ground. The gilding outlines an ungilded, lozenge-shaped *tengahan* in the center and, following the original pattern, covers the four corners of the initially uniformly patterned main field and the wide, fourfold, surrounding border. The border consists of an outer *kemadha* enclosing three smaller, floral arabesque bands. The corners of the cloth are marked by two squares, each embellished with a floral motif. The wide border and the glazing indicate this cloth was meant for Sumatra, where these features were determinants of quality. The size of a Sumatran head cloth was generally ten to fifteen centimeters smaller than that of its Javanese counterpart, probably due to the fact that the former were made commercially, that is, for maximum profit on sale. As usual on Sumatra, the cloth was left unhemmed.

MAKER

The invention of the copper stamp around 1850 greatly facilitated the manufacture of batik with repeated geometric motifs. It is found on cloths made in Peranakan workshops in Lasem for export to Sumatra, where dealers in the ports of Jambi and Palembang ordered variations, according to the demands of their customers. Such special orders came to be called by the name of the harbor, that is, *kain Jambi* or *kain Palembang.*

This head cloth was made for the Palembang market. The telling feature is the special undulating line with flowers and leaves in the border. Red too was favored in the market in Palembang, where the *prada* would have been added. The glue was applied with wooden pattern stamps;[1] the stamps were adapted, as can be seen here, from the batik pattern itself. Originally this cloth had no *tengahan.* In Java that area was left as a plain, cream field; on *iket kepala* for the Sumatran market the *tengahan* was often decorated with a pattern that differed from the rest of the cloth. In this case the difference is the gold.

Minangkabau Muslim man from west Sumatra wearing a head cloth from Lasem with stylized floral motifs, c. 1900.

WEARER

An abstract motif such as this was calculated to appeal to Muslim Sumatrans, who might have used this as a head cloth on ceremonial occasions. This particular cloth was probably used as a *tutup cerana* (covering for food or gifts), as so much of the surface was gilded. Had it been meant as a head cloth, only the half that remained visible after folding would have been gilded. This type of motif was also used by Minangkabau men in west Sumatra, where it was folded in a particular manner called *saluak* .[2]

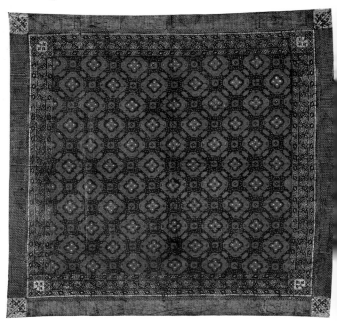

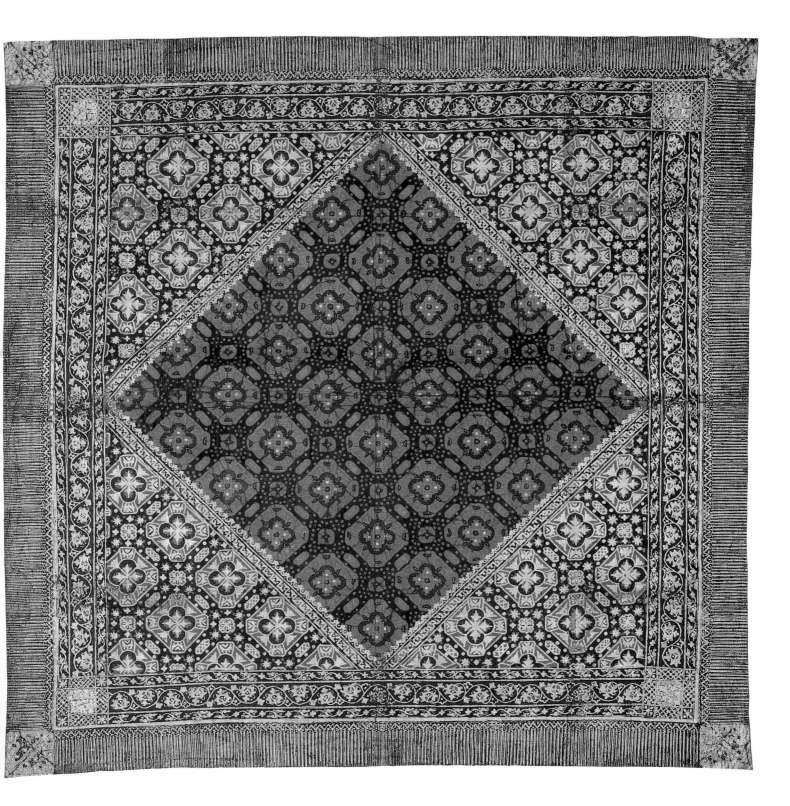

Catalogue no. 75
Wall hanging
or tablecloth
Java, Sidoarjo, c. 1943
Hand-drawn wax resist
on machine-woven
cotton; synthetic dyes
105.8 x 120 cm
(41 5/8 x 47 1/4 in.)
Los Angeles County
Museum of Art,
Inger McCabe Elliott
Collection,
M.91.184.6

Five small pieces of cotton were pieced together by hand before the batik design
was applied to this *Djawa Hokokai* cloth in bright blue, dark green, and golden
soga brown with touches of cream on a deep blue ground. The center is dominated by two finely detailed phoenixes enclosed within floral rings. Bouquets of
dahlias or zinnias held together by flowing ribbons decorate the corners, while
smaller clusters adorn the intermediate spaces. Chrysanthemums are recognizable in the inner floral border. The unusual outer border consists of a wide band
of geometric motifs in *nitik* technique.

MAKER

Comparable in style with batik of the best quality from Peranakan entrepreneurs
in Sidoarjo, this *Djawa Hokokai* wall hanging was probably a product of such a
shop. It may have been produced as a sample to be shown to the Japanese, who
supplied the entrepreneurs with cotton when ordering batiks. In this case the
cloth consists of five bands exquisitely sewn together by hand. The borders were
also perfectly hand-hemmed. The cloth was glazed by rubbing with the side of
a wine bottle, making the details more striking.

FUNCTION

This intricate cloth may have been meant as a wall hanging or tablecloth, although
there is no extant information concerning the use of such cloths made for officers
of the occupying Japanese army.

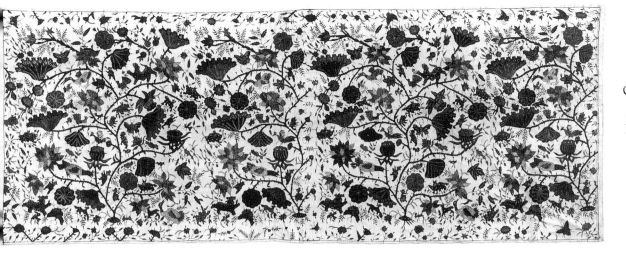

Catalogue no. 76
Canopy (?), *langit-langit*
Java, Cirebon, c. 1950
Hand-drawn wax resist
on machine-woven
cotton; synthetic dyes
106.7 x 164.1 cm
(42 x 64⅝ in.)
Los Angeles County
Museum of Art,
Inger McCabe Elliott
Collection,
M.91.184.440

Four abundantly flowering lotus trees, sprouting from small, rocky islands, spread side by side from top to bottom across the *badan*. Butterflies, birds, and mythical Chinese animals hide among the foliage; ducks stand underneath. An interesting feature are the babies clambering in the branches. A maze of floral creepers and fern fronds form a second layer. The filler motifs follow the crowded style that was current during the 1950s. A border of fine floral elements encloses the *badan* and a plain *seret* edges all four sides. The motifs have been top-dyed in blue on red in an effort to imitate the traditional Lasem color style, the result of which is a rather flat shade of brownish black on a cream ground. Elements belonging to a variety of local styles have been combined in this cloth, giving it a hybrid character.

MAKER

Cotton became scarce on several occasions: the American Civil War, World War I, the Japanese occupation, and the period after the declaration of independence in 1945. This batik must have been made in a Peranakan workshop during the latter. It consists of two pieces sewn together by machine. Both pieces show a narrow band of colored weftlines and an embroidered number 16. The cloth is too short to be worn by an adult as a *kain panjang*. The design, a tree of life with animals and small children, is depicted twice in its entirety and twice in part, as if it were intended for a longer cloth.

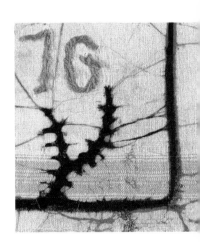

FUNCTION

The unusual size of this cloth indicates that it may have been meant as a hanging behind the bridal seat or as a canopy over a Peranakan matrimonial bed. In spite of the hybrid style, the motifs—trees of life, ducks, and butterflies—possess traditional symbolic associations with marriage as does the watchful *qilin*. The trees bloom not only with flowers, representative of daughters, but also produce a "crop" of baby boys, the ideal of a Chinese family.

A family altar in a Peranakan
home with a batik *tok wi*
hanging in front of the table.
Lasem, 1981.
Photograph, Rens Heringa

NOTES

1. Paramita R. Abdurach-
an, *Cerbon* (Jakarta: Yayasan
Mitra Budaya Indonesia;
Penerbit Sinar Harapan,
1982), 154.

2. Rens Heringa, interview
with Nian Djumena, Jakarta,
1994.

3. Abdurachman, *Cerbon*,
31.

Ceremonial Cloths

Batik Pasisir served religious purposes, both as apparel and as ritual object. Two types can be distinguished: the first responsive to the ritual needs of Muslims in Java and Sumatra; the second, playing a role in Peranakan ancestor worship.

Islamic tradition discourages the depiction of living creatures, so batiks appropriate for use by Muslims were decorated with abstract, often calligraphic designs (*tulisan Arab* or *kaligrafi Arab*). The writing is often illegible, as the person waxing the motifs may not have been able to read or write Arabic script. In spite of this, the texts impart magical and protective powers, as they are supposed to consist of some of the one hundred names of Allah or the *Sahadat*. The calligraphic texts generally form highly stylized magical squares and octagons or birds and animals, their symbolism deriving from Sufi precepts, which were easily accommodated by existing Indonesian ideas. Probably due to the role played by Peranakan Muslims on the Pasisir, some of these motifs show Chinese influence. Originally these cloths were only made as hangings or ceremonial coverings.[1] When they came to be used as clothing, it was forbidden to wear them on the lower body, as sitting upon such texts would defile them.[2]

The Peranakan ritual cloths, decorated in a more naturalistic style, were no less meaningful. Their inspiration was often found in embroidered silk pieces brought from China.[3] The motifs consist of animals derived from Chinese mythology or the Chinese zodiac or saints and gods from the Chinese pantheon and often retain the significance of the originals. The *tok wi* (throne for the ancestors) cloth was used to decorate the altar in the inner hall of Peranakan family residences, where their ancestors were honored. As each occasion required its own colors and motifs, Peranakan families often owned a series of such cloths. Blue-black with white *kelengan* cloths served during mourning; bright red, for festive occasions, primarily weddings. Pairs of phoenixes and lotuses in red also graced the hangings that decorated the bed and doors of the bridal chamber.

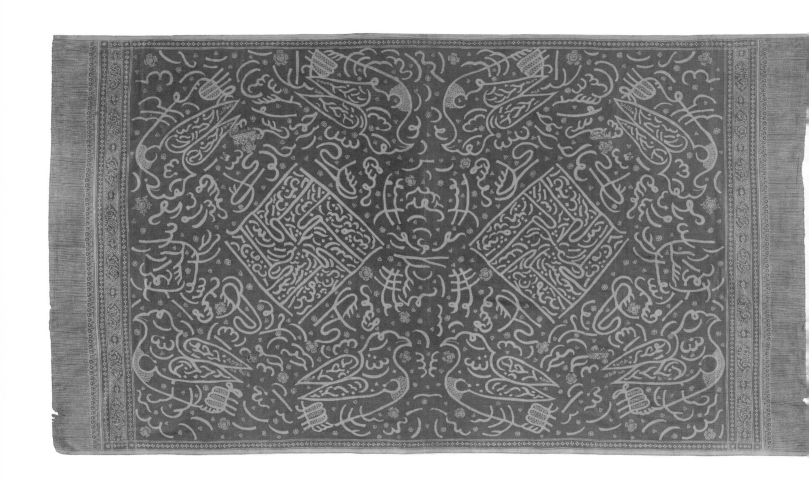

NOTES

1. Hansjörg Mayer, ed., *Die Gärten des Islam* (Stuttgart: Staib and Mayer, 1993), 214–15, 219, 244; Inger McCabe Elliott, *Batik: Fabled Cloth of Java* (New York: Clarkson N. Potter, 1984), 140–43, 216–17. Most of the *tulisan Arab* batiks in the Elliott book are described as having been produced in Cirebon, but three are attributed to Palembang. It is not unlikely, however, that the three, while acquired in Palembang, were not actually made there. Jakarta antique dealers, using the term *batik Palembang*, contribute, as noted earlier, to certain misunderstandings about origins.

2. Judi Achjadi, "Batiks in the Central Javanese Wedding Ceremony," in *To Speak with Cloth: Studies in Indonesian Textiles*, ed., Mattiebelle Gittinger (Los Angeles: Museum of Cultural History, 1989), 154.

3. Barbara Leigh, "The Theme of the Heavenly Garden: Gold Thread Embroidery in Aceh," in *Weaving Patterns of Life: Indonesian Textile Symposium, 1991*, eds., Marie-Louise Nabholz-Kartaschoff et al. (Basel: Museum of Ethnography, 1993), 182.

Two diamond shapes composed of Arabic calligraphy and forming apotropaic *banji* motifs dominate the center of this cloth, surrounded by eight calligraphic doves. The maze of script covering the rest of the main field may contain hidden motifs, that are, however, difficult to distinguish. A sprinkling of *bintang* (stars) shimmers among the script on the heavily oiled, deep-red ground. The ends are decorated with a *kemadha* and a wide band of medallions, which, like the main field, is enclosed by a border of simple, four-petaled flowers.

MAKER

This type of batik, probably made by a Javanese entrepreneur in Cirebon for either local use or export to Sumatra, is called *tulisan Arab* (Arabic script). Because of the Islamic reticence toward depicting living creatures, painters and woodcarvers in Cirebon specialized in zoomorphic calligraphy in Arabic script, which itself added a second layer of meaning. *Tulisan Arab* on batiks always has a religious connotation and was believed to protect the wearer. It was used on banners, jackets for warriors, wall hangings, *kudhung, iket kepala,* and *selendang.*[1]

FUNCTION

The symbolic interpretation of cloths such as this was similar on Java and Sumatra, although their functions differed. The combination of red and ivory (*gumading*), which on the Pasisir was considered a dark variety of red and white, was reminiscent of the *sindur* cloth used at Javanese weddings; at the ritual meeting of bride and groom on the threshold of her family house, the young couple was symbolically "carried" in this *selendang* by the bride's mother.[2] The male (white) and female (red) were thus received as a unit into the family. The symbols on this particular cloth express additional Islamic ideas. According to Sufism, the swastika refers to the passing of time and regenerative cycle, hence, its appropriateness at weddings. In Muslim families two swastikas were generally placed on the heads of the couple to indicate their subservience to Islam. The doves represent the *Sahadat* but are also associated with prayers for the couple's well-being, which fly up to heaven. The small stars refer to the heavenly paradise that the couple experiences on earth during the wedding.[3]

While the same symbolism obtained in Sumatra, the cloth found different use. It may have served as a *lelangit* (firmament) stretched over the bridal throne, where the couple sat in state. The small repairs in the four corners of this cloth may attest to this function.

Catalogue no. *77*
Wall hanging
or covering,
hiasan dinding
Java, Cirebon, c. 1900
Hand-drawn wax resist
on machine-woven
cotton; natural dyes
81.5 x 141.8 cm
(32 1/8 x 55 7/8 in.)
Los Angeles County
Museum of Art,
Inger McCabe Elliott
Collection,
M.91.184.502

Catalogue no. 78
Wall hanging,
biasan dinding
Java, Cirebon, c. 1900
Hand-drawn wax resist
on machine-woven
cotton; synthetic indigo
90.1 x 227.8 cm
(35 1/2 x 89 5/8 in.)
Los Angeles County
Museum of Art,
Inger McCabe Elliott
Collection,
M.91.184.431

The main field of this cloth is solidly covered with Arabic script, which surrounds three prominent, eight-pointed figures. The flaming starbursts in their centers enclose a character that was possibly meant to represent the name of the Prophet. A sharp point protrudes from each of the four corners. Numerous double-bladed swords, the miraculous *Dhu'l-Faqar* given by Muhammad to his son-in-law, Ali, in order to protect the faith, are depicted throughout. Lozenges with a *celuki* (Chinese carnation motif) also occur throughout. The main field is enclosed by a narrow border of starflowers. The ends show the ubiquitous *kemadha*.

MAKER

This *tulisan Arab* batik was probably made in a Javanese workshop in Cirebon for local use or export to Sumatra.

FUNCTION

This cloth, with its "heavenly" blue ground, was possibly used as a *lelangit* over a marriage bed or as a hanging over a bridal throne, as it is faded on one side. Such cloths also functioned as *tutup cerana*, although this particular example seems too large for such use. Despite all present-day denials, the role played on the north coast by Chinese Muslims lives on in the *celuki* motif. The blue-and-white *kelengan* is appropriate for its apotropaic properties. In Java octagonal shapes enclosing a ninth point are often associated with the *Wali songo*, the nine saints who introduced Islam to Java. The layout of the cloth, which is reminiscent of Persian carpets, may originally have had cosmological overtones.[1] The borders of the cloth may thus be seen as presenting a view through the sky door with octagonal mountains (or mosques) rising up into a sky that reverberates with the name of Allah.

NOTE
1. For carpet symbolism see Schuyler V. R. Cammann, "Symbolic Meanings in Oriental Rug Patterns," *Textile Museum Journal* 3, no. 3 (1972): 5–42.

NOTES

1. H. C. Veldhuisen, field notes, Cirebon, 1971.

2. Paramita R. Abdurach-man, *Cerbon* (Jakarta: Yayasan Mitra Budaya Indonesia; Penerbit Sinar Harapan, 1982), 154, 136.

3. C. A. S. Williams, *Outlines of Chinese Symbolism and Art Motives*, 3d ed. (New York: Dover, 1976), 138.

4. Ibid., 152–53.

The lower section of this altar cloth shows a huge dragon rising from undulating waves and clutching a large ball. To its left is a tiger; to its right, a leopard; below each of these, a phoenix. Lotuses sprout from the waves; clouds float in the air. The upper section depicts a scene with five human figures, a horse, and two flowering trees flanking a temple. A wide border of meandering *banji* motifs encloses both scenes.

MAKER

The format on this Peranakan batik is the same as those on hand-embroidered altar cloths made in China and imported to Java. Many scenes were adopted from these cloths, but Peranakan entrepreneurs created a style of their own. It is a remarkable fact that altar cloths are always hand-drawn. This was a necessity occasioned by the sheer diversity of pictures, many too large for a single stamp. The filler motifs on this batik are typical of *batik Cirebon*, as indeed are the small clouds. At the beginning of the twentieth century the same style was imitated in Tegal, which is situated between Cirebon and Pekalongan. Peranakan entrepreneurs from Cirebon contracted with relatives in Tegal when orders overwhelmed their capacity for timely production. Later those entrepreneurs undertook to produce batiks competitively on their own.[1]

FUNCTION

This batik was used as a hanging for the front of the ancestral altar in a Peranakan home. A wide band of red cotton at the top and white cotton bands at the sides adapt it to this purpose. The color, red, indicates that this cloth was for use on festive occasions. The dragon may represent the mythical *singa barong* of Cirebon, emblem of peaceful coexistence.[2] Alternatively, it may represent the *naga murka*, the irate dragon that guards against greed and gluttony. The ball, constant appurtenance of dragons, is variously described as the sun, the moon, or the pearl of potentiality.[3] The mythical animals in the corners do not follow the usual configuration, wherein the birds are depicted in the upper corners (compare catalogue no. 80).

The scene in the upper section represents godly figures to the right of the temple and mortals to the left as if in a *wayang* play. Though it may represent a well-known Chinese story, its meaning, which might clarify the cloth's function, remains obscure. Standing on clouds to the right, are three of the eight immortals. The first, with the fan, may be Zhong Li-quan, who holds the secrets of the elixir of life. The figure in the middle, because of the fly-brush in his hand, is probably Lu Dong-bin, who is worshipped by the sick.[4] The object held by the third figure is not clear. The figures to the left may have come to the temple for healing. The figure in front approaches the door; his servant holds an umbrella and is followed by his horse.

Catalogue no. 79
Altar cloth, *tok wi*
Java, Cirebon,
c. 1910–20
Hand-drawn wax resist
on machine-woven
cotton; synthetic dyes
103 x 108.6 cm
(40½ x 42¾ in.)
Los Angeles County
Museum of Art,
Inger McCabe Elliott
Collection,
M.91.184.409

Catalogue no. 80
Altar cloth, *tok wi*
Java, Pekalongan,
c. 1950–60
Hand-drawn wax resist
on machine-woven
cotton; synthetic dyes
94.5 x 105 cm
(37 ¼ x 41 ⅜ in.)
Los Angeles County
Museum of Art,
Inger McCabe Elliott
Collection,
M.91.184.559

A bearded figure looms in a central roundel, which is further embellished with floral sprigs and leafy boughs. The upper corners show two white phoenixes; the lower, two *bai-ze*, mythical composite animals usually referred to as *qilin* in Java. The borders are decorated with floral scrolls and lucky symbols, among others the gourd bottle, containing the elixir of life. This is the emblem of the magician Li Tie-guai, one of the eight immortals, and also the sign associated with herbalists. In the upper section two seated figures flank the Chinese character for good fortune; they are in turn flanked by a fan, which represents Zhong Li-quan, who is said to have had the power to raise the dead with his fan, and a large artemisia leaf, or mugwort, which wards off illness. Beyond those are two lively dancers or musicians.

MAKER

The batik, pieced together and sewn by machine, must have been made in a period when cotton was scarce. This was true of the Japanese occupation, but even around 1950 the best-quality Dutch cotton was still hard to come by

because of import restrictions imposed by the Indonesian government. Dutch cotton cloth was exported to Malaysia instead for batik production there; some of this found its way into Indonesia with smugglers. A stamp from the firm Salomonson on one of the two constituent segments gives some information. It bears the trademark Toko Rotterdam, indicating the bolt was seventeen yards; the quality is noted as *cap cent*, though the number 2 below this informs us that there are fewer threads per square centimeter than on cloth marked with a 1. The spelling of *cap* is significant: it was *tjap* for the Indonesian market; *cap*, for Malaysia. So, we may assume this cotton was smuggled.

The Peranakan workshop could not have been prosperous because leftovers were sewn together for a small batik.

FUNCTION

The bearded man is difficult to identify, but he may represent a generic ancestor, the batik designer using as a model the historical figures portrayed in one of the popular Chinese operas often performed on special occasions. It is also possible that he is a deity in the garb of a high-ranking Chinese official, such as Lu Dong-bin. The birds and animals in the corners represent female and male properties and in this combination possibly stand for the family.

Catalogue no. 81
Hanging, *mui li*
Java, Cirebon, c. 1920
Hand-drawn wax resist
on machine-woven
cotton; synthetic dyes
104.7 x 201.8 cm
(41 ¼ x 79 ½ in.)
Los Angeles County
Museum of Art,
Inger McCabe Elliott
Collection,
M.91.184.46

NOTE
1. C. A. S. Williams,
*Outlines of Chinese Symbolism
and Art Motives*, 3d ed. (New
York: Dover, 1976), 34, 170.

In the central roundel of this rectangular cloth two Chinese lions, an adult and a cub, play with a large ball. A mystic knot tied with festive ribbons and the fungus of longevity fill in the rest of the circle, which is guarded by two light and two dark bats and two standing dragons. At either end of the cream cloth a flowering lotus tree grows out of a small rock. Two phoenixes carry the peony of early summer, their emblem, in their beaks. Two small elephants stand at the top. A three-fold border surrounds the scene on three sides: rolling waves form the inner border, while the outer edge shows rows of *gigi walang*. A wide red band of cotton material has been sewn onto the top of the cloth.

MAKER

This is a good example of an original batik design with Chinese symbols which departs from the tradition of Chinese hand-embroidered cloths. A wide range of filler motifs has been used, and most of these, such as the *banji*, are not typical of *batik Cirebon*. These factors lead to the conclusion that the batik was made around 1920, when the distinctive motifs of the various batik centers were being imitated all along the north coast. The quality of the deep, saturated red indicates the use of *garancine*, a synthetic dye of the early decades of the twentieth century which closely resembles natural red.

FUNCTION

This red and white *mui li* (door curtain), with its many auspicious symbols, served as a hanging over the entrance to the nuptial chamber during a Peranakan wedding. The flowering lotus trees contain the wish for many sons, also implied by the lion cub playing with its parent. The dragons, bats of happiness and longevity, and elephants, symbols of strength and sagacity, guard the scene. The phoenix indicates early summer, which corresponds in human life to the time for marriage.[1]

Catalogue no. 82
Handkerchief,
sapu tangan or *toka*
Java, Cirebon, c. 1880
Hand-drawn wax resist
on machine-woven
cotton; natural dyes
69.9 x 69.9 cm
(27 1/2 x 27 1/2 in.)
Los Angeles County
Museum of Art,
Inger McCabe Elliott
Collection,
M.91.184.374

A phoenix occupies the roundel in the center of this small but intricate cloth. The four corners are home to a tiger, a lion, a deer, and a *singa barong*. All four are presented with their attributes, an apotropaic coin, abundantly flowering creeper, fungus of longevity, and scrolls of wisdom. Four potted plants, flanked by deer, fill the spaces in between. Butterflies with open wings embellish the corners. The borders combine intermittent *banji* scrolls and floral branches, enclosed by two smaller rows of *banji*. The sparce filler motifs in the animals and bird in the main field of this ceremonial cloth indicate that they were possibly meant to be gilded.

MAKER

The filler motifs in the deer and lion suggest a Peranakan workshop in Cirebon as the source of this batik. The same type of *sapu tangan* was produced all along the north coast. They were used, not as handkerchiefs, but flung across the left shoulder as chatelaines. Remarkable is the fact that this type of batik was only produced by Peranakan in designs most closely associated with Peranakan tastes, although they were used not only by Peranakan women but until the late nineteenth century by Javanese and Indo-European housekeepers as well. Indo-European entrepreneurs only made small handkerchiefs with European designs along the borders.

WEARER

This small, rectangular, blue-and-white *sapu tangan*, with three finely hand-hemmed sides, might have been worn by a Peranakan bride, possibly on the third and last day of the traditional wedding. Among the Peranakan of Singapore and Malaysia and among ethnic Sumatrans the bridal *sapu tangan* evolved into a form that is a mere remnant of the original batik version: a triangular cloth resembling a neatly folded handkerchief. These cloths were heavily embroidered with gold thread and sequins.[1] Such cloths, now mere accessories, were a vestige of the chatelaine. In this particular example the central motif, the female phoenix, indicates the bride. The male animals and the female flowering plants may stand for the relatives surrounding her, each offering a wish for her well-being. The small deer indicate her ancestors.

NOTE
1. Ho Wing Meng, *Straits Chinese Beadwork and Embroidery: A Collector's Guide* (Singapore: Times Books International, 1987), 118; Rens Heringa, field notes, Sumatra, 1990.

GLOSSARY

•

Rens Heringa

ABBREVIATIONS

A ARABIC

C CHINESE

D DUTCH

I INDONESIAN

J JAVANESE

M MALAY

alas-alasan (J): resembling a forest. Traditional central Javanese motif depicting wild creatures of the sky, land, and water. Symbolizes the cosmos and fertility.

ang kin (C): piece of red cloth. Tasseled silk sash, often red, bound around the waist to keep the hip wrapper in place. Also called *udet*.

ayam puger (J): chicken in a coop. Traditional Javanese motif worn by maidens during the period of confinement before marriage. Also worn by young bachelors.

badan (I/J from A): body. The main field of a batik cloth.

baju (I/M): jacket, tunic; from *bazu* (Persian): shoulder garment. Collarless tunic with a slit at the neck, first worn by half-caste women.

baju Cina (M): jacket in Chinese style. Man's collarless jacket with hip pockets, closed with buttons in the front.

bang-bangan (J): rendered red. Traditional Pasisir color combination with motifs in red on a cream ground.

bang biru (J): red [and] blue. Traditional Pasisir color combination with motifs in red and blue on a cream ground.

bang biru hijau (J): red, blue, [and] green. Traditional Pasisir color combination with motifs in red, blue, and green on a cream ground.

banji (J), from *wan-zi* (C): ten thousand. An apotropaic swastika motif symbolizing prosperity.

banji serong (J). *Banji* motifs placed at an angle.

batik Belanda (M/I): Dutch batik. Term used for floral designs created by Indo-European entrepreneurs in Pekalongan.

batik cap (I/J/M): stamped batik. Batik cloth waxed by means of copper stamps.

batik Jambi (J/M/I). Batik made in the port town of Jambi on the east coast of Sumatra.

batik kombinasi (I/M): combination batik. Stamped and hand-waxed patterns combined.

batik-lurik (J). A checked, handwoven cotton cloth from Tuban in which the lines are used as a grid for dotted, geometric batik motifs.

batik tulis (I/J/M): written batik. Batik cloth hand-waxed with a *canting*. See *canting*.

bilik (I/M): plaited bamboo wall. Pasisir term for traditional Javanese background motif resembling plaiting. See *gedekan*.

bintang or **bebintangan** (I/J/M): star or constellation of stars. Term often used in Sumatra for abstracted floral motifs.

boenga rampai (I): mixed flowers. Designs of the 1950s and 1960s intended to express feelings of national unity. See *pantjawarna*.

booh (J/M), from *boog* (D): arch, bow. Border along the selvages on Indo-European batik cloths.

buah delima (I/M): passion fruit. Because the passion fruit has many seeds, this motif is considered an emblem of fertility. Also called *salakan*.

buketan (I/M): decorated with bouquets; from *boeket* (D). Hence, *buketan Panselen*, batik with bouquets in the style of Lies van Zuylen, and *buketan Semarangan*, batik decorated with bouquets and intended for sale in Semarang. (*Panselen* is an oral corruption of Van Zuylen.)

canting (I/J). Small, spouted copper container with a reed handle, used to apply designs in melted wax to the surface of cloth.

canting cap (I/J/M): *canting* stamp. Copper stamp for making batik. Also simply *cap*.

canting nitik (M/I): *canting* tap. Utensil with a four-lobed spout used to create tiny, four-lobed motifs. See *nitik*.

ceblong (J): tadpole. One of the *tanahan Semarangan* repertoire of backgrounds.

celuki (J): carnation. Hence, *celuken* (J), decorated with carnations. Traditional Pasisir motif inspired by Persian designs. Also *cluki* and *teluki*.

cempaka mulya (J). Flower of the *kamboja* tree, which is planted in Javanese cemeteries, abode of the ancestors. As a traditional Pasisir motif, it may have ancestral connotations. It was worn by the mothers of Peranakan bridal couples.

cemplongan (J): pinpricker. Comblike utensil with rows of fine needles used in Indramayu to make pinpricks in the waxed background of a batik cloth. Also *complongan*.

cemukiran (J). Pointed, slanting motifs surrounding the plain area in the center of a *kemben* or *kudhung*. Associated with arrows or flames and providing protective powers.

cenderawasih (I/J): bird of paradise. Motif related to phoenix symbolism. See *feng huang*.

cinde (I/J). Silk fabric from Sindh (Gujarat). The term is used in the archipelago for *patola* cloth. Also *cindai*. See *patola*.

cocohan (J). Pinpricks applied to the waxed background of a cloth, resulting in small, colored dots.

colet (J). Application of synthetic dyes with a brush to small areas outlined in wax.

custcleeden (D): coastal cloths. Woven, painted, printed, and resist-dyed Indian textiles traded for spices throughout the archipelago by the Dutch.

dam-daman (J): resembling a checkerboard (*dambord*) (D). Background motif with a checkered effect.

destar (J/M): turban. Term used by devout Muslim men for *iket kepala*.

Djawa baroe (I): new Java. Batik style popular during the first decades of the Indonesian Republic.

Djawa Hokokai (i/j): Java Service Association. Founded by the Japanese during the occupation. Complex batik style that originated during that period. Also *Jawa Hokokai* (modern Indonesian.)

dlorong (j): beam, girder. Pasisir term for slanting or vertical bands of motifs. Also *dlurung*. See *geblak*.

Encim (c): aunt. Hokkien term of address for young married women. Also refers to a batik style worn by such women.

feng huang (c): phoenix. According to Chinese symbolism, the mythical bird is considered a female symbol, while it is a male emblem in Java. As a pair these birds connote conjugal bliss. A traditional Pasisir motif, the female is depicted with long, serrated tail feathers and the male with curling plumes.

galaran (j): resembling a bamboo mat. Traditional Javanese background motif consisting of fine, straight lines.

gandawari (j): sweet, wafting fragrance. Border section in the *kepala* of a traditional hip wrapper. Originally the abstracted motifs stood for the fusion of male and female properties.

ganggeng (j). Creeper trailing on the surface of inundated paddy. Traditional Pasisir motif symbolizing fertility and regeneration.

garusan (j). The high gloss given to a batik cloth by rubbing with a shell or wine bottle.

geblak (j): thrown backward. Alternating diagonal bands, one of which contains floral motifs.

geblak tempel buketan (j). Slanting bands with an overlay of floral bouquets. Traditional Javanese motif.

gedekan (j): resembling a plaited bamboo wall or mat. Traditional Javanese background motif. See *bilik*.

gigi walang (j/m): cricket's teeth. Border motif, used either along the selvages or in the *kepala*, with apotropaic properties. Also *gigi balang* (j/m): border that throws out. Pasisir Malay term used for the Peranakan version of this style.

glatik (j): rice bird. Motif used in both batik and weaving which stands for the harvest and bloom of life.

grinsing (j): against illness. Ancient Javanese textile type known to ward off bad influences. An apotropaic Javanese motif resembling snakeskin and generally used in backgrounds. Also *gringsing*.

gumading (j): resembling ivory; from *gading* (j). Deep shade of yellow exclusively found in the oiled backgrounds of naturally dyed, traditional Cirebon batik.

hiasin dinding (i): decoration for a wall. A large cloth, often decorated with batik and hung on the wall behind a bridal throne or used as a wall hanging by urban Indonesians or foreign residents.

iket kepala (j/m): head wrapper. A head cloth worn by nominally Muslim men. Also called *udeng*.

irengan (j): blackened, lying fallow. Traditional Pasisir color combination with free-flowing motifs in black on a cream ground or with geometrical motifs in cream on a black ground, worn by older women.

isen (j): fillers. Denotes the small motifs that decorate the principal patterns.

jarit (Pasisir Javanese): woman's hip wrapper.

kabaya (m). Loose garment with wide sleeves made of white calico, originally worn by women of mixed Portuguese or Chinese descent. During the nineteenth century termed *baju top* in Java. Also *kebaya*.

kain (i/j/m): [length of] cloth. The word is generally combined in a phrase that may refer to a specific style, a place of production, or even the locality to which the cloth was to be transported.

kain buntungan (j): chopped off, mutilated, lying fallow. Hip wrapper in traditional Pasisir style, lacking the *kepala* and meant to be worn by postmenopausal women.

kain dua negeri (I/J/M). Batik cloth made in two different production centers, one on the Pasisir and one in central Java.

kain gendongan (I/J/M). Large, rectangular cloth in which a small child can be carried.

kain Jambi (J). Term used in Java to indicate Pasisir batik exported to Jambi, Sumatra. See *batik Jambi.*

kain lama (M): old or antique cloth. Term used in Jambi for antique cloth imported from the Pasisir.

kain Palembang (J). Term used in Java to indicate Pasisir batik exported to Palembang, Sumatra.

kain panjang (I/M): long cloth. Open, rectangular cloth that is wrapped around the hips by both men and women.

kain porselen (J/M). Cloth resembling a porcelain plate. The motifs are dyed in several shades of blue on white.

kain prada (I). Cloth decorated with gold dust or gold leaf.

kain Rembang (M). Term used in Bali for red-and-white cloths imported from the eastern Pasisir port of Rembang.

kain sembagi (J). Cloth decorated with floral patterns. Until the end of the eighteenth century imported into the archipelago from India. Hence, *sembagen*, motifs resembling these patterns. See *kalamkari.*

kain simbut (Sundanese): blanket, covering. Early form of ceremonial resist-dyed cloth. Until the first decade of the twentieth century made in Sundanese villages in the west of Java.

kain sisihan (J/M): cloth [with] dissimilar halves. The *kepala* at either end of this traditional Pasisir cloth differ in color and motif. Originally this type of batik was meant to be worn by bridal couples just before the wedding.

kain songket (I/J/M). Silk cloth decorated with supplementary gold weft.

kain tanah liat (M): clay cloth. Term used among the Minangkabau in west Sumatra to denote reddish-brown silk batik imported from Java.

kain tiga negeri (I/M). Batik cloth made in three different production centers on the Pasisir and in central Java, combining the motifs and colors of all three.

kalamkari (Hindi). Resist-dyed, multicolored cotton cloths produced in India and Persia and imported into the archipelago until the end of the eighteenth century.

kaligrafi Arab (I): Arabic calligraphy. Patterns consisting of Arabic script worn by Muslims as *kudhung, selendang,* or head cloth. Also called *tulisan Arab.*

kalong (J): fruit bat. Chinese and Peranakan emblem of longevity. Motif used by elderly persons.

kawong (J). Ancient geometric motif. According to some informants, an abstraction of the halved fruits of the sugar palm. Originally one of the central Javanese forbidden motifs, later used as a background motif in Indo-European cloths. Also *kawung.* See *larangan.*

kayu tingi (I/J). Bark of various mangrove species, which gives a reddish-brown dye. On the Pasisir specifically used as an over-dye on blue.

kebayak (J): short jacket. Open in front and with long sleeves tied at the wrists, worn by Javanese women.

kelengan (J): dyed blue-black. Traditional Pasisir color combination with motifs in blue on a cream ground. Worn by Peranakan women in mourning.

kemadha (J): small weir. End border on a *kudhung, iket kepala,* or *selendang* consisting of a wide band of vertical stripes.

kembang manggar (J). Flowering stalk of the coconut palm. Traditional Javanese motif, used as background on Indo-European cloth. Associated with marriage.

kembang sungsang (J). Flower of the poisonous *Gloriosa superba* creeper. Traditional Pasisir apotropaic motif.

kembang teratai (I/J): red lotus. Motif symbolizing fertility and prosperity.

kemben (J): breast cloth for women.

kemuning (J). Small, white, fragrant flower used ceremonially and as a motif on Indo-European cloths.

kepala (I/J): head. Section at one or both ends or bisecting a batik hip wrapper, decorated with a motif that differs in color or pattern from that of the *badan*.

kepala dlorong (J): slanting *kepala*. Indo-European *kepala* style comprising slanting or vertical motif bands.

kepala pasung (J): *kepala* [in the form of the] root of the nose. Pasisir term for classic *tumpal*, bisecting the *badan*.

kepala tumpal (I/J). Design in the *kepala* comprising rows of triangular motifs. Generally denoted in the literature as *tumpal*. Alternative regional terms include *kepala pasung*, *pucuk rebung*, and *sorotan*.

kotak seribu (M): one thousand pigeonholes. Motif consisting of small, decorated lozenges or squares. Specific to Cirebon, where it has cosmological overtones.

kroncong (J): jewelry making a tinkling sound. Set of three pins connected by a small chain, used to close the *kabaya*. Also called *peniti kabaya* (M).

kudhung (J). Rectangular cloth, slightly wider than a *selendang*, worn as a head and shoulder covering by Muslim women.

kupon (J): resembling a butterfly; from *kupu* (J). Motif associated with marital bliss.

langit-langit (I/J/M): the heavens. Canopy for a bed or marriage throne. Also *lelangit*.

lan hua (C): orchid. Motif on Chinese and Peranakan batiks, symbolizing love and beauty as well as numerous progeny.

laran (C): wax-dyeing process. Resist technique resembling batik, made by tribal groups in China.

larangan (J): forbidden, restricted. Sumptuary laws restricted the wearing of certain motifs to the aristocracy of the central Javanese courts. These motifs were designated as *larangan*.

Laseman (J): in the style of Lasem. Free-flowing variants of traditional Pasisir floral motifs, possibly originating in Lasem. Also refers to the specific red color originally made and used in Lasem.

limaran (J), from *limar* (J). Silk cloth with diaper pattern. Hence, motif consisting of lozenges.

lok can (Pasisir Chinese): blue silk; from *juan* (C): silk. Silk shoulder cloths, originally blue and white, produced by Peranakan workshops and exported to Sumatra and Bali.

lung (C): dragon. In China the dragon is the emblem of the male. In Java it represents female and chthonic properties. Traditional Peranakan motif.

lung (Pasisir Javanese): plant tendril. One of the *tanahan Semarangan* repertoire of backgrounds. See *ukel*.

lung ganggeng (Pasisir Javanese). Creeper trailing on the surface of inundated paddy. One of the *tanahan Semarangan* repertoire of backgrounds.

lung-lungan (Pasisir Javanese): profusion of tendrils. Hence, vine or creeper. Traditional Pasisir motif associated with fertility and regeneration. See *semen*.

mana suka (I): liked by everybody. Designs of the 1950s and 1960s expressing the democratic character of dress in the new Indonesian Republic.

melati (I/J): jasmine flower. Because of its pure white color and its fragrance, used ceremonially. Hence, *melaten* (J), resembling *melati*; motif associated with weddings.

mengkudu (I/J). Red dye obtained from the roots of the *mengkudu* shrub. Source of the bright red color found on Pasisir batik.

mui li (C): red curtain. Often decorated with batik and hung over the door of the nuptial chamber during a Peranakan wedding.

nitik (J): to tap, mark with dots. Hence *batik nitik*, batik marked with dots. Traditional central Javanese patterns consisting of clusters of dotted, geometric motifs. Also adopted into the Indo-European repertoire as a motif for borders and bands. Also *nitbik*.

paden (I/J): resembling rice plants. One of the *tanahan Semarangan* repertoire of backgrounds.

pagi sore (I/J/M): morning/late afternoon. A diagonally bisected format with a light half (morning) and dark half (late afternoon) for, respectively, evening and daytime wear.

pantjawarna (I/J from Sanskrit): five-colored. Hence, multicolored. Color combination— white, red, yellow, blue, and sometimes green— connoting a ceremonial unification of separate parts. Design of the 1950s associated with the Indonesian concept of unity in diversity. Also *pancawarna*. See *boenga rampai*.

papan (I/J): board, plank. Rectangular section of the traditional Pasisir format, forming the *kepala* together with the row of triangles. The latter (row of triangles) is associated with male quali-ties; the former (*papan*) is considered female.

parang (J): rocky outcrop; cleaver, dagger. Traditional central Javanese motif of slanting bands with stylized daggers.

parang klithik (J): medium-sized *parang* [motif].

parang menang (J): cape of victory, winning dagger. The capes or daggers in this motif all point in a single direction.

parang rusak (J): jagged, rocky outcrop; broken dagger. Motif said to resemble such an outcrop or dagger, originally restricted to the use of the ruler.

parang seling kawong (J). Alternating *parang* and *kawong* motifs arranged diagonally.

parang sonder (J): *parang* [with] dancing scarves. The daggers have been transformed into stylized scarves.

pasir (I/J): grains of sand. One of the *tanahan Semarangan* repertoire of backgrounds.

patola (Gujarati). Silk cloth decorated with the double-ikat technique in Gujarat. Imported into the archipelago until the late eighteenth century, it was highly valued for ceremonial purposes. See *cinde*.

pending (J). Woman's belt with silver or gold segments.

perang Lombok (I/M): the battle for Lombok. Motif depicting military scenes. Associated with colonial power.

pinggir (I/J): border, edge. Border enclosing the *badan* of the traditional Pasisir hip wrapper. Also called *sikilan*.

piring aji (J): holy or magic plate. Batik pattern. In a different version called *sembagen buk*.

poleng (J/Balinese): checked pattern. Black-and-white checked motifs believed to have apotropaic properties.

prada (J). Gold leaf applied to batik.

rawan (J): resembling a marsh. Traditional Pasisir background motif consisting of wavy lines.

ren-renan (J): replete with thorns. Spiky extensions typically seen on traditional motifs from the eastern Pasisir.

sapu tangan (I/M): hand wiper. Square cloth, often decorated with batik, used as a ceremonial handkerchief by a bride. See *setangan*.

sarung (I/J/M): sheath. Cloth sewn to form a tubular skirt. Always includes a *kepala* section. In Western sources the term *sarong* is often used indiscriminately for both the flat and tubular cloths.

sawat (J): sexual drive. Motif depicting two bird wings flanking a tail, commonly included in *semen* patterns to stress their fertile properties. A representation of the Garuda bird associated with Javanese rulers.

saya (Portuguese): underskirt. Wide, gathered skirt made of Indian chintz, worn by women of mixed Portuguese-Indian descent who belonged to the VOC elite.

sekar jagat (J): flowers of the universe. Traditional Javanese pattern consisting of a free-form patchwork decorated with free-flowing and abstract motifs.

selendang (I/J/M). Narrow, rectangular cloth, worn diagonally across a woman's shoulder.

seluar (Pasisir Javanese), from *shalwar* (Persian) or *shilwar* (Hindi). Baggy trousers, worn just below a man's knee. Introduced into the archipelago by Muslims.

semanggen (J): resembling a clover leaf. Traditional Pasisir motif used in borders. One of the *tanahan Semarangan* repertoire of backgrounds.

sembagen huk (C/J). Motif combining the florals of Indian import cloth with the Chinese mythical bird *huk*. The motif, depicting a phoenix in an egg, was originally associated with the coming of Islam.

semen (central Javanese): profusion of sprouts. Traditional central Javanese pattern associated with fertility and regeneration.

semen ukel (J). Design of the central Javanese *semen* type with a background of *ukel* motifs, doubling the regenerative properties.

seret (J): border, circle. Selvage borders on Javanese batik.

setangan (M), from *sapu tangan* (I/M): hand wiper. A square cloth carried as a handkerchief or used as a chatelaine by women or as a head cloth by Muslim men.

sidhangan (J): divided by diagonal lines. Unpatterned, lozenge-shaped section in the center of a batik *kemben*. Such a cloth can only be worn by a married woman.

sikilan (J): resembling extremities [arms and legs]. The borders of a traditional Pasisir hip wrapper. Also called *pinggir*.

sindur (J). Cloth with a red center and white borders, which symbolizes fertility through the combination of female and male colors. Used by the mother of a bride to cover the couple during a Javanese wedding ceremony.

singa barong (J): mythical lion. Motif typical of Cirebon.

soga (J): Reddish-brown natural dye that contains the bark of the *soga* tree combined with varying ingredients, depending on the region in which it is made. As a result *soga* occurs in various shades.

tanahan (J/M): ground. Pekalongan term for the background motifs or colors of a batik. In central Java called *latar*.

tanahan polos (I/M): unpatterned ground, plain-colored ground.

tanahan Semarangan (J). Style of intricately layered backgrounds meant for customers in Semarang.

tapih (I/J). Rectangular, wraparound cotton hip wrapper for women.

tapih cinde (J). Rectangular, wraparound cotton cloth with multicolored, geometricized motifs, imitating those on *cinde* cloth. These resist-patterned fabrics were imported from India until the late eighteenth century. Also *tapicinde*.

tapih sarasa (J). Rectangular, wraparound cotton cloth with multicolored, free-flowing, floral and faunal motifs; imported from India until the late eighteenth century. Also *tapisarasa*.

telacap (J): cape, promontory. Alternative term for the *tumpal* motif in a *kepala*.

tengahan (J/M). Central, often unpatterned rectangular or lozenge-shaped area of a *kudhung* or *selendang*.

tengkuluak (Minangkabau). Elaborately wrapped women's headdress often consisting of an imported Pasisir batik.

terang bulan (M): full moon. Style with wide, contrasting side borders.

tiron (J): imitation of. Indicates a synthetically dyed copy of a naturally dyed style from a particular area.

toka (M), from *touca* (Portuguese): handkerchief. Used by the lady of the house as a chatelaine. Also *cantelan dompyong* and *sapu tangan*.

tok wi (C): seat [for the] ancestors. Cloth often decorated with batik to cover the ancestral altar in a Chinese family home.

tritik (J): joined in long rows. Resist-dyeing process in which designs are reserved by sewing rows of small stitches, after which the thread is gathered before the dyeing. Once the color has been applied, the stitching is removed, showing the patterns.

truntum (J): to put forth buds. Traditional central Javanese motif consisting of a geometrically applied layer of star-shaped flowers, symbolic of peace of mind. Generally worn at a wedding by the parents of the bride and groom. Also used as background motif in Indo-European designs.

tumpal (Old Javanese/I/J): edge, border of another color. Triangular motifs usually encountered in single or double confronting rows in the *kepala* of a traditional Pasisir batik. Associated with the tree of life or the world mountain, both emblems of the axis of the universe.

tutup cerana (M). Covering for a ceremonial betel nut tray or food tray. In Sumatra men's head cloths are often used for this purpose.

ukel (central Javanese): plant tendril. Traditional central Javanese background motif used in *kain tiga negeri*. Also called *lung*.

ungkeran (Pasisir Javanese): profusion of tendrils. Hence, vine or creeper. Traditional Pasisir motif associated with fertility and regeneration.

wos utah (J): scattered rice. Traditional central Javanese background motif symbolizing fertility and prosperity.

wungon (J): purplish. Term used for an over-dye combination of red and light blue seen on traditional Pasisir batik.

DESIGN FORMAT AND STYLISTIC VARIATIONS OF THE *KAIN PANJANG* AND *SARUNG*

◆

Harmen C. Veldhuisen

The manner in which the design of a hip wrapper was sectioned, that is, its format, originally served as a marker of social stratification: free women wore the *kain panjang* with one row of *tumpal* forming half a *kepala* at each end of the *badan*; slaves, the *sarung* with the two rows of *tumpal* joined together, forming a complete *kepala* bisecting the *badan*. The various ways in which the borders and *kepala* of a *kain panjang* contrasted with each other indicated the wearer's marital status. An intermediate format, the *sarung* with the *kepala*, again consisting of two *tumpal* rows, positioned at one end of the unsewn cloth, came to serve as the main form of dress for women who wanted to distinguish themselves from slaves. After the official abolishment of slavery

Design Format

Kain panjang

Kain panjang kepala tumpal
Traditional style, Pasisir

CATALOGUE. NO. 2

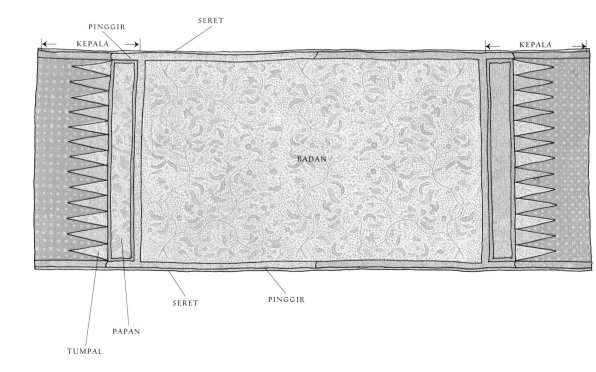

in 1860, all *sarung* formats were considered mainly as comfortable, less formal alternatives to the *kain panjang*. Around the mid-nineteenth century gradual changes in the *kepala* came to indicate ethnic distinctions between Pasisir Javanese, Peranakan, and Indo-Europeans. In the *sarung kepala gigi balang* and the *sarung kepala buketan* the *kepala* was positioned about one hand's width from the end of the cloth. During the early decades of the twentieth century an addition to the *kain panjang* repertoire, the *pagi sore*, was worn principally by Peranakan women.

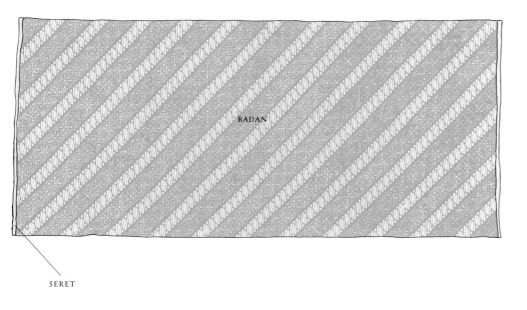

BADAN

SERET

Kain panjang
Traditional style,
central Java
Los Angeles County
Museum of Art,
M.73.73.17

Kain panjang
Indo-European style,
Pasisir

CATALOGUE NO. 34

BADAN

SERET

BOOH
(BOW BORDER)

Sarung **(Pasisir)**

Sarung kepala pasung
Traditional style

CATALOGUE NO. 5

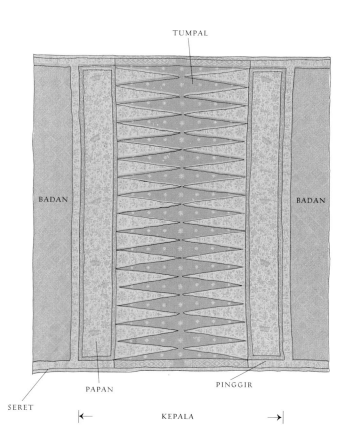

TUMPAL

BADAN

BADAN

SERET

PAPAN

PINGGIR

KEPALA

Kain panjang pagi sore
Peranakan style, Pasisir

CATALOGUE NO. 57

PAGI   SORE

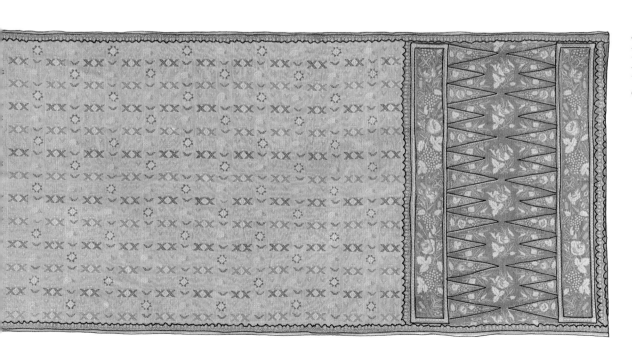

Sarung kepala tumpal
Indo-European and
Peranakan style

CATALOGUE NO. 19

Sarung kepala gigi balang
Peranakan style

CATALOGUE NO. 16

Variations in the Indo-European-style Kepala

Vertical rectangle, introduced 1860s

CATALOGUE NO. 18

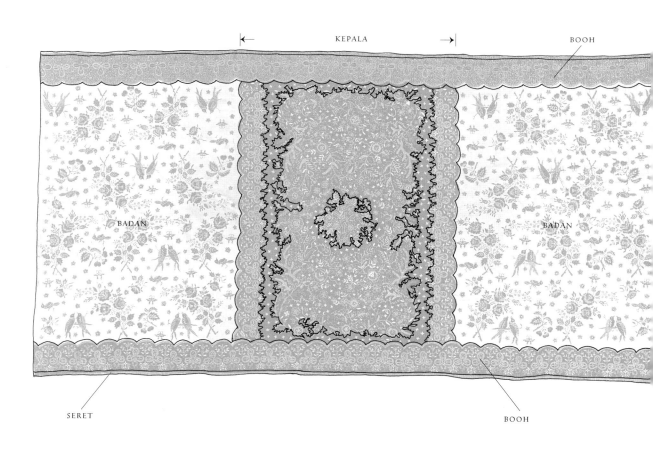

KEPALA

BOOH

BADAN

BADAN

SERET

BOOH

Broad diagonal bands,
introduced 1880s

CATALOGUE NO. 25

Vertical or diagonal
bands, introduced
1890s

CATALOGUE NO. 32

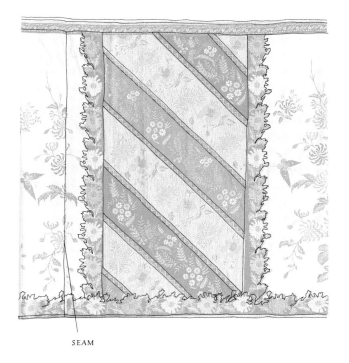

SEAM

A stiff floral
arrangement, introduced
c. 1900

CATALOGUE NO. 28

SEAM

Tree with one or two birds, introduced c. 1900

CATALOGUE NO. 45

SEAM

A multiflowered bouquet, introduced 1910s

CATALOGUE NO. 49

APPENDIX 2

PLACEMENT OF THE *Kepala*
◆
HARMEN C. VELDHUISEN

Each batik format was wrapped and worn in a distinctive manner.

1. Kain panjang kepala tumpal

(CATALOGUE NO. 2)

The cloth is wrapped around the hips, placing one end center front and winding toward the right. The *tumpal* end covers the left thigh, and most of the plain section of the *kepala* is folded inwards.

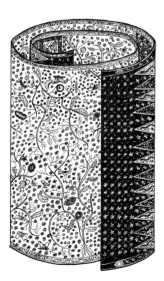

seam

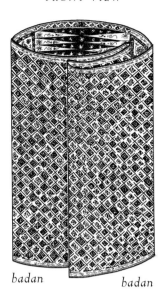

badan   *badan*   *kepala*

2. *Sarung kepala pasung*
(CATALOGUE NO. 5)

This was the only format in which the *kepala* was worn at the small of the back. The superfluous material of the tubular cloth is wrapped left over right in front with the seam hidden under the fold.

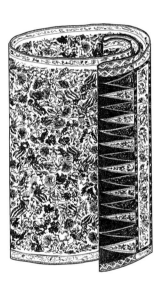

3. *Sarung kepala tumpal*
(CATALOGUE NO. 6)

While similar in appearance to the *kain panjang kepala tumpal* when worn, the *sarung kepala tumpal* shows one row of *tumpal* at the left thigh; the other is folded underneath.

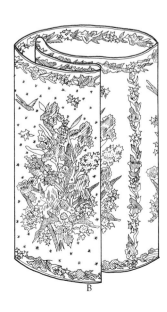

A   B

4a. *Sarung kepala gigi balang*, Peranakan style
(CATALOGUE NO. 16)

4b. *Sarung kepala buketan*, Indo-European style
(CATALOGUE NO. 49)

The Peranakan and the Indo-European *sarung* are folded in similar manners, at approximately three-quarters of the *kepala*, with most of the design showing. However, the Peranakan *sarung* is wrapped left over right, whereas the Indo-European *sarung* is wrapped right over left.

MATERIALS AND TECHNIQUES
•
RENS HERINGA

The batik methods practiced on the Pasisir have differed traditionally in many ways from those of central Java. The greater part of the descriptive literature concentrates on the latter, although details of the Pasisir process can be found scattered among these sources.[1] The distinctions, occurring primarily in the dye process, are nevertheless rarely articulated. To complicate matters, the governing elite on the north coast, when making batiks for their own use, adhered to the central Javanese waxing and dyeing methods due to the fact that these aristocratic families were originally appointed by and often related to the rulers of the central Javanese Principalities.

Materials

Cotton

Toward the end of the eighteenth century machine-woven English cloth came to replace the handwoven Indian fabrics that for at least one hundred years had served as the base material for batik worn by the Javanese aristocracy. The heavy quality of English muslin, with its high thread count, was especially appreciated on the Pasisir, where, as a rule, handwoven cotton had been used. After 1830, with the eastern Netherlands developing as an industrial weaving area, the Dutch, aided by substantial government subsidies, succeeded in establishing supremacy in cotton imports into the archipelago. This situation continued until 1942 and the commencement of war in the Pacific, though due to their much lower prices considerable competition from Japanese cotton imports into the archipelago had been felt for several decades.

Regardless of where it was produced, the fabric was sold by the piece in widths of 38–42 inches (approx. 1–1.1 m), specially woven to form the height of a hip wrapper, and mostly in lengths of 15 yards (13.7 m). Prime-quality fabric, the so-called *primissima*, measured 16 1/2 yards (15 m).[2] Two particular types were famous in Java: the first identified by its trademark *cent*, or *sen* (the local pronunciation of *cent*), the smallest denomination Dutch coin, a picture of which, *cap sen*, was stamped on each length; the second known by its trademark *cap jangkrik*, or grasshopper. The bolts of *primissima* could be recognized by red and light brown weft stripes, the so-called heading, woven into the face plait, which formed the outer section of the piece when it was rolled.[3] The number 16, embroidered in red with a tambour needle, constituted a second mark of identi-

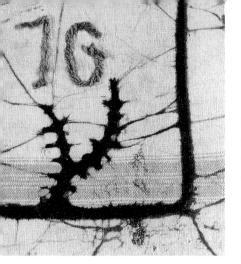

FIGURE 65
Cat. no. 76 (detail).

Although most entrepreneurs insisted that they removed the weft lines and number 16 from the end of the bolt, these are periodically encountered, partially obscured by motifs and colors, on high-quality nineteenth- and early twentieth-century batiks.

fication. Both the weft stripe and the numerals 16 were visible on top of the bolt when its blue paper wrapping was removed (FIGURE 65). Affluent entrepreneurs bought fabric wholesale in the bustling textile markets of the larger batik centers. The entrepreneur decided how many items would be cut from each piece, taking into consideration flaws in the material and frequently skimping on the length allocated to each item (FIGURE 66). The piece was sufficient for five *kain panjang*, six *sarung*, or a combination of the two, alternated with *iket kepala* and *selendang*. Only batiks made from the highest-quality fabric consistently had full measurements: a length two times the width for a *sarung* and two and a half times for a *kain panjang*. Less prosperous workshop owners could obtain material already cut into individual lengths in smaller retail shops, often paying in installments.

Silk

A small percentage of Pasisir batik—*sarung*, *selendang*, or *celana* (trousers)—is made on a silk base. This fabric was imported from China in bolts called *bantal* (pillow), which were measured by weight and sold at 18–22.50 Dutch guilders per kilogram.[4] Pongee silk and crepe de Chine are the finest quality encountered.

Wax and Dyes

Wax

For centuries the best-quality beeswax has come to Java from Lombok, Timor, and other islands in eastern Indonesia. For each phase of waxing the pure beeswax was combined with additives such as dark blue wax recovered during the boiling process (see below), white or yellow mineral wax, resin, and buffalo grease. The colored mixtures enabled a clear distinction at each new phase of waxing. Pasisir batik, because of its plain, light-colored or even white or cream backgrounds, required special wax mixtures that adhered closely to the base cloth. Crackled breaks (*remukan*) that might occur in the waxed backgrounds during the often prolonged dye process could thus be avoided.

Dyes

Natural dye materials were used to achieve the bright colors of *batik Pasisir*. The main traditional Pasisir colors were various gradations of blue in combination with a range of reds from scarlet to reddish brown. An overdye combination of red and blue resulted in a deep blue-black. Accents of green and yellow served to enliven the palette. The blues were all derived from the indigo shrub (*Indigofera tinctoria*), which was extensively cultivated all over Java. An extract of its leaves, made into a paste, was usually obtained from special indigo makers. In the workshop the required amount was diluted with water and thoroughly mixed with quicklime and molasses to set the long and complicated indigo dyeing process in motion. On the Pasisir the addition of fermented sticky rice (*tapai ketan*) or cassava (*tapai pohong*) served to achieve deeper shades.

Tints of red and reddish brown were produced with various tree roots and mangrove bark, imported from other islands in the archipelago and purchased

FIGURE 66

Cloth is unpacked on the back porch of a workshop owner's house in Kampong Karet, the batik area of Batavia, and cut into the appropriate lengths for hip wrappers, shoulder and head cloths. The man in the foreground scores the edge of the cloth with a knife; the man to his left tears the material.* Copy photograph, Henk Beukers

* This and other photographs marked with an asterisk are from J. D. Daubanton, *De Batikindustrie op Java: Haar ontstaan en ontwikkeling, bewerking der goederen, gebruikte materialen en voortbrengselen* (Rotterdam: Internationale crediet- en handels-vereeniging Rotterdam, 1922).

in their natural state in the market. Most important for Pasisir batik was the root of the *mengkudu* tree (*Morinda citrifolia*), producing a strong, bright red. *Kayu tingi* (*Ceriops candolleana*) was used for a darker brownish red.[5] In the workshop each of these materials was finely pounded and heated in secret mixtures, which also included leaves or roots containing alum as a mordant.

Yellow was either brushed on with a solution of *kunir* root (*Curcuma longa*) or dipped in a bath containing the root of the *tegerang* tree (*Cudranus javanensis*). Green was mostly achieved through an overdye of *tegerang* on a light indigo, though a variety of ingredients have been reported from different locations.[6]

The Indo-European entrepreneurs were particularly innovative, experimenting with natural dye materials to achieve a more varied palette. Around 1890 the first synthetic aniline dyes, German made, were imported into the archipelago, followed by an increasing range of powdered naphthol and diazo dyes, which by the 1930s had become the medium of preference (FIGURE 67).

The Canting

The manufacture of the wax pen, or *canting*, cut from a thin copper sheet and welded into a small container with a spout, has traditionally been a male profession. Until the early twentieth century itinerant *canting* makers traveled along the north coast filling orders. Each region in Java used to have its particular model, of which only the central Javanese types are still in use. The spouts are fashioned in different sizes in order to bring variety to lines and dots (FIGURES 68A–C).

FIGURE 68A

Some *canting* have more than one spout to draw the double lines that often delineate borders.
Koninklijk Instituut voor de Tropen, Amsterdam

FIGURE 67

A shop owned and run by Peranakan selling batik ingredients in the village of Kalitengah, near Cirebon, June 1981. Such materials are available in even the smallest towns. A variety of wax mixtures, powdered synthetic dyes, generally produced by European chemical companies (e.g., Hoechst in Germany and Ciba in Switzerland), and large containers of mordants and fixatives are sold in bulk or in small quantities.
Photograph, Rens Heringa

FIGURE 68B

The *canting nitik*, with its four-lobed spout, produces separate dots, in a crosslike formation.
Koninklijk Instituut voor de Tropen, Amsterdam

FIGURE 68C

The dotted, geometric *nitik* patterns on this batik signed by Maria Paulina Carp resemble a woven supplementary-weft pattern.
Photograph, Henk Beukers

FIGURE 69

FIGURE 69

Cloth was kneaded with a mixture of water, burnt rice straw (*merang*), and oil from the seeds of the *jarak* tree (*ricinus*) during the day and hung to dry at night. Such arduous work was undertaken by an oiling laborer (*kuli nge-tel*). Repeated for three to four weeks, the process slightly loosened the yarns of the fabric for the wax and dyes to penetrate easily. Koninklijk Instituut voor de Tropen, Amsterdam

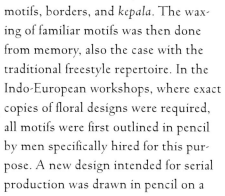

Process

Cloth preparation

After repeated rins-ing to remove the sizing applied in the weaving mill, the fabric under-went a lengthy treatment with mordants in preparation for the natural dyes (FIGURE 69). Once the use of synthetic dyes was adopted, this step was omitted.

Waxing

Pencil guide lines were drawn on the fabric with a wooden ruler (*blebes*) for traditional geometric motifs, borders, and *kepala*. The wax-ing of familiar motifs was then done from memory, also the case with the traditional freestyle repertoire. In the Indo-European workshops, where exact copies of floral designs were required, all motifs were first outlined in pencil by men specifically hired for this pur-pose. A new design intended for serial production was drawn in pencil on a piece of tracing paper. The *pengobeng* (hired woman who waxed batik), facing a source of natural light, pinned this to the back of the white cotton, so that the pattern showed through the cloth and could be copied in wax. After the *pengobeng* had repeated the design many times, she could draw it from memory (FIGURE 70).

Four waxing phases followed. Hung over a bam-boo rack (*gawangan*), the cloth underwent the initial step of waxing: the outlines (*klowong*) of the first-layer, or largest, motifs were applied to both sides of the cloth. The second layer of somewhat smaller motifs was drawn in the spaces between the larger designs, again on both sides of the cloth. The first-layer motifs were next embellished with intricate filler patterns (*isen*); this, the finest and most cre-ative part of the waxing process, determined the quality of the batik. Finally, the background areas were covered (*nutup* or *nembok*) with wax by means of a wide-spouted *canting* or even with a brush, again

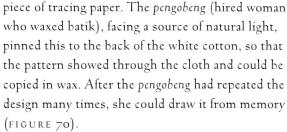

FIGURE 70

Ciebon, 1992. The waxing process was executed by *pen-gobeng*, each assigned her tasks in accord with her spe-cific skills. The wax was heated in an iron pot (*wajan*) on a small charcoal brazier (*anglo*) or kerosene stove (*kompor*) standing in the mid-dle of a group of wo-men, so that each could scoop it into her *canting* easily. Photograph, Harmen C. Veldhuisen

on both sides of the cloth (FIGURE 71). In Lasem and Indramayu as a last step these waxed back-grounds were pierced by pinpricks (*cocoban*) (FIGURES 72–74). Each step required a particular skill, so the cloth passed through the hands of several *pengobeng* of varying levels of proficiency.

FIGURE 71

Pengobeng waxing back-grounds*
Copy photograph, Henk Beukers

FIGURE 72

Indramayu, July 1981. The waxed backgrounds of the tra-ditional batiks of Lasem and Indramayu are pierced by young girls with small pin-pricks (*cocoban*), which will appear in the background in blue or red. Photograph, Rens Heringa

FIGURE 73

The special utensil used by the Indramayu girl in figure 72, the *cemplongan*, consists of forty needles embedded in a block of wood, which made decoration with *cocoban* more efficient. Photograph, Rens Heringa

FIGURE 74

Cat. no. 6 (detail). The *coco-ban* in the background of a Lasem batik show more flu-ent lines, as the pinpricks are applied one by one

Dyeing

Though the dye mixtures were hot after being prepared, they had to cool before being applied to prevent the wax from melting. On the Pasisir the lightest color was invariably dyed first, to be followed by stronger tints, in contrast to central Java, where the process moved from dark to light shades. On traditional Pasisir batik only red and blue dyes were used. For a red-on-white or red-on-cream *bang-bangan* cloth the dye process was finished after the application of red. For a bright red and blue *bang biru* cloth, bright red would always be dyed first. Blue would be applied after an intermediate waxing of the areas to remain red, while some parts might be left uncovered to achieve accents of black where the two dyes fused. The dyeing of indigo in large troughs was heavy work, executed by the *kuli medel* (blue dyers) (FIGURE 75). An extensive series of dippings was needed to reach the deeper shades of blue, for instance, when a blue-on-white *kelengan* was intended. For a combination (other than *bang biru*) in which blue was dyed first, only *kayu tingi*, producing a brownish red, was suitable, as *mengkudu* (FIGURE 76) does not take when top-dyed over blue.

Removing the wax

Wax was removed in vats of boiling water (FIGURE 77), to which alum had been added. On the Pasisir this step was traditionally carried out after the application of each new color. This meant that the cloth had to be waxed all over again after being rinsed and dried (FIGURE 78). In the central Javanese system a partial rewaxing would be combined with a mere scraping of wax in particular areas. As a result, a Pasisir batik shows a range of clearly contrasting colors, while central Javanese colors blend into each other.

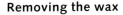

Complex dyeing methods

The Indo-European entrepreneurs introduced and perfected a more complex dye sequence, applying various shades of a single color. Each sequentially darker shade of red or blue occasioned the intermediate steps of boiling, drying, waxing, and dyeing.

Finishing Treatments

Various embellishments could be applied to finished batiks.

Gilding

During the nineteenth century batik meant for ceremonial use was often decorated with a layer of gilding (*prada*). In Pekalongan a small brush made of squirrel's whiskers was used to cover or outline the resist-dyed patterns with an adhesive mixture of yellow ocher powder, lamp oil, and buffalo blood. The next day, when the sticky substance was almost dry, gold powder was brushed on. In other production

FIGURE 77

Removing the wax (*nglorod*) in vats of boiling water, during which the cloth must be raised and lowered continuously to prevent the wax from adhering once again to the surface of the cloth. Koninklijk Instituut voor de Tropen, Amsterdam

FIGURE 78

Behind the workshop batiks are dried on bamboo racks after boiling and additional rinsing.*
Copy photograph, Henk Beukers

FIGURE 75

Kuli medel doing the heavy work of dyeing indigo in huge wooden vats. Following a few hours of immersion, the cloths are draped over bamboo to let the color develop under the influence of light as they drip dry.*
Copy photograph, Henk Beukers

FIGURE 76

The powdered root of the *mengkudu* plant mixed with dried *jirek* leaves (*Symplocos fasciculata*) as a mordant were the ingredients used to dye cloth red. The cloth was spread across on a broad, flat container to be sprinkled and rubbed for three consecutive days with the dye paste, a method still in use with synthetic dyes.*
Copy photograph, Henk Beukers

FIGURE 79

Cat. no. 82 (detail; for color
see catalogue entry). On a
cloth intended for gilding,
motifs were generally drawn
without filler details, as seen
in some areas of the *qilin* in
this ceremonial handkerchief
for a Peranakan bride.

centers egg white was used as the adhesive, while in
Sumatra thin gold foil cut to match batik motifs
replaced the powdered gold (FIGURE 79).

Glazing

Glazing (*garusan*) to impart a silklike sheen was
applied particularly to shaded pastel Peranakan
batiks in the 1920s and 1930s (see cat. no. 61). The
cloth was laid on a flat surface and sprinkled with
wax scrapings, which were rubbed evenly into the
fabric with a smooth shell attached to a flexible
length of bamboo.[7] The side of a wine bottle
achieved the same result.

Labor-saving Techniques

In order primarily to bring the price of batik within
reach of a larger public, various techniques were
devised to speed up the process. A few of these methods are mentioned here, though they were not characteristic of the production of the sorts of high-quality cloths represented in this catalogue.

Copper stamps

The first technical innovation was the *cap*, or copper
stamp (FIGURE 80), which came into existence
around 1840–50 in response to printed European
imitations of batik flooding the Javanese market.
Until a few decades ago such stamps were generally
restricted to the manufacture of lower-quality cloths
and emergent fashion trends, both of which
demanded production in large quantities. Each

FIGURE 80

Cap were cut into narrow
strips from thin copper sheets
and welded into a heavier
copper frame with a handle
on the back. Geometric
motifs were particularly suited
to *cap*.*
Copy photograph, Henk
Beukers

design needed stamps of various sizes and shapes for
the patterns on the *badan* and its background, the
borders, and the *kepala* as well as their mirror images
for the reverse. Only well-financed workshops with
large production capacity could afford this investment. In most cases the stamped patterns were combined with hand-waxed details and *isen* (FIGURE 81).

FIGURE 81

Workshop of The Tie Siet,
Pekalongan, June 1981. The
heavy *cap* are handled by the
tukang cap (stamping laborer),
always a man, who works on a
padded table. He uses both
hands, one to align the
imprints neatly, the other to
bear down on the *cap*.
Photograph, Rens Herenga

FIGURE 82

Workshop of The Tie Siet, Pekalongan, June 1981. Relatively unskilled and therefore low-paid, young women occupy themselves with *colet*.

Photograph, Rens Heringa

Painting

A more recent innovation is *colet*, the painting with synthetic dyes of small areas, previously outlined in wax, a specialty of Peranakan workshops (FIGURE 82). The use of small amounts of concentrated dye enable the use of a variety of colors at low cost (FIGURE 83).

Development of these techniques

Further development of stamping and painting has led to a revaluation of the batiks produced with these techniques. Elaborate procedures have become possible: *Semarangan* backgrounds overlayed with floral bouquets are in some cases entirely executed with stamps. After the borders and *kepala* are stamped and colored by *colet*, the pattern of the *badan* and finally the often extremely complicated backgrounds follow. Paper guards are used to prevent the spoiling of previously dyed areas. Finally the colored areas are waxed over and a single dip in dye imparts the background color, thus considerably speeding up the process and still yielding a rich-looking result

Notes
1. J. E. Jasper and Mas Pirngadie, *De batikkunst*, vol. 3 of *De inlandsche kunstnijverheid in Nederlandsch Indië* (The Hague: Mouton, 1916), ch. 2–6.

2. J. J. B. Ostmeijer, *Handleiding bij het schatten samengesteld ten behoeve van het personeel van den pandhuisdienst* (Batavia: Albrecht, n.d.), 263.

3. M. Simon Thomas and P. den Otter, "Twentse tjaps," *Textielhistorische Bijdragen* 34 (1994): 107.

4. Ostmeijer, *Handleiding bij het schatten*, 248.

5. Rens Heringa, "Dye Process and Life Sequence: The Coloring of Textiles in an East Javanese Village," in *To Speak with Cloth: Studies in Indonesian Textiles*, ed. Mattiebelle Gittinger (Los Angeles: Museum of Cultural History, University of California, Los Angeles, 1989), 113–20.

6. Jasper and Pirngadie, *Batikkunst*, 40–50.

7. Ostmeijer, *Handleiding bij het schatten*, 279.

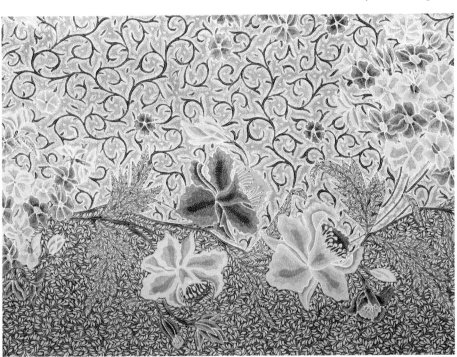

FIGURE 83

Cat. no. 61 (detail; for color see catalogue entry). The flowers in the elaborate hand-drawn *tanahan Semarangan* background of this batik have undergone a special treatment: small areas of color were hand-painted along the outlines. Combined with the shaded filler motifs, this resulted in a three-dimensional effect.

SELECTED BIBLIOGRAPHY

ABDURACHMAN, PARAMITA RAHAYU. "Dermayu Batiks: A Surviving Art in an Ancient Trading Town." *Spafa Digest* 8 (1987).

DJUMENA, NIAN S. *Batik dan Mitra; Batik and Its Kind* (bilingual). Jakarta: Penerbit Djambatan, 1990.

ELLIOTT, INGER MCCABE. *Batik: Fabled Cloth of Java.* New York: Clarkson N. Potter, 1984.

GEIRNAERT, DANIELLE C., and RENS HERINGA. *The A.E.D.T.A. Batik Collection.* Paris: Association pour l'Etude et la Documentation des Textiles d'Asie, 1989.

GELMAN TAYLOR, JEAN. *The Social World of Batavia: European and Eurasian in Dutch Asia.* Madison: University of Wisconson Press, 1983.

GITTINGER, MATTIEBELLE, ed. *Indonesian Textiles*, 1979 Roundtable on Museum Textiles. Washington D.C.: Textile Museum, 1980.

GITTINGER, MATTIEBELLE. *Master Dyers to the World: Technique and Trade in Early Indian Dyed Cotton Textiles.* Exh. cat. Washington, D.C.: Textile Museum, 1982.

GITTINGER, MATTIEBELLE, ed. *To Speak with Cloth: Studies in Indonesian Textiles.* Los Angeles: Museum of Cultural History, University of California, Los Angeles, 1989.

HANSSEN, LINDA. "Ceremoniële Doeken van de Minangkabau: Textiel als Metafoor voor Sociale Ordening." Masters thesis, Utrecht University, 1995.

HERINGA, RENS. *Een schitterende geschiedenis: Weefsels en batiks van Palembang en Djambi.* Exh. cat. The Hague: Museon, 1993.

HERINGA, RENS. *Spiegels van ruimte en tijd.* Exh. cat. The Hague: Museon, 1994.

HOLMGREN, ROBERT J., and ANITA E. SPERTUS. *Early Indonesian Textiles from Three Island Cultures: Sumba, Toraja, Lampung.* Exh. cat. New York: Metropolitan Museum of Art, 1989.

JASPER, J. E., and MAS PIRNGADIE. *De batikkunst.* Vol. 3 of *De inlandsche kunstnijverheid in Nederlandsch Indië.* The Hague: Mouton, 1916.

KAT ANGELINO, P. DE. *Batikrapport.* Batavia: Landsdrukkerij, 1930–31.

KHAN MAJLIS, BRIGITTE. *Indonesische textilien: Wege zu Göttern und Ahnen.* Cologne: Wienand, 1984.

MAXWELL, ROBYN J. *Textiles of Southeast Asia: Tradition, Trade and Transformation.* Melbourne: Oxford University Press and Australian National Gallery, 1990.

NABHOLZ-KARTASCHOFF, MARIE-LOUISE, ET AL., eds. *Weaving Patterns of Life: Indonesian Textile Symposium* (1991). Basel: Museum of Ethnography, 1993.

RAADT-APELL, M. J. DE. *De batikkerij Van Zuylen te Pekalongan: Midden-Java 1890-1946.* Zutphen: Terra, 1980.

ROUFFAER, G. P. "Beeldende kunst in Nederlandsch Indië." *Bijdragen van het Koninklijk Instituut voor Taal-Land- en Volkenkunde van Nederlandsch-Indië* 89 (1932).

ROUFFAER, G. P. "De voornaamste industriën der inlandsche bevolking van Java en Madoera." *Koloniaal-Economische Bijdragen* (1904).

ROUFFAER, G. P. *Over Indische batikkunst, vooral die op Java.* Haarlem: n.p., 1900.

ROUFFAER, G. P., and H. H. JUYNBOLL. *De batik-kunst in Nederlandsch Indië and haar geschiedenis.* 3 vols. Utrecht: A. Oosthoek, 1900–1914.

SOLYOM, BRONWEN, and GARRETT SOLYOM. *Fabric Traditions of Indonesia.* Exh. cat. Pullman, Washington: Museum of Art and Washington State University Press, 1984.

VELDHUISEN, HARMEN C. *Batik Belanda 1840–1940: Dutch Influence in Batik from Java: History and Stories.* Jakarta: Gaya Favorit, 1993.

VELDHUISEN-DJAJASOEBRATA, ALIT. *Batik op Java.* Lochem: De Tijdstroom, 1973.

VELDHUISEN-DJAJASOEBRATA, ALIT. *Bloemen van het heelal: De kleurrijke wereld van de textiel op Java.* Amsterdam: Sijthof; Rotterdam: Museum voor Volkenkunde, 1984.

VÖLGER, GISELA, and KARIN VON WELCK, eds. *Indonesian Textiles, Symposium 1985.* Vol. 14 of *Ethnologica.* Cologne: Rautenstrauch-Joest Museum, 1991.

WILLIAMS, C. A. S. *Outlines of Chinese Symbolism and Art Motives*, 3d ed. New York: Dover, 1976.

ACKNOWLEDGMENTS

This project would not have been possible without the dedication and assistance of many people. First, I would like to thank the authors. Peter Carey, Trinity College, Oxford: although we have never met, he has been a model of professional cooperation. Primary authors Rens Heringa, Leiden, and Harmen C. Veldhuisen, Rotterdam, selected the pieces for the catalogue, providing the focus for this study of *batik Pasisir* and bringing their combined expertise to every aspect of this volume. From New York City, Inger McCabe Elliott has consistently offered suggestions and encouragement.

I want to thank the museum for providing me with funds from the Andrew W. Mellon Curatorial Support Endowment, which enabled me to examine batik collections in Europe in 1993. On that trip I was graciously shown textiles in museum storerooms by the following people: in the Netherlands, Rogier M. A. Bedaux, chief curator, and Maria Laman, conservator, the Rijksmuseum voor Volkenkunde, Leiden; Rita Bolland, curator emeritus, the Tropenmuseum, Amsterdam; and Alit Veldhuisen-Djajasoebrata, curator of Indonesian art, the Museum voor Land- en Volkenkunde, Rotterdam; in Germany, Carl Wolfgang Schumann, director, Deutsches Textilmuseum, Krefeld; and Brigitte Khan Majlis, curator, Rautenstrauch-Joest Museum, Cologne; in Switzerland, Marie-Louise Nabholz-Kartaschoff, keeper of Asian textiles, Museum für Volkerkunde, Basel; in France, Monique Drosson, former assistant curator, Musée de l'Impression sur Etoffes, Mulhouse; and in England, John Guy and Rosemary Crill, assistant cura-

232
.

tors, Victoria and Albert Museum, London. Steven Vink, head of documentation at the Koninklijk Instituut voor de Tropen, Amsterdam, and Petra van Bergen-Godthelp of the Koninklijk Instituut voor Taal-, Land- en Volkenkunde, Leiden, accommodated numerous requests for photocopies. During my stay in Leiden, D. J. Stuart-Fox, librarian at the Rijksmuseum voor Volkenkunde, was particularly generous with his time and considerable knowledge of publications on Indonesia. Rudolf Smend and his wife, Karin, of Cologne, and J. van Daalen of Utrecht showed me their extensive collections of batik. Warm hospitality was extended to me by my friend and colleague Brigitte Menzel during the many days I spent in Krefeld and Cologne. Appreciation must be given to the National Endowment for the Arts. Without its initial funding this project might never have been realized. I owe a debt of gratitude to the Costume Council, support group of the Costumes and Textiles department for their generous fundings of catalogue-related travel and the introductory video for the exhibition. I would also like to thank Mattiebelle Gittinger, curator of Southeast Asian textiles at the Textile Museum, Washington, D.C., advisor to the project in its early stages. Lee Chor Lin, National Museum, Singapore, kindly assisted with a last-minute photo request.

Closer to home there were many here at the Los Angeles County Museum of Art who provided assistance in one form or another. Earl A. Powell III, then director, ably represented the museum in discussions with the collector and provided encouragement for this project. Edward Maeder, former curator of costumes and textiles at LACMA, charmed Ms. Elliott as only he could do. The museum is now being ably led by Andrea Rich, president and CEO, and Graham W.J. Beal, director and executive vice-president, whose joint support has been vital to the final realization of this project. Sandra Rosenbaum, Kaye Spilker, Sharon Takeda, J. Danielle Sierra, Gail Stein, and Cynthia Cavanaugh, my colleagues in the department of costumes and textiles have been sympathetic and supportive throughout this long process, rendering assistance when needed. Mitch Tuchman, our editor in chief, Jim Drobka, head graphic designer, and Peter Brenner, supervising photographer, all helped to make this catalogue a reality. Jay McNally did an outstanding job of photographing the batik textiles, while textile conserators Catherine McLean and Cara Varnell along with Kaye Spilker expertly prepared the pieces for photography and display. As always it was a pleasure to work with senior graphics designer Amy McFarland, who turned black typescript on white pages into glorious color. Marilyn Bowes, Marc Shroetter, Celia Taylor, and Alice Wolf assisted with the daunting task of unrolling (and rerolling) the batiks on several occasions. I wish to thank Museum Service Council volunteers Siuin Morrissy, Sam Shaffer, and Martha Weiskal for their help. I would like to acknowledge the assistance of Leslie Bowman, Beverley Sabo, and others of the exhibitions department. Art Owens, Lawrence Waung, Bill Stahl, Michael Tryon, and the technical services staff of the museum worked hard to create an outstanding presentation of the textiles. My gratitude is extended to Jane Burrell, acting head of education, and Mary Beth Bresolin, Jeff Defalque, Joan Klopenburg, Laura Schroeter, and Elvin Whitesides for their excellent teamwork on the exhibition's video component. Renee Montgomery, registrar, and Mark Mitchell, budget manager, were helpful in many difficult moments. Exhibition designer Bernard Kester's love of textiles made working with him a pleasure. Barbara Pflaummer and her staff in the department of media and public affairs, along with Melody Kanschat, Tom Jacobson, Joan Van Hooten, Sonya Levy, and Greg Murphy in our membership and development office, and Cim Castellon, museum shop manager were encouraging and support-ive. Virtually everyone at the museum was involved with this project at one time or another, and I wish to thank them all.

Rens Heringa would like to thank the colleagues at museums, too many to mention here, who showed her textiles in their storerooms over the past twenty years. For this project special thanks go to Indonesian friends and informants for sharing their knowledge of batik. Among others, Mr. and Mrs. Hamid Algadri, Nian Djumena, Liem Giok Hwa, Myra Sidharta, and Ratmini Soedjatmoko in Jakarta; K. R. T. Hardjonegoro (Go Tik Swan), R. A. Paptini Partaningrat, and Mimi Soendoro in Surakarta; and Ate Tan-Loa in Rijswijk. Help in obtaining illustrations was extended by Steven Vink of the Historical Document Department of the Koninklijk Instituut voor de Tropen in Amsterdam, that insti-tute's staff, and the staff of the Royal Institute of Linguistics and Anthropology in Leiden. Practical help came from Bruce van Rijk and Tineke Mook at the Instituut Indonesische Cursussen in Leiden.

Harmen Veldhuisen wishes to acknowledge the years of cooperation of the relatives of many of the batik entrepreneurs who are among the subjects of this book, those who are mentioned as well as those who wished to remain anony-mous. He thanks the batik collectors Eiko Adnan Kusuma and Nian Djumena, Jakarta; Rudolf Smend, Cologne; Carl Wolfgang Schümann, director of the Deutsches Textilmuseum, Krefeld; and the batik dealers Adrian Idris and Daly Adjas, Jakarta, for their helpful discussions. Grateful appreciation goes to Greet de Raadt-Apell for tracing informants in the Netherlands; his wife, Alit Veldhuisen-Djajasoebrata, who commented on the Dutch text; Rosemary Robson, Leiden, for translating his manuscript; Jan Prins, Vlaardingen, for his gift of photographs; Martinus Ader, Rotterdam, for solving computer problems; and the Museum voor Land- en Volkenkunde, Rotterdam, for their fax facilities.

My deepest appreciation goes to my husband who encouraged me through-out this endeavor.

Dale Carolyn Gluckman
Associate curator of costumes and textiles

238
·
Index

EDITOR
Mitch Tuchman

DESIGNER & ILLUSTRATOR
Amy McFarland

PHOTOGRAPHER
Jay McNally

PRODUCTION ASSISTANCE
Theresa Velázquez
Matthew Stevens

TRANSLATOR
Rosemary Robson

INDEX
Kathleen Preciado

PHOTO ILLUSTRATION
Michael Conway/Atlas Design, LLC

PRINTER:
Toppan Printing Co., Ltd., Singapore

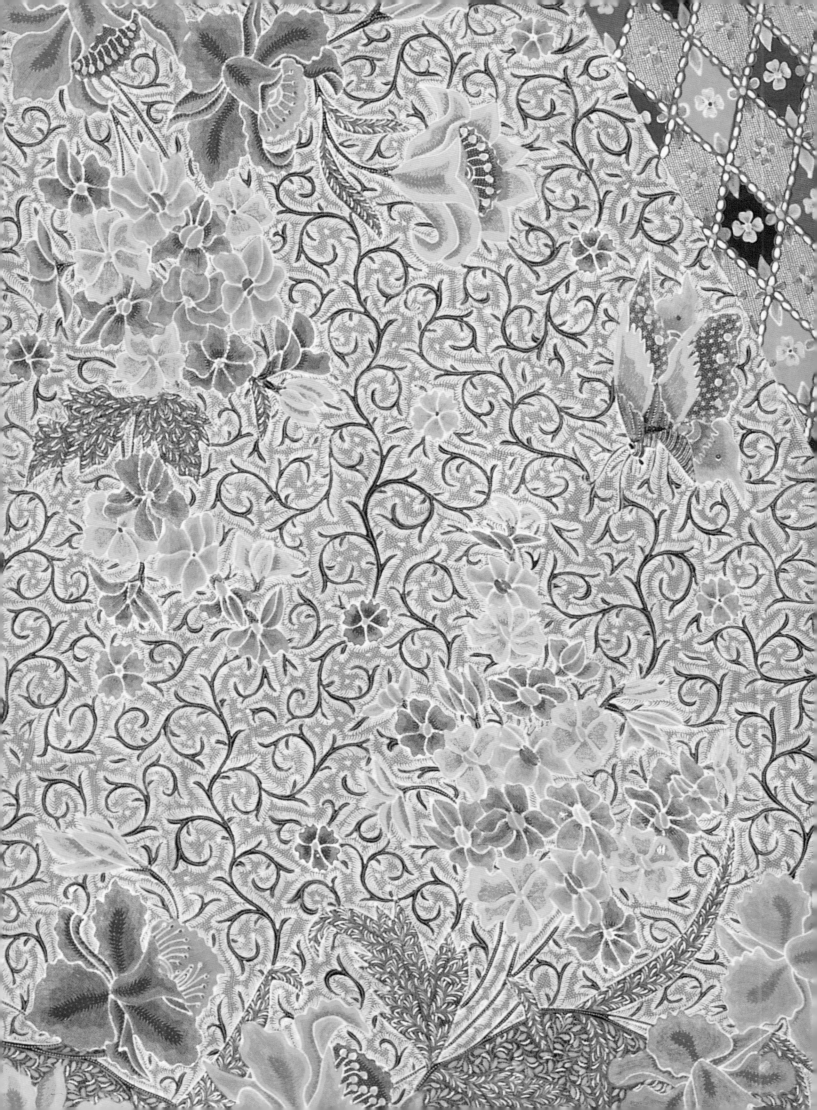